Praise for *Becoming SRE*

SRE is ever-evolving, which makes it exciting to both study and adopt; however, due to this constant change, it can be difficult to know where to begin. *Becoming SRE* is the definitive guide to help you start your journey, as well as guide you on your way.

—*Alex Hidalgo, Principal Reliability Advocate at Nobl9 and author of* Implementing Service Level Objectives

An essential guide to transforming yourself or your organization into the SRE mindset, and accomplishing the change you want in your systems. This book is sure to expand the SRE canon from a trilogy to a tetralogy.

—*Liz Fong-Jones, Field CTO at Honeycomb and coauthor of* Observability Engineering

Prepare for a fun and winding adventure! *Becoming SRE* unfolds the story of site reliability engineering in a fresh and inspiring way. Each chapter unlocks a gem of wisdom, revealing the quintessential mindset, culture, and practices that are core to being an SRE. You'll face the dragons of complex systems, service levels, toil and failure, and learn why SREs are obsessed with them. If you're beginning your career in SRE, practicing your career, or just launching it in your business or organization, you'll find this book a treasure, packed with guidance, relatable stories, and a good dose of fun.

—*Jason A. Cox, Director of Global SRE, Disney*

If you took the years of SRE expertise held by David and the cast of characters quoted in this book and compressed it down to its most compact form, you would get this book. *Becoming SRE* represents the messy business of SRE in book form, meeting readers where they are and bringing them along with stories, analogies, footnotes, and charm.

—*Amy Tobey, Senior Principal Engineer, Equinix*

Becoming SRE gets to the heart of why SRE is a critical role for production services, and how to develop the right SRE practices for your business.

—*Salim Virji*

Becoming SRE

*First Steps Toward Reliability
for You and Your Organization*

David N. Blank-Edelman

Beijing · Boston · Farnham · Sebastopol · Tokyo

Becoming SRE

by David N. Blank-Edelman

Published by O'Reilly Media, Inc., 1005 Gravenstein Highway North, Sebastopol, CA 95472.

O'Reilly books may be purchased for educational, business, or sales promotional use. Online editions are also available for most titles (*http://oreilly.com*). For more information, contact our corporate/institutional sales department: 800-998-9938 or *corporate@oreilly.com*.

Acquisitions Editor: John Devins	**Indexer:** WordCo Indexing Services, Inc.
Development Editor: Virginia Wilson	**Interior Designer:** David Futato
Production Editor: Clare Laylock	**Cover Designer:** Karen Montgomery
Copyeditor: nSight, Inc.	**Illustrator:** Kate Dullea
Proofreader: Doug McNair	

February 2024:   First Edition

Revision History for the First Edition

2024-02-12:   First Release

See *http://oreilly.com/catalog/errata.csp?isbn=9781492090557* for release details.

978-1-492-09055-7

[LSI]

Table of Contents

Part III.   Becoming SRE for the Organization

Preface

No one ever told us we had to study our lives,

make of our lives a study, as if learning natural history

or music, that we should begin

with the simple exercises first

and slowly go on trying

the hard ones, practicing till strength

and accuracy became one with the daring

to leap into transcendence, take the chance

of breaking down the wild arpeggio

or faulting the full sentence of the fugue.

—And in fact we can't live like that: we take on

everything at once before we've even begun

to read or mark time, we're forced to begin

in the midst of the hard movement,

the one already sounding as we are born.

> —Excerpt from "Transcendental Etude" by Adrienne Rich in
> *The Fact of a Doorframe: Poems Selected and New 1950–1984* (Norton, 1984)

Where Are You Right Now?

Hello, Dear Reader. I start this book with that particular excerpt from Adrienne Rich's poetry because it does a far better job than I could of acknowledging that you are coming to site reliability engineering (SRE) and this book with a particular and existing context already playing out. Perhaps you are in the midst of a reliability crisis at work, being asked to lead a team, in the midst of a career change, or entering a new career. I'm picturing you in the middle of the hard movement, and I promise to keep that in mind as we get started together with SRE.

You are currently reading a book primarily for people getting started with SRE in some capacity or another. You may have a ton of experience with adjacent operations practices, software development, or just plain IT, and that's great; we'll make use of all of that. But I don't make a lot of assumptions about your prior SRE knowledge.[1]

It has been a real gift over the last five-plus years to talk with many people who are right on the edge of a diving board, nervously peering over the edge as they prepare to jump into SRE. Sometimes I get to talk to people midflight who have just jumped and want to discuss what they should do when they encounter the water. Some are white-knuckled on the ladder, trying to decide if they should climb or climb higher than before. Others need help explaining to the rest of their organization the value of this whole process of getting better by diving, then climbing back up again, and then diving and climbing again. Some want to know how to judge a good dive. Some want to know if scuba divers could be repurposed to become a diving team (because they also have *dive* in the name). This metaphor is starting to groan under its own weight, but you get the idea.

I'm incredibly grateful to have been able to talk with each and every one of these people who shared their stories around SRE. Doing so allowed me to see firsthand that even with the splendidly growing amount of material on SRE available, there is still a great desire for information on how to get started with SRE. A surprisingly, even delightfully, high percentage of people I've talked to about SRE have read *Site Reliability Engineering: How Google Runs Production Systems*, edited by Betsy Beyer et al. (O'Reilly, 2016). Many have also read *The Site Reliability Workbook: Practical Ways to Implement SRE*, edited by Betsy Beyer et al. (O'Reilly, 2018). And gosh, some had even read my book *Seeking SRE: Conversations About Running Production Systems at Scale* (O'Reilly, 2018) before we talked. And yet, they still wanted to talk about how to get started.

Much of the material in those books makes assumptions about your knowledge or deeper understanding of modern operations practices. This book doesn't. This is why there is the crucial Part I, "Introduction to SRE" that you will want to read first.

Navigating This Book

This book is structured to address two separate but equally pressing questions: How do *I* (personally) get started? And how does *my organization* get started?

---

1 If you actually are an experienced SRE, shhh, don't tell anyone, but there's great stuff in this book for you, too, including advice on how to build a team or a culture around you. But let's keep this little secret between the two of us, OK?

There are three parts:

- Part I, "Introduction to SRE" (prerequisite for all that follows)
- Part II, "Becoming SRE for the Individual"
- Part III, "Becoming SRE for the Organization"

In my experience, there is some important common ground shared between the individual and the organizational SRE launchpads. And that's where we will start, with the information needed to get off the ground both as an individual and as a collective. For example, in both situations, you won't get very far if the people involved don't have a good grasp of the SRE mindset, so there's a whole chapter (Chapter 2) dedicated to just that topic.[2]

After we've covered this ground, you will have a choice of adventure: do you want to read about getting started as an individual or getting started as an organization first? You can read either Part II or III first, depending on your immediate interest. I would, however, counsel you to go back (or forward) to read the other part, just by virtue of the fact that individuals make up organizations and organizations take what individuals can do to the next level. The other part, whichever one is the "other" for you, will enrich your understanding of your initial part. To wrap things up and further welcome you to the SRE community, I'll throw in some wisdom from people who have been in the biz for a while.

We Are Going to Need a Bigger Boat

As mentioned earlier, there are now a number of really good books and other resources on SRE or with useful advice for SRE. I will not be attempting to rewrite them in an effort to make this a complete omnibus of SRE information. Even if I could convince my editor to allow me to write something many times beyond our agreed-upon page limit, it would do you no service if I paraphrased (less well) those works instead of just directing you to the original. The one thing I can do is to point you, compass-like, directly at the most useful references for learning more or diving deeper into a topic we have discussed—and that's what I will do.

So fair warning: this book will contain a metric ton of pointers to other books and resources (including, but not solely, from this publisher).

---

2 And if for some reason you are forced to read just one chapter in this book, then Chapter 2 is probably the one.

I'm Not the Lorax

While I'm in the mood to provide warnings and caveats, let me add this important one:

I'm not the Lorax.[3] I don't speak for the SREs.

Well, certainly not all of them.

This book contains my best efforts to represent SRE as I have learned about it from smart people. It contains opinions I have formed as the information filtered through my brain. You may disagree with those opinions or other material in this book. Nothing would make me happier than to hear that you engaged with the book to the point where you wanted to talk to me or someone else about the things you read that you disagree with. SRE should be a conversation, not a doctrine. Not all SRE implementations and interpretations look the same. This book is not the one true way to think about or talk about SRE (nothing is); it is just my best take. I look forward to hearing yours.

---

3 Dr. Seuss, *The Lorax*, Random House, 1971.

> ## This Book Is Full of Voices
>
> While the word *conversation* is still ringing in your ear, I have another last explanatory note that may be helpful to you as you read this book.
>
> You will find that I mention, quote, reference, and drop many names as we go. In the process of researching, writing, and reviewing this book, I spoke to lots of people. When they said something smart, I put it in the book and tried to give them credit by name. If you find yourself wondering, "Who are all of these people?" now you know.

Ready?

I hope I haven't scared you away yet, because we have sooooo much good stuff to talk about together. Sit down next to me and let's get started *Becoming SRE*.

Convention Used in This Book

The following typographical convention is used in this book:

Italic
    Indicates new terms, URLs, email addresses, filenames, and file extensions.

O'Reilly Online Learning

O'REILLY® For more than 40 years, *O'Reilly Media* has provided technology and business training, knowledge, and insight to help companies succeed.

Our unique network of experts and innovators share their knowledge and expertise through books, articles, and our online learning platform. O'Reilly's online learning platform gives you on-demand access to live training courses, in-depth learning paths, interactive coding environments, and a vast collection of text and video from O'Reilly and 200+ other publishers. For more information, visit *https://oreilly.com*.

How to Contact Us

Please address comments and questions concerning this book to the publisher:

O'Reilly Media, Inc.
1005 Gravenstein Highway North
Sebastopol, CA 95472
800-889-8969 (in the United States or Canada)
707-827-7019 (international or local)
707-829-0104 (fax)
support@oreilly.com
https://www.oreilly.com/about/contact.html

We have a web page for this book, where we list errata, examples, and any additional information. You can access this page at *https://oreil.ly/becoming-sre*.

For news and information about our books and courses, visit *https://oreilly.com*.

Find us on LinkedIn: *https://linkedin.com/company/oreilly-media*.

Follow us on Twitter: *https://twitter.com/oreillymedia*.

Watch us on YouTube: *https://youtube.com/oreillymedia*.

Acknowledgments

The word *Acknowledgments* is a little weak for me. Not only do I acknowledge, but I also greatly appreciate, respect, and hold in the highest regard the people mentioned in this section and their contributions to this book. I am honored and thrilled to be working with and learning from them.

This book would not have been possible or even half as good without:

- The people who contributed their ideas, hopes, and dreams on SRE in conversations during my research: Ben Lutch, Ben Purgason, Dave Rensin, John Reese, Joseph Bironas, Narayan Desai, Niall Murphy, Tanya Reilly, Tom Limoncelli, and the many other people in the SRE field who have shaped my thinking over the years.

- The crack team of tech reviewers: Amy Tobey, Celeste Stinger, Jess Males, Kurt Andersen, Niall Murphy, Patrick Cable, and Richard Clawson.

- My editors (in order of their contact with the book): John Devins, Virginia Wilson,[4] Clare Laylock, and Carol Keller.

- The illustrators and graphic design magicians for the book cover and figures in this book: Kate Dullea and Karen Montgomery.

- My family, who have somehow figured out how to be both patient and supportive of me as I wander in the desert of yet another book project. Love you dearly.

- You, the reader. Authors ain't nothin' without you.

Coping

Looking back at each of my past books, I realize that I have always included a little note about what allowed me to cope (mbira, yoga, etc.) during that time/project and the people who helped me do that thing. I think it is about time I give coping its own due. This time the book writing was easy, but the world was hard. Really hard. For everyone. But I don't have to tell you. What helped me then and what continues to help me now—as banal as it sounds—is bread baking (both at home and professionally). Who would have thought bringing together flour, water, salt, and a starter could be so healing? For this book I have to thank Earnest and Junior, the two bakers who welcomed me into a bakery at 4:30 a.m. and patiently helped me chase my sourdough dreams.

---

4 I sincerely hope she doesn't edit this out because she is humble to a fault, but Virginia, my development editor, is the bestest. Virginia's the person I worked most closely with on this text; she is a really fabulous editor and, well, the bestest.

Introduction to SRE

First Things First

Welcome to the book! Let's level set about what site reliability engineering (SRE) is and where it comes from.

What Is SRE?

There are a number of definitions for *site reliability engineering* you can find in the world. Here is the best one I have been able to construct over the years:

> Site reliability engineering is an engineering discipline devoted to helping organizations sustainably achieve the appropriate level of reliability in their systems, services, and products.

If I am presenting this definition to an audience, I usually say that there are at least three words in that definition whose presence, if understood correctly, will lead you to a decent grasp of SRE. If given the chance, I will ask that audience, "Which three words do you think are the most important in this definition?" Please feel free to pause here and reread the definition above and answer that question for yourself before you read any further.

I ask this question not just because I like audience interaction, but also because it offers diagnostic insight into the crowd itself. In Chapter 4, I will go deeper into what you can learn from this diagnostic. But in the meantime, let's look at the three words I would choose first if asked this question.

Reliability

Pretty easy first guess, right? Reliability is central to everything we do in SRE (heck, it's right in the name). One way to stress the importance of reliability is to note that an organization can spend millions in the local currency to build the best software with the spiffiest features, hire a great sales team to sell it, staff up a crack team of support people to support it, and so on, but if the software isn't up when a customer attempts to use it, all of that money and effort goes in the trash (or down the toilet, whichever metaphor is more striking to you).

When you have issues with reliability, your organization can suffer a loss of:

Revenue
> This is especially true if the system that is down is critical for making money.

Time
> Employees are dealing with an outage instead of planned work.

Reputation
> People won't want to use a service they find flaky and will happily switch to a competitor.

Health
> If your environment is constantly on fire, if on-call people are regularly woken up, if your staff always has to spend their time on work instead of their friends or family, there can be serious impact on health.

Hiring
> People in this industry talk to each other. If it gets around that your workplace is one big "tire fire," it will be very difficult to hire new people.

Appropriate

I believe one key idea that SRE either introduced or highlighted in the operations discussion is the notion that only in the rarest situations is 100% reliable a desirable or even possible goal. It's not possible in many cases because, in this interconnected world, chances are very high that your dependencies aren't 100% reliable. Being more reliable than your dependencies can sometimes be achieved through clever planning and coding, but not always.

SRE focuses instead on practices like service level indicators/service level objectives (SLIs/SLOs),[1] to help you determine, communicate, and work toward an appropriate level of reliability in your systems.

---

1 I highly recommend that you seek out Alex Hidalgo's book *Implementing Service Level Objectives: A Practical Guide to SLIs, SLOs, and Error Budgets* (O'Reilly, 2020) on the topic.

Sustainable

This word entered the definition later than the rest when it became clear that in order for an operations practice to be successful, it had to be sustainable. Sustainability harkens back to the "loss of health" issue with reliability. Reliable systems are built by people. If the people in your organization are burnt out, exhausted, unable to connect with the people in their lives outside of work or engage in self-care, they won't be able to build reliable systems. Many people learn this the hard way; please don't be one of them if you can help it.

(Other Words)

There are a few other words from this definition that I will just mention here to foreshadow our upcoming discussion in Chapter 4: *engineering*, *discipline*, *helping*, and *organization*. See you in that chapter soon!

Origin Story

While I believe it is useful to know about the origin of SRE and how it came into being at Google (roughly in the 2003 timeframe), that's not my story to tell. Ben Treynor Sloss, the progenitor of SRE, provides his official version in *Site Reliability Engineering* (also referred to as the *SRE book*), edited by Betsy Beyer et al. (O'Reilly, 2016).

Instead, I'd like to tell you about the first time I began to really understand the topic because it may help you too. It connects with the Google origin story because it happened to be the time Treynor Sloss explained his understanding of SRE to the first public gathering devoted to the topic. I'm a big believer that the stories we tell ourselves are crucial for understanding our identity, so this was a pretty big moment.

On May 31, 2014, in Santa Clara, California, I watched Treynor Sloss give the keynote address called "Keys to SRE" (*https://oreil.ly/cSXef*) at the very first SREcon.[2] I recommend you watch it too.

---

2 Full disclosure—I'm one of the cofounders of SREcon.

In that talk he showed a single slide that jump-started my understanding of SRE. Figure 1-1 shows a snapshot of the slide.

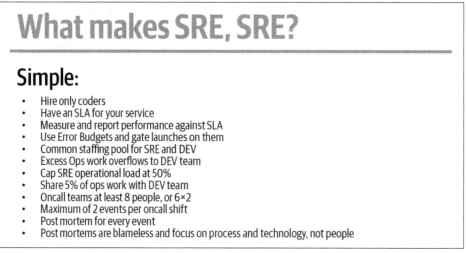

Figure 1-1. A slide from Ben Treynor Sloss' keynote address at SREcon14, used with permission

Figure 1-1 is the list I started with and is still a great place for anyone to start.

Looking back at this slide now, nine years later as of this writing, I'm struck by how many of these items have held up over time and which things seem to depend on the Google context in which they were born. Since this talk was given, there's been quite a bit of nuance added (one might say at least three books' worth; see the SRE resources in Appendix C), which is perhaps a really good reason why you are reading this book too.

SRE and Its Relationship to DevOps

Whenever I talk to people who are trying to get their head around site reliability engineering, I can almost guarantee that the discussion at some point will find its way to questions like these: How do DevOps and SRE compare? What's the relationship between them? And would it be reasonable to have both at the same company? These are nontrivial questions that I have spent years trying to find satisfying answers to. This is why I decided to crowdsource Chapter 12 of *Seeking SRE* on this topic. I didn't have a great answer at that point, and I really hoped someone else would.[3]

---

3 One of my favorite answers was from Michael Doherty, who said, "Site Reliability Engineering: we don't know what DevOps is, but we know we're something slightly different." It's not one of the official answers above, but I can't argue with it.

With the help of the responses from that chapter and some subsequent soul-searching and research, I finally came to an answer I liked. Once I realized that it was going to take more than one approach to really answer these questions, I was able to construct a multipart explanation that works for me. I hope it does the same for you. Allow me to lay out all three parts with a little bit of commentary on each.

Part 1: SRE Implements Class DevOps

This comes from Chapter 1 of *The Site Reliability Workbook* (O'Reilly, 2018) and subsequent messaging from Google. For the nonprogrammers reading this, it is meant to say that SRE is one implementation[4] of the general DevOps philosophy. This is not my favorite comparison for a few reasons:

- Nonprogrammers can't quite understand the phrasing or nuances in it.
- I don't think I know of another implementation of DevOps beyond the "default" one that evolved over time and practice in the wild, so that seems a little suspicious.
- It implies a historical connection back in the mists of time at SRE's origin (or at least a dual discovery) that I haven't seen evidence to support.
- I'm still not sure if I buy it.

The reason I keep this idea about SRE and DevOps around (besides that it comes from people smarter than me) is it does capture the similarities, or at least the resonant frequencies, that are shared by the two modern operations practices.

Part 2: SRE Is to Reliability as DevOps Is to Delivery

So, I don't know about you, but periodically I have a crisis of faith around DevOps. This particular time I had realized that I could not find a description of DevOps or DevOps practices that would help me immediately be able to distinguish it from other operations practices in the world. I wanted words that would immediately differentiate it from anything else so that I could unambiguously pick it out of a lineup ("#3, that's DevOps! I'd know it anywhere!"). I looked over all of my resources and my hand-curated collection of DevOps acronyms, but still didn't succeed.

---

4 In particular, it's a prescriptive one since DevOps has, in many ways, gone out of its way to avoid dictating any specific methodology or tools. Whether it has succeeded in doing so might be another fun conversation to have.

For SRE, I could say, "SRE is about reliability." If someone asked, "What's the operations practice that focuses on reliability?" the easy answer would be SRE. This led me on a quest to ask the DevOps luminaries, "If SRE is about reliability, what is the one word for DevOps?"

I went from luminary to luminary (all of whom were very nice), carrying my lantern, until finally I received an answer from Donovan Brown that felt good. For him, DevOps was all about *delivery*. Delivering value to customers, delivering software, etc. Finally, I had the word I was looking for.

SRE is to reliability, as DevOps is to delivery.

I can live with that.

Part 3: It's All About the Direction of Attention

This final piece of the puzzle comes from my friend Tom Limoncelli, who was kind enough to submit this as an answer to my call for submissions for the *Seeking SRE* crowdsourced chapter I mentioned earlier. Figure 1-2 is a picture from that chapter (modified from the original at his request).

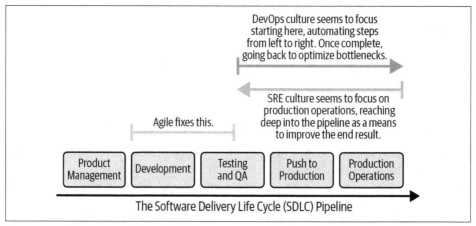

Figure 1-2. The Limoncelli model of SRE, DevOps, and Agile strategies. Modified from the original in Seeking SRE *(O'Reilly, 2018).*

In some ways, I like this model best because it explains a number of overlaps in practice between DevOps and SRE that seem to not overlap in attitude or intent. I'll give examples of this in a moment, but here's my best summary of Tom's theory:

1. The DevOps story begins with a developer typing code into a laptop. DevOps concerns itself with (among other things) what it is going to take to deliver that code to production so customers can reap the most value from it. The direction of attention is from laptop to production.[5] You might surmise this is one reason why continuous integration and continuous delivery (CI/CD) systems have such a prominent place in the DevOps tool chest, skill set, and presence in hiring ads.

2. SRE starts in a different place. It starts (and indeed, the SRE mindspace resides) in production. What does an SRE have to do to create a reliable production environment? Answering that question involves a gaze that looks "backward" from production, asking this question step by step, until the developer's laptop is reached.

3. The direction of attention is different. The same tools might be used (for example, a CI/CD pipeline), but for a different reason. DevOps and SRE will both engage heavily in creating a monitoring system, but they might do it for a different reason.[6]

And this leads us to the answer to the question above: Can/should SRE and DevOps cohabitate at the same organization? For me, the answer is yes.[7] While there might be some overlap in tooling and sometimes skills, they focus on different things and provide different benefits to an organization.

Onward to SRE Fundamentals

Now, if someone asks you, "So, what's SRE?" you have the building blocks to tell them. I'll have lots more to say about this in Chapter 4. But now that we've talked a little about SRE definitions and history, let's move forward to some actual SRE fundamentals that will be core to our understanding of the topic and the rest of this book.

---

5 With stops along the way to store it in a repository, and tests to make sure it is safe to deploy it so that customers can start reaping value from it.

6 I've never seen this studied, but my instinct suggests that they would monitor different things as a result. This would be a fun thing to research.

7 Well, given suitable conditions like org size (a new startup may not need both), company culture (if SRE fits in; see later in this book), and need (hire for what you need, not to collect them all).

CHAPTER 2

SRE Mindset

It starts with curiosity.

How does a system work? How does it fail?

For SRE, the primary question is not, "How is it supposed to work?" but rather, "How does it *really* work? How does it really work in *production*?"

Here's a little example scenario: your frontend talks to a database. But what happens when it can't? What happens when multiple instances that shouldn't be running talk to that database at the same time? What if the database responds 20%…34%…60% slower than it did when the code was (presumably) tested? How does the code know it is talking to the right database? What are the implicit dependencies? I could fill this entire chapter with nothing but questions like these because understanding how a system really works is an exercise in intense curiosity.

In this chapter, I am going to explore a fundamental question on which much of this book turns: What is the SRE mindset? What are the qualities that define it, how does it differ from other mindsets, how do we begin to think in this direction, and so on?

This is an easy question to ask but a hard one to answer, so I reached out to a sizable group of some of the smartest SREs I know to get their take on the subject (and the SRE culture topic we will discuss in Chapter 3). I've included their answers with my own but attributed their responses as appropriate, so you will find this chapter cites other people more than usual (to give credit where credit is due).

The SRE mindset is going to be foundational to the rest of the book, so you will see a fair amount of foreshadowing in this chapter.

Understanding a System as a System (the Question)

In talking with Dave Rensin about this, he posed the following scenario:

Imagine Pat is walking into the data center and trips over a power cable. (Oscar left the cable on the floor while racking and testing a new server.) The cable unplugs and the server loses power.

When the server loses power, the database server instance (provisioned to run on that server by the automation/orchestration that Susan set up) goes down. This database server held an important shard of the data for the application; the sharding was configured by Yasmin.

The backend for the application (written by Neeraj) slowly starts to lock up as threads busy-wait trying to reach the data they need to continue processing. The response time of Sarah's frontend for the application begins to get slower and slower as connections to the backend hang and then time out. The monitoring system (set up by Liz) notices there is a problem at this point and sends out an alert to all the members of the team, but that alert is delayed in reaching some of them. Finally, the load balancer (configured by Sam) just starts handing out error 500s like candy.

A customer trying to purchase a widget on the website gives up in frustration and purchases it from a competitor.

Question. Who is responsible for this outage (and loss of a sale)?

So, who is responsible for this loss of business? Think about this question and talk amongst yourselves. Dave's answer is in the sidebar "Understanding a System as a System (the Answer)" on page 15.

Zooming Out to Maintain a Systems Perspective

The set of questions at the beginning of this chapter about a database connection could be a little misleading because I started with the camera in our mind's eye zoomed in very close. Focusing on the minutiae of a database connection can be worthwhile, but when I say, "How does a system work?" I am also referring to:

- The entire application, with its development and deployment processes
- The entire service, which includes that application code plus the ancillary automated or sidecar processes (e.g., log collectors or cleanup scripts)
- The service and the infrastructure it runs on
- The physical overlay for the infrastructure (running in how many areas around the globe?) and the connections between these pieces

- The sociotechnical context in which the service and the infrastructure run
- The organizational context that this sociotechnical context resides in

All of these things and more are taken into account when I say that the SRE mindset has a systems focus.

The SRE mindset is concerned with the big picture and the little picture. When we are trying to understand how a system works, we are frequently zooming in to the micro level and out for the wide macro shot. We will follow the problem at whatever level of detail is necessary.

Creating and Nurturing Feedback Loops

I will develop this idea in considerably more detail in the upcoming chapters (e.g., in Chapters 10 and 15), but this subject deserves to be mentioned early. The SRE mindset is firmly rooted in the notion that reliability is improved through feedback loops. It is our role as SREs to create and nurture these feedback loops whenever we can. Someone with an SRE mindset is always on the lookout for places where there is potential to create or support this iterative movement toward reliability.

Keeping the Focus on the Customer

How does a system work? How does it fail?

Answering these questions from a perspective that considers many different scopes that compose "a system" is important, but there's another crucial axis we have to discuss to properly describe the SRE mindset: How does a system work...*for the customer*? How does it fail...*for the customer*?

You will see this discussed all throughout this book, but let's take a moment to be extra, extra explicit about this point. While I haven't met an SRE who wasn't interested in how systems and technologies work or fail in the abstract, the people I've found who've had the most impact are those who are most curious about the impact on the customer.[1] They are always probing how the customer will perceive something and how the system is meeting the customer's expectations.

When I teach people about SLIs and SLOs, I always start with the exhortation that "reliability is measured from the customer's perspective, not the component perspective." To drive this home, I run people through the following thought experiment:

---

1 *Customer* in this context is broadly defined. Could be external, could be internal, could be another service that calls yours. As the old blues standard goes, "we all gotta serve somebody."

Imagine you have provisioned 100 web servers to act as the frontend pool for the service you run. Sometime later, when the service is in production, there is an issue in the data center. Perhaps there is a power issue, or maybe the wrong firmware was automatically installed, and 14 of these servers burst into flames (metaphorically) and no longer work. Now you have 86 working servers and 14 dead servers.

Here's the quiz. Keeping in mind that there are 86 working servers and 14 in a failed state, this situation is:

A. No big deal; you can deal with it at your leisure.

B. Something that warrants your immediate attention; you should stop what you are doing and tend to it.

C. An existential crisis; even if it is 2 a.m., you should scramble everyone including the C-level executives until it is resolved.

Take a moment to think about this before you continue reading. I've given this quiz to countless numbers of people over the years, so I have a pretty good guess as to which answer you will choose on average. If you are one of those people who has seen this quiz already, try asking a colleague. If you do find yourself in an audience where I ask this, be sure not to give away the answer—just pause and watch how others mull over the question and respond.[2]

The answer? *It depends*. If the system has been engineered such that no customers have noticed a problem, the answer could very well be A. If there is a degradation in service visible to customers, very likely B. If things have been built such that the service is dead in the water and there is an interruption in revenue at a key time, you bet you might be waking up the CEO at home.

After you get over any residual irritation from being asked a bit of a trick question, I'd like you to consider that the information I gave you was factually correct (86 servers up, 14 servers down). It is almost certainly the information you would have received from your monitoring system first. An SRE mindset, which is focused on how the system works for the customer, leads you to the correct answer of *it depends*.[3] When I talked about this scenario with John Reese for this chapter, he noted that SREs are always trying to ascertain "What is the intention of the system from the customer's perspective?"

---

2 In Chapter 4, we will explore ways to talk to people about SRE who are not familiar with it. In that chapter, I note that how people parse my definition of SRE can often be diagnostic. Observing how other people think through this quiz is also often similarly useful in telling you something about their working environment and experiences.

3 It also leads us to make sure our monitoring system is watching for and clearly representing problems from the customer's perspective.

Understanding a System as a System (the Answer)

In the sidebar "Understanding a System as a System (the Question)" on page 12, I laid out a scenario from Dave Rensin that asked this question: Who is responsible for this outage (and loss of a sale)?

Answer: the system.

That's right, pointing at a named individual doesn't get you a better understanding of the issue or a place to address the outage. This scenario illustrates pretty clearly why a crucial component of the SRE mindset is systems thinking.

Now, I know some readers are going to balk at how forced or contrived this example is. *It's never everyone's and no one's fault at the same time.* You are partially right; it is contrived.

But for fun, I encourage you to put this book down and look at the public details for the Microsoft outage in their South Central US region in 2018 (one of their worst). The official report has rolled off their status page, but a news report on the outage (*https://oreil.ly/_ceV4*) and an official developer blog entry (*https://oreil.ly/h3kPD*) gives most of the salient details.

As described in Microsoft's public announcements, weather systems in the area led to issues with power that led to issues with data center cooling. Those issues caused hardware issues that took out servers and then services, which had unexpected cascading impact to core services outside of the region. Many, many services and clients were impacted (for example, the outage triggered bugs in Outlook client retry logic, which didn't help).

Just reading the report they published at the time will make you wince over and over again. Many of the individual components in the story were operating exactly as they were designed to, yet systems as a whole were falling over.

The natural next step is to contemplate the causal chain(s) for this outage and what Microsoft should do to address them. Was the issue the bad weather in San Antonio that took down so many services worldwide? Was it issues with a data center cooling system that caused Outlook clients to begin to DDoS the messaging servers? A pathologically reductionist view might lead you to conclude this was all an HVAC problem, and all of Microsoft should have spent the rest of 2018 working on HVAC to prevent this from happening again. But that sounds ridiculous, right?

At a certain point, you are likely to come to the same conclusion about responsibility as I gave for the example in these sidebars: it's the system.

Relationships (to People and Things)

I've just floated the idea that the SRE mindset is defined by a certain relationship with our customers. In many ways, we can be defined by the relationships we have in this life. To that end I'd like to point out a few other key relationships for SRE.

SRE's Relationship to (Other) People

The first is relatively simple and quick to state: SREs are relentlessly collaborative. We know reliability as it manifests in the real world is a collaborative endeavor. We can't do what we do without working shoulder to shoulder with the wide variety of colleagues in the orbit of the systems we care for. For someone demonstrating the SRE mindset, collaboration is the default.

A more advanced variation of this idea that I'd encourage you to ponder: we also collaborate *with our customers* on reliability.[4]

A related aside on collaboration that ties to a recurring theme in this chapter: in addition to our strong ethical and values-based rationale for craving collaboration with a diverse and inclusive set of people, the SRE mindset also recognizes that it provides the best data and results. SREs are always in search of good data that can help their reliability efforts.

Welcome to Our Neurodivergent Colleagues!

The topic of diversity and inclusion as it relates to SRE is a rich one (it came up a number of times in *Seeking SRE*, but I would love to see a more extensive treatment). One aspect of this that came as a surprise to me when researching this chapter involves cognitive diversity.

With no prompting or prior indication, three separate people mentioned to me the compatibility between neurodiversity—especially around ADHD—and SRE. It was suggested that both the work was well suited to people with ADHD and that people with ADHD were some of the best at this work.

I bring this up for one reason: if you are part of the neurodivergent community and are contemplating entering site reliability engineering, welcome!

---

4 There's a hint of a Zen koan in this statement. Meditating on "how can I collaborate more with my customers on reliability?" will lead you to some very interesting places.

SRE's Relationship to Failure and Errors

One idea that helps differentiate the SRE mindset from other mindsets is our relationship to failure and errors in general. Let's discuss each in turn.

All throughout this book, you will find an implicit attitude toward failures that I want to make explicit here. It's not that we welcome failure to the point where we are overjoyed by outages and want to cause them ourselves,[5] but remember this: *How does a system work? How does it fail?*

The SRE mindset is different from most other mindsets in that it treats failure as an opportunity to learn. Learning from failure is a core component of the SRE mindset and as such has an entire chapter devoted to it (Chapter 10).

SRE has a relationship to errors (especially transient errors) that I have not seen elsewhere. In most other contexts, especially previous operations contexts, errors are something to be stamped out—to be eliminated entirely—at every turn. Most people want their systems to be error-free and will set that as an explicit goal (even if they will never achieve it). SRE treats errors as *signal*, and we *like* clear signals. Real data can help us focus our attention.

Let me tell you a story to illustrate this point. Many moons ago at an SREcon conference, I was sitting in a sunny courtyard eating breakfast with John Looney before the sessions began. Someone I had never met joined our table, and we made introductions. We started chatting about the things we were working on. This new person, whose name and affiliation have been lost in the mists of time, was describing a new CI/CD platform for software deployment that he and his team had been building and were in the final stages of putting into place. It sounded pretty snazzy. As I recall, he was particularly proud of the features they had included to help reduce and, ideally, entirely remove the errors that would be deployed to production.

Shortly after this, he had to leave early to get to a session, so John Looney and I sat quietly together in the sun sipping our hot beverages. As best I recall, John said something like "Hmm, if I were building this, I'd let some errors get through. I'd want to know what was going wrong or what would go wrong with my service." This comment stuck with me, and every once in a while, I'd think about it. It was several years later when I finally understood what he meant and how this reflected a different relationship to errors than I had ever considered.

---

5 Chaos engineering, <cough, cough>.

Without thinking about it,[6] John had demonstrated that, to an SRE, errors aren't necessarily the adversary. He wasn't saying, "Errors are great; let's make more of them!" He was acknowledging that errors were already, and always would be, present in the system. With an SRE mindset, errors can serve the larger purpose of helping us understand that system.[7] This requires "surfacing" the errors in addition to any efforts to eliminate them. Again: *How does a system work? How does it fail?*

There are a few other aspects of an SRE mindset that are buried more deeply in this story. One key aspect is that of *ownership*. A distinguishing facet of the SRE mindset is the strong sense of ownership SREs have over the services they run. They will go to all edges of the system or wherever else it takes them in pursuit of a problem or an understanding.[8] This isn't to suggest that others don't feel a sense of ownership, just that SREs will automatically scope as wide as they need to in order to care for their systems. "Not my code, so not my problem" is seldom heard from SREs. If there is a problem with a service, it is *their problem*—their puzzle to solve—and they will pursue it wherever it takes them.

Welcome to the Barbershop (Yak Shaving)

I feel somewhat compelled to mention the downsides of the SRE mindset when applicable. SREs can be prone to yak shaving. If you haven't heard this term before, I'm delighted to introduce it to you.

Yak shaving refers to situations that go something like this: you have a task to perform that requires installing a piece of software. Doesn't matter what software, it can be anything you need for a specific task.

In order to install that software, you need to upgrade a shared library on that machine.

You discover this necessitates upgrading the OS.

The new version of the OS requires a bigger system disk, so you first have to clear some space in the storage area that holds your disk images.

---

6 You may be amused to hear that some number of years later, I went back to John to discuss this conversation and what I had learned from it. He had no recollection of it at all. Just goes to show you that some of our best teachers do it without thinking. Be sure to spend time with people like that.

7 When I brought this story up to Narayan Desai while discussing this book, he said (paraphrased) "Oh, yeah, in some ways errors are just a social construct." Gosh, I love SREs.

8 John Reese reminded me of the SRE adage of "no haunted graveyards." A poorly understood system can have issues buried in it that will come out and haunt you at the worst of times. SREs will work hard to exorcise them. This adage also highlights the difference between diagnosis and mitigation. Narayan Desai notes that SREs are "less likely to whack it with a pipe wrench until the errors stop."

In the process of upgrading the OS, you discover there is a mandatory upgrade to the organization's provisioning software, so you handle that first.

Unfortunately, that new version doesn't play nice with your current virtual network configuration, so you need to address that before your upgraded machine will boot.

But that requires…

And so on and so on until at some point, you look down at your hand and see you are holding an electric trimmer. You look up and see you are standing in front of a yak. You are about to shave a yak, and while you know you had a perfectly good reason to be doing this, you can barely remember how you got here. This is yak shaving.

My little yak-shaving story[9] was a bit on-prem-y and small in scope, but I guarantee you that it would be easy to tell a similar one about cloud resources or systems at scale. The SRE mindset around ownership and chasing a problem no matter where it leads also means that sometimes we are prone to spending quality beauty care time with a yak. Over time you get better at deciding when yak shaving is important and when it isn't.

One side effect of this aspect of the SRE mindset is that SREs tend to be generalists by nature (Narayan Desai calls them "a hedge against specialization"). This isn't to say that SREs don't go really deep into a specific area or specialize on a topic, as, say, storage SREs will tell you. Pursuit of "how does a system work" often calls for a generalist. Reliability is an emergent property of a system. Working with emergent properties (security is another one) involves meeting the challenge wherever and whenever it presents itself.

The Mindset in Motion

A chapter about the SRE mindset would be incomplete without some discussion of how the basic questions evolve as you get further into SRE, so let's look at that topic together as a way of drawing this chapter to a close. Here are some future-looking variations of our basic questions:

How does a system work? → How will the system work if we scale it?
Helping services to scale is a core strength of SRE, but it doesn't necessarily start there. I usually suggest people engage with smaller systems before they work their way up.

---

9 It occurs to me that there is an echo here from the previous sidebars in this chapter about tripping over a power cord in a data center. Hmm…

How does a system work? → How can the system work with less operational load?
This is where the topic of "toil" comes into play—be sure to read Chapter 5 by Vivek Rau, in *Site Reliability Engineering* (O'Reilly, 2016). As Dave Rensin says, SREs are angered by toil and the almost allergic reaction it provokes in them. They will identify it and seek to reduce it as much as possible in the systems they encounter.

How does a system work? → How can the system work reliably for more people?
This question touches on a theme that multiple people expressed to me when discussing the SRE mindset for this chapter, each from a different angle. Tanya Reilly talked about "SRE and empathy," Joseph Bironas said "make the world a better place and take people along with you," and John Reese mentioned "lowering boundaries." SREs deeply care about making things better, both for the people who contribute to a production environment and for those who consume something from it.

Similar to the book *Grover and The Everything in the Whole Wide World Museum* by Norman Stiles et al. (Random House, 1972), there are so many examples behind this door that I am hesitant to start listing them lest they become an entire chapter. Here are a paltry few examples of things SREs will put in place to make things better for the people involved:

- For people who create things that go *to* production: better release tools (self-service) for developers, SRE-managed monitoring libraries that make it easy to send observability data to the central monitoring system, easy-to-use documentation tools that work even when nothing else does, and easier onboarding

- For people who consume things *from* production: content delivery network (CDN) setups that provide a good experience far from the "home" or "standard" service geo region, building accessibility testing tools into the CI/CD process, privacy engineering work, and making sure a service can "degrade gracefully" if it needs to

How does it fail? → How does the system fail when the service/product succeeds?
Success can be as much of a threat to the reliability of a system as an inadvertent defect. Customers can't tell the difference between your website being completely down because of a bug or because it had insufficient capacity to handle the load being thrown at it.

How does it fail? → When will it cease to work as needed?

Dave Rensin also points out that at some point, every system will outlive its suitability. SREs pay attention to that runway and are thinking about how to replace it (ideally, with something better) before that runway runs out. This is another form of failure in answer to the question "How will it fail?" that doesn't get talked about nearly as much as errors and outages.

There are a few things we can learn from the (admittedly incomplete) list above. First, the SRE mindset is in it for the long game. Second, everything we've touched on in this chapter has layers and levels that advance and evolve. If any of this has made you curious (see what I did there?), join me for the rest of this book.

CHAPTER 3

SRE Culture

The hardest thing about writing a chapter on SRE culture is that everyone and no one knows what *culture* is. It is one of those "squishy" words that we understand in context, but defining it can be difficult.[1] The second-hardest thing about writing a chapter on SRE culture is being able to clearly differentiate between "SRE culture" and any other kind of culture so that you can say, "Yes, this is specific to SRE culture; I can tell this is SRE culture and not something else."[2] The third-hardest thing about writing a chapter on SRE culture is being able to express why you should care about this topic at all.

But those are all my problems, not yours, and this book is about your problems (though if you care about culture in your organization, you have the same problems). The good news is we can tackle both together. To do so, let's start addressing each of these challenges, albeit in reverse order. First up: why SRE culture matters.

Happy Fish, um, People

Why should you care about SRE culture? Because the only way for the SREs on your team to thrive is if you understand and foster the sort of environment that SREs require. When you have (or desire) a nascent or aspirational SRE team, you have the same sort of concerns you might have caring for some new tropical fish. You want to

---

1 I'm fond of the definition in sociologist Dr. Ron Westrum's article "A Typology of Organisational Cultures" (*https://oreil.ly/5e3HR*) (*BMJ Journals*, Vol. 13). He defines *culture* as "the organization's pattern of response to the problems and opportunities it encounters," but that is a deeper insight than the colloquial understanding of the word. Most people think of *culture* in terms of shared behaviors and values in an organization.

2 SRE culture versus DevOps or sysadmin culture would be a considerably more challenging ask.

know what they eat, how warm their water should be, what else should be in their tank, and how big of a tank they need to thrive.[3]

Ask yourself: what conditions and environment, that is, what culture, is most likely to lead to happy SREs? This question is important both for organizations and individuals to be constantly asking.[4]

How to Create a Supportive Culture for SRE

Rather than pretending that there is a complicated formula or patented process available to create a supportive culture for SRE, here's a (perhaps overly simplistic) start: reread Chapter 2 on the SRE mindset. After each section, see if you can come up with one or two conditions or preconditions for supporting each aspect of the mindset. That advice may seem like "culture left as an exercise to the reader," but there is an important reason for that. I believe culture is *highly* situational and org specific. It is the very act of you reviewing those aspects and applying them to your local conditions that will give any value at all to what I have to say here. But so it doesn't seem like I am leaving you stranded, let's take a look at a hypothetical example to get you started.

In Chapter 2 (with lots more details to come in Chapter 9), we talked about how SREs have an almost physical aversion to toil and as a result will work every reasonable chance they get to eliminate it. A healthy SRE culture supports this by:

- Giving SREs the opportunity to eliminate toil when they see it as an explicit goal when planning work. Encourage people to scratch this itch.
- Celebrating the elimination of toil internally (Toil Hunter-of-the-Month Club awards?) and externally. You definitely want to report these wins to management and the rest of the org explicitly in whatever your regular "here's what SRE has been doing" communication[5] consists of.

---

3 Pretty good analogy, no? I bet you have other questions you might add to this list to extend it.

4 We usually think of culture as an organizational concern, but it's not uncommon to have a new SRE implementation consisting of a single person or a handful of people. In those cases, the development of the culture intentionally or unintentionally falls on those individuals, so they care about this question too.

5 Don't have one? Put this book down and start writing one with the goal of sending it first thing next week to your management chain and as much of the org as would be appropriate. Get into a rhythm of sending it regularly. Trust me on this one.

- Investigating or writing toil-elimination tools. If you are in an org that allows for the adoption of third-party tools (open source, etc.), set aside time for investigating and discussing tools in the ecosystem that might help eliminate a class of toil. For example, you might locate a tool or a framework that would make self-service or automated changes possible for a system you run. If your org has rules or an ethos of "must be invented here," then work toward building similar tools to address multiple sources of toil at once.

The previous example is written from an organizational perspective, but the same basic idea works from an individual perspective as well. Let's say there aren't "SRE teams" to plan for; there is just you, or maybe you and a colleague, starting out doing SRE work. In those cases—often and ideally—you have some capacity to choose what to work on. My suggestion is to build some time into your schedule to explicitly address some aspect of toil in your environment.

And after you do so and have even a small win, don't hesitate to crow about it to your management chain and others in the org. I know that there are some readers who visibly cringed when they read "crow about it." Many of us prefer to work quietly in the background, making things better rather than communicating broadly about the work we have done. As one of those people, I totally get it. That being said, I have also learned that if we don't make (our) work visible, no one else will. That visibility can have a significant impact on the success of your nascent SRE efforts.

This is more than just a suggestion on how to pass your time at work. Establishing a specific focus on toil elimination early on[6] does several things to lay the groundwork for SRE culture. It also ensures you will devote time to something you enjoy doing— which is crucial to making the hard work you have ahead of you sustainable. It sets up an intentionality, which is going to be important going forward.

---

6 Kurt Andersen, a reviewer of this book, makes the point that it is important to have management support for this work to have unbreachable boundaries, regardless of other priorities that might attempt to intrude upon the team/individual.

> ## Fish Food
>
> In Chapter 2 I noted the generalist aspect of SRE and the sort of brains it attracts. It's a little difficult to determine the causal direction (Do people whose brains work a certain way gravitate toward generalist work? Or does generalist work bring out a particular way of thinking?) but the end result either way is a set of cultural imperatives necessary to keep SREs happy—arguably the most important of which is this:
>
> *Any SRE culture you create (intentionally or unintentionally) has to support curiosity.*[7]
>
> I would also argue, again because of that brain thing, that an SRE culture should provide a certain level of novelty to maintain interest. That imperative doesn't get its own bulleted list because if you pay sufficient attention to curiosity, this property of novelty will naturally emerge.

Culture as a Vehicle or a Lever

The second reason for caring about culture is admittedly a bit more utilitarian than the first one of "keep SREs happy." The term Joseph Bironas used in a conversation we had was *vehicle*, where we are using culture as a means of transportation to get our organization—or even us as individuals—to where we want to go. There's some subtlety in this suggestion, so let me make sure the idea is clear. We know that the actual work of SREs in an organization can help improve things (like reliability) for that organization. The suggestion here is that on top of this, if we nurture the right SRE culture, it will also have a positive impact on the organization. It is another lever we can use to move the world.

I realize this (and quite frankly almost everything about *culture*) is kind of abstract, so let's pick a super-simple example to explore this idea. One aspect of our systems that doesn't get enough attention is documentation. Every SRE I know has at least one story about documentation and how its absence or skew from reality impacted the reliability of some system. If you are a connoisseur of postincident reviews, you know how often documentation (and the lack thereof) plays a role in outages.[8]

---

7 I am prepared to defend the statement "Sustained reliability depends on curiosity" and the ramifications it has on SRE.

8 You usually find it mentioned explicitly in the more candid, often internal, postincident reviews ("We lacked documentation on..."). Over time, you'll find you develop an eye for spotting the implicit or glaringly absent cases too ("Hmm, you would think that would have been documented...").

SREs know the presence or absence of documentation can make a significant difference at many decision points during the running of a service. This knowledge gets translated into a cultural imperative[9] sometimes stated as "it isn't done until it is documented." When you have SREs or SRE teams within an organization that think and behave this way with everything they touch—especially by modeling this value—it can have a profound influence on the rest of the organization, trending it toward more and better documentation. Here, we see SRE culture has helped move the organization (like a vehicle or a lever) in the right direction.

Your First Tasks

Back in my pre-SRE days when I was running the systems group for a computer science department at a university, I would give my new student hires two tasks as their first projects:

1. Find something in our online documentation that was missing, unclear, or in some way needing improvement, and make it better.

2. I would gleefully announce, "Good news, it is map day!" Map day consisted of taking our online database of all the machines on our network (both on desks and in the server room) and making sure it was correct by visiting all of the locations in our building and cross-checking it with reality. This was usually done by a pair of new student hires over the period of a week (so it was not exactly map "day," but no one seemed to notice).

The first task had all of the positive effects you might wish for: a new hire had to read and engage with our documentation (and often the subject of the documentation itself) at a deep enough level that they could improve it. They indirectly learned about our documentation standards and mores. They were immediately contributing to making something better in our world.

The second task may seem like some combination of tedious and quaint, but it served a number of purposes beyond just keeping the data current. It forced the new staff to visit and ideally engage with all of the on-prem users of our network, often offering them a glance at what sort of things they used our systems to do. It gave them some knowledge of where we kept things in the server room and how we organized our network.

As a related aside, every once in a while, a student would decide (with my support) to write a tool or some code to make this manual process easier for them. It would be fun to track the toil-reducing students down and see how many of them became SREs.

---

9 And sometimes an engineering imperative; see Chapter 19, "Do Docs Better: Integrating Documentation into the Engineering Workflow" in *Seeking SRE*.

Nostalgia aside, I bring up these two tasks because you might be well served by giving your new hires variations of them. Documentation improvement and environment discovery are swell projects. The first projects someone receives when joining an organization are often a signal about the organization's culture, so choose wisely.

What Do You Want SRE to Be/Do?

If you subscribe to "SRE culture as vehicle/lever," and if you are trying to be active and intentional in the creation of your SRE culture, then you quickly run into some of the most substantial identity questions SRE has to offer. The idea that SRE culture helps shape organizational and individual behavior/impact relies on second- or third-order effects (i.e., you do something that influences something else, which hopefully has the effect you want or perhaps influences something that influences something else that eventually brings the desired result) at its core. That's actually not the hard part. The hard part of the "SRE culture as vehicle" model is that it forces you to decide where you want to go.

This statement isn't particularly profound, but that doesn't make it any less hard. If someone tells you to procure a vehicle, your first questions are going to be "Where do you want to go, and what do you need to do with it? Do you need a boat (or are you going to need a bigger boat)? Do you have to get somewhere fast? Are you carrying a lot of people with you? Does it have to look pretty (a showpiece)? How stealthy does it have to be? Is it the first of what will be a fleet?" I bet you and I could generate questions spurred by this analogy until the cows came home and we'd still not exhaust the topic.

Though I am a big fan of Rilke's take on questions,[10] you are still going to have to answer some fairly existential questions about SRE and its desired impact in your organization before it can be effective. And that's why the idea of "SRE culture as vehicle/lever" is so darn hard.

Figuring out "What do I want SRE to be here?" as an individual or "What do we want SRE to do here?" as an organization is a much larger topic. I promise that I take on these tasks later in the book, so you won't be hanging on that cliff indefinitely. In order to stay on the topic of SRE culture in this chapter and provide useful advice on that topic, let's agree to make the (perhaps aspirational) assumption that you have a

---

10 "I would like to beg you, dear Sir, as well as I can, to have patience with everything unresolved in your heart and to try to love the questions themselves as if they were locked rooms or books written in a very foreign language. Don't search for the answers, which could not be given to you now, because you would not be able to live them. And the point is, to live everything. Live the questions now. Perhaps then, someday far in the future, you will gradually, without even noticing it, live your way into the answer." —Rainer Maria Rilke, *Letters to a Young Poet*, 1929.

few substantive answers to these questions in your pocket already and you want to know how to translate them into a supportive culture.

Thinking About Assembling the Culture You Want and Need

In the 1980 TV series *Cosmos*, Carl Sagan said, "If you wish to make an apple pie from scratch, you must first invent the universe." Teenager me didn't know quite what to make of that statement; I just knew it was profound. Since that time, I've come to understand this quote as a meditation from Sagan on how making something as simple as an apple pie requires us to bring together ingredients (flour, sugar, fats, the fruit of a tree, etc.) that themselves came from component elements, which themselves came together from even smaller pieces, and so on, all the way back to hydrogen atoms and smaller. Each step of the way engages some pretty sophisticated processes necessary to combine their component elements.

I bring up this Sagan quote because I find it useful when thinking about building culture to give yourself the leeway to not only break things into relatively small parts but also to focus on the processes that bring them together. In the Sagan example, just asking, "What does it take to grow a fruit tree?" sends you down an incredibly rich path.

A little closer to home, asking a question like "What does it take to provision a reliable and useful dev environment?" can quickly fill up several whiteboards worth of space. If you actually try this whiteboard experiment (and I suggest you do— though it doesn't have to be this exact question), something interesting should happen.

When you stand back to admire your handiwork, I would expect you to be able to walk back up to your whiteboards and circle representative sections that reflect SRE approaches, values, priorities, etc. For example, it would not surprise me if you were able to find words like *self-service*, *well-documented*, *extensible*, *instrumented/observable*, *mirrors production*, and *accessibility* on those whiteboards.[11] When you go looking for these qualities, you are hunting for the SRE cultural overlay. Once you have this overlay identified, the next question to ask is, "How do we get more of that in our lives?"

Congratulations, you are starting to build culture.[12] Culture, like reliability, can also be an emergent property.

---

11 That was just a list off the top of my head; your list could be very different. Also, different decompositions or scenarios will yield different lists.

12 Kurt Andersen recommends Edgar H. Schein's book *Organizational Culture and Leadership* (Jossey-Bass, 4th ed., 2010) as a good resource on this topic.

Wait, Are We the Baddies?

I want to acknowledge that sometimes an exercise like the one I described doesn't go nearly as well as you'd hope. You fill up a couple of whiteboards and then, when you go back to look for a cultural overlay, you find you have been prioritizing less desirable approaches/values/etc. Or perhaps worse, you attempt to find SRE values on the whiteboards and you can't find any.

If you find yourself in either of these situations, paradoxically, I would treat it as good news. You now have a very clear and strong signal that the plans you are making have an absence of the SRE culture you desire. The good news is SREs thrive on clear and strong signals. Go SRE the heck out of this problem.

I Still Don't Know Where to Start

If everything I've said so far still feels too distant or abstract for where you are, either as an individual or as an organization, and you are thinking, "Just tell me one concrete place to start," I've got your back. As much as I would like to just quote Douglas Adams in *The Hitchhiker's Guide to the Galaxy*[13] and move on, I have a better idea, courtesy of a conversation I had with John Reese, one of the original Google SREs.

Reese suggests that if you want to build an organizational structure that is a factory for building SRE culture, you could do no better than focus intently and intentionally on your incident handling and review. Incidents and their mitigation, analysis, review, and obviation are our "What does it take to grow a fruit tree?" analog from the Sagan quote. If you break down each of the concepts in play here[14] and then work diligently and skillfully to address the questions they (and your actual incidents) pose, it will put your attention on the areas of engineering (reliability engineering) where SREs can make a difference in an organization.

---

13 "We'll be saying a big hello to all intelligent lifeforms everywhere and to everyone else out there, the secret is to bang the rocks together, guys." —Douglas Adams, *The Hitchhiker's Guide to the Galaxy*.

14 By *concepts*, I mean the various concepts in the constellation of things that play into incident handling/ analysis/remediation. For example, just off the top of my head: observability/monitoring (how did we know what is going on?), release engineering (how did it get into production?), fault tolerance (could it have fixed itself?), and communication (how is information exchanged?). There's a much longer list I could construct if so inclined.

Sisyphus Peered into the Mist

The statement "work diligently and skillfully to address..." in the main text has a hidden assumption that I unfortunately have not found to be universally true. It makes the assumption that you or your organization truly want to improve the reliability of your systems and not just keep the status quo (at a dull roar). That is not always the case. I know that is a strange statement to make in this book in particular, but it is the day-to-day reality in many, many environments (including at every famous company you can name). I feel pretty safe in predicting you will find yourself in this situation at some point.

So what do you do when you come to the unpleasant realization that the context you are in cares less about improving reliability than you do? Let's set aside the glib answers of "Bounce! Bounce now out of that situation!" and "Do the right thing anyway." Both of them can be fine answers, but let's talk about the middle path for a moment.

First off, it is reasonable to acknowledge "this situation sucks, and I don't like it," showing some compassion to yourself and your coworkers. Then it is time to engage your SRE mindset to start asking questions like:

- What are the signals I have here that tell me this? How will I know when things are getting better or worse?
- What do I know about the larger system in play here? (What's the larger context organizationally, financially, politically, etc.?)
- What are the dependencies and incentives in play?
- What levers can I pull directly? What levers can I pull indirectly or as a second-order effect that can impact this situation?

If a cold, hard look at the situation with this approach still leaves you despondent, then maybe your thoughts can return to the glib answers like "Bounce!" But if you do see a lever you can pull, a thing you can influence, or an experiment (even with people) you can run, try that. Better yet, if you have colleagues who feel the way you do, talk to them and try it together.

SRE the heck out of this problem.

Incidents also tend to be what we might call a "forcing function" that might cause you to start growing your own fruit trees. For example, returning to a previous subject, your analysis of your latest incidents might be sending you a clear signal that your documentation or the delivery of your documentation is lacking. It takes less than a handful of situations in which an outage was prolonged, either because the documentation was lacking or you couldn't actually get to your documentation because something was down, before you and others might decide SRE should lead a charge to improve documentation org-wide.

While I agree with Reese that incident handling and review could be a powerful engine for generating an SRE culture, I do feel compelled to mention a few caveats. When SRE takes on incident handling and analysis for an organization as their primary function, especially in isolation from the rest of the organization, this has a very real potential to devolve into an "SRE handles all on call—they will now be the pager monkeys whose job it is to follow a script at 2 a.m. when the service goes down" situation. This is not a theoretical warning; I've seen it happen. It can happen even when people have the best of intentions ("We'll take on call so we can learn your system and how it can fail"[15] is a common intention).

How do you avoid the incident-handling train going off the rails and not delivering the SRE culture you hope for? Later in this book (for example, in Chapters 12 and 15), I'll talk more about how SRE efforts can fail, but let's tee some of that up here. Besides generally being on guard for this happening now that you know it can happen, there are a number of warning signs.

One key warning sign for me is found in the question "Who is getting smarter and what are we doing about it?" My fond hope for you is that your postincident reviews are currently yielding new and useful information about your systems and how they can fail.[16] Let's just assume they are.

Who in the organization is learning from them? If you said, "Just SRE at this point," there is your first red flag. Put this book down and go work on that. Your car is in reverse; any gas you give it at this point will send you in the opposite direction of the culture you are hoping to create.

If the answer is closer to "SRE and engineering personnel and relevant stakeholders are getting smarter," then move on to the next question: "What is SRE and the rest of the organization doing with this knowledge?" If the answer is "basically nothing," then you have your second red flag. Now you are deep into questions around SRE's access and capacity to make reliability-improving changes (either directly or indirectly), given your organizational context. And I do mean "changes," not just "access and capacity to tread water."

While I think it is possible to deal with these concerns at the same time as trying to create an SRE culture, it can be like pushing a shopping cart with a broken front wheel. Every time you push it forward, it may tend to pull in a direction that you

---

15 I feel somewhat compelled to point you to Niall Murphy's Chapter 30, "Against On-Call: A Polemic," in *Seeking SRE*, where you will hear a number of similar innocuous-sounding sentiments challenged.

16 If not, start there and then come back to this culture stuff. There's more info about postincident reviews all throughout this book, including in Chapter 10 on learning from failure, so plenty of help awaits.

don't particularly want to go in. If you think SRE is on call because it is the single biggest lever to trend reliability in the right direction, but if the service owner thinks the biggest value you offer is that developers don't have to get woken up or spend their valuable time on dealing with outages, then the mismatch is setting your efforts up for derailment.

I will talk more about these things later in the book, but perhaps the shortest distillation of a strategy for prevention is "Use your words, especially early in the process." Now that you have a better idea of what you want and don't want from the incident response and analysis engine, communicate that clearly (and often) internally and externally with all of your SRE efforts.[17]

Nurturing Your Nascent SRE Culture

OK, cool, so let's assume that with the help of the other ideas in this chapter (or perhaps despite them), you have started down the road to creating the culture you desire. How do you nurture and grow that culture in yourself and in your organization?

I have two answers to this that I have seen be really helpful for organizations (and the individuals in them).

The "book club" or "graduate seminar" idea

Many organizations host a "Postmortem of the Month" or "Design Document of the Month" gathering where a group of interested people pick a write-up of an outage or a proposed system architecture, give it a close read, and then discuss it as a group of peers. These write-ups don't even have to be from your own organization to foment a valuable discussion.[18]

It is important to note that discussions on these topics must be divorced from your regular process of reviewing postincident write-ups or design documents. You can't say, "Oh, we already talk about an outage after it happens, so we got this covered." The reason why you can't double them up is that the management, accountability, and, quite frankly, residual emotional overlay in that situation makes it very difficult to have the sort of dispassionate learning experience desired for this effort.

---

17 I just want to acknowledge that advice to "go talk to people" could on its face feel someplace between glib and impossible. I remember when my parents would advise me to "just go to your teacher and say such-and-such," and how incredibly divorced from any possible reality I could inhabit that advice felt. My hope is that much of this book will give you pragmatic framing and accessible words. Hold on, help is coming.

18 There are pluses and minuses to reviewing internal materials. On the plus side, internal-only documents are likely to be more candid and detailed than externally published material. On the minus side, you may not have as great a diversity of situations to discuss. Also, it can be harder to have a dispassionate discussion of an event you participated in or a design you helped create.

The basic process for one of these "book clubs" or "graduate seminars" is pretty simple. Here's one version: an organizer picks the object of discussion and disseminates it to the group members a few weeks ahead of time so everyone has the opportunity to read it over before the meeting. In the meeting, the group spends the first N minutes laying out the facts, ideally at a high level of detail.[19] Then it is time to stack up questions: "How did X happen? How did X part of the system behave this way? And why did they decide to use X instead of Y here in the architecture?" Three of my favorites to ask are:

- What is missing from the write-up we have here?
- What do we still not know, or what may we never know?
- Why wasn't this worse? (This is for outages; hat tip to John Allspaw.)

Then the group is off to the races. I don't know about you, but this sounds like a super-fun time to me. This is one way both to make SRE happy and to begin to create the kind of "culture as vehicle" we mentioned earlier as we foster effective analysis around incidents.

Though I have seen this idea applied in practice more often at slightly more mature organizations, there is no reason why you couldn't start a group now. If you are in a situation where there isn't a group of peers to gather (i.e., you are taking this on as an individual, perhaps because you are a team of one or two), there are still two options: self-study or finding an external group to join (there are meetups, perhaps virtual, who get together for this sort of thing).

"Rotations" or "exchange programs"

This one is a little harder to pull off because it requires more management and organizational buy-in, but I know of no better way to inoculate an entire organization with SRE culture than this. The basic idea is that individuals on an SRE team take turns temporarily rotating into positions in other groups/teams, and/or individuals on external teams work for some time as SREs on your team. There are lots and lots of variations on this idea because the details can be highly situationally dependent.

---

19 Both so the entire group can level set, but also, quite frankly, for the people in the room who didn't read the document or didn't read it closely ahead of time. I mean, that never happens, but just in case.

For example, here are two of the variables you can tweak:

Length of rotation

Some companies arrange substantial time periods for these rotations. For example, Google's Mission Control program lets a software engineer (SWE) spend six months as an SRE. My only advice here is that you do really need a reasonable amount of time in a position for this idea to offer any value. A single "take my SWE colleague to work" day is much less likely to offer the culture-nurturing benefits you desire than a rotation of a month or more.

Level of embedding

With a rotation, ideally you want to be able to step into someone else's role or to have them step into yours. To make that happen, there has to be enough of a shared skill set to make this viable. If that isn't possible, "shadowing" arrangements are possible, albeit suboptimal. I say suboptimal because they are often a drain on the person being shadowed. If at all possible, you really want the person rotating in to be seen as contributing to the group, at least at the level you would expect from a new hire. If that is not possible, you may need to get creative here (perhaps refer back to the sidebar "Your First Tasks" on page 27).

I have yet to hear about a healthy rotation effort in an organization that didn't yield good cultural impact.

Keep On Keeping On

Work on SRE culture is a never-ending effort. I don't think this is much of a surprise because, like every other desirable emergent property, culture overlays most everything. While I get to end this chapter, you don't get to end your work in this direction. At best, you might get a few pauses or a brief break from the work. The good news is that at a certain point in a successful SRE culture effort, you will start to hear back echoes of your work from other parts of the organization. Others will start to pick up what you are putting down. They will ask you for more of what you are trying to promote, and that will feel really good. Enjoy!

CHAPTER 4

Talking About SRE (SRE Advocacy)

Welcome to a highly meta chapter in which we are going to be talking about talking about SRE.[1] Effective SRE advocacy turns out to be crucial for both individuals and organizations, for reasons we will see in a minute. In this chapter, we're going to explore the craft of SRE advocacy and what resources you have available to hone it for both vantage points. We will talk about the kinds of stories that matter and how to pick the most effective ones, and I will offer a whole slew of tips on the subject. This chapter is about the stories we tell ourselves.

Why It Matters, Even Early in Your Experience with SRE

Without fail, you will at some point have to explain to others what SRE is and why it matters. That point invariably comes much sooner than you would expect,[2] which is why this chapter is right up front with the rest of the introductory material.

When I say explain it to others, I mean people who run the gamut from your grandparents to your CEO. Sometimes you will just be satisfying someone's curiosity at a cocktail party, but it's equally likely you will be in a position of singing for your supper as you have to justify SRE's presence in your organization and why someone should continue to pay for it.[3] It is also very common to have to explain to another group in your org what SRE is and why it would be in their best interest to engage

---

1 You know what you must do. Find someone who does not have this book yet and talk about this chapter. The fate of the meta metaverse is in your hands.

2 Like "day one" sooner. In addition to wanting to prepare you for this situation, I strongly feel that the process of talking about SRE with other people will immediately strengthen your own understanding of SRE, which is yet another reason to think about this early in the book. It also lives here because advocacy has a foot in both individual and organizational contexts.

3 There's plenty more discussion on handling the business aspects of SRE in Chapter 13.

with you. I don't believe I am exaggerating when I say that the survival of SRE at a company is predicated on the strength of its advocacy.

I believe that survival is probably a strong enough motivator for you to pay attention to advocacy, but I will throw one more reason into the mix: identity. I'm convinced that the stories we tell ourselves are a major way identity is formed. I'm very confident that what SRE means personally and organizationally matters to you (or you are in the wrong book, my friend).

When It Matters

So when is SRE advocacy particularly important? I've already mentioned a few scenarios, but let's explore this question a little further. In my experience, SRE advocacy is crucial in the personal context when dealing with hiring and career changes. Not only do you have to sell yourself and why you personally will improve your potential employers' lives, but part of the sell has to include why your SRE approach/mindset can make a difference.

If you are applying for a job at an organization that already has an SRE story (weak or strong), this is your moment to determine whether your SRE story matches theirs. I'd strongly suggest that you pay very close attention to how well they are able to articulate their SRE story in the hiring process. If they can't be clear or consistent in their description to you of SRE and its purpose, that will give you a really good signal about how effective they are at expressing this to others in the organization.

Organizationally, I've seen SRE advocacy be crucial in two settings: during the early stages of SRE and when attempting an expansion of influence. The first setting is pretty obvious; if you are trying to establish SRE in an organization, there's a lot of education and justification that has to take place. We'll talk about this more in this chapter, but how SRE gets framed in discussions can have a significant impact on how people will treat it going forward.

The second setting where advocacy is crucial is the expansion phase. I might say it like this: "Cool, you've been able to set up a new SRE group. Now you have to get others to play with you. How are you going to do that?"[4] Effective advocacy is how you are going to do that.

I realize that everything I have said so far in this chapter makes it sound like advocacy is a do-or-die proposition—it's true, I actually believe that. The good news is that this entire book is chock-full of ideas, resources, and guidance to support your advocacy efforts. Pretty please use everything you can from it to support those efforts.

---

4 Remember that relentlessly collaborative thing?

Get Your Story (and Audience) Straight

For me, SRE advocacy (well, any advocacy) starts with a story I want to tell.[5] The reason why I start with a story is that humans are wired to be story-receiving machines. It is one of the best ways we know to relate complex, multivariate information. It may not be obvious at first glance, but that is exactly what the concept/definition of SRE is—a collection of some pretty sophisticated ideas bound together. And when you begin to discuss it, different people zero in on different aspects of it based on their background and prior experience.

This is why I came up with a precisely vague[6] definition that I could hang all of this on to frame the conversation. This is the definition of SRE we saw in Chapter 1; let me repeat it here for convenience:

> Site reliability engineering is an engineering discipline devoted to helping organizations sustainably achieve the appropriate level of reliability in their systems, services, and products.

As I mentioned before, whenever I speak to people using this definition, I usually ask them to pull out the keywords they notice (like *reliability* and *appropriate*). Each one of those words is a door into an entire room's worth of discussion; letting others choose means the listener gets to choose the doors that stand out to them. I have used this definition over and over again, as it seemed to work well to draw people into a discussion.

---

5 Later in this book, I describe storytelling as a core skill to have as an SRE—here's one context where that is very clearly the case.

6 By *precisely vague*, I mean the definition is intentionally vague enough to encompass a wide range of work toward reliability without being so vague as to be applicable to all engineering.

My talks with groups are usually one part me passing air over my larynx, two parts open discussion/Ask Me Anything. I try to get a sense of my audience's situation and how I can help. To my surprise, over time, something weird happened with the talks that used this interactive definition—something I didn't expect.

I started to notice a pattern. While it wasn't completely predictive,[7] I found that different audiences would pull out different words based on their current organizational challenges. During the Q&A period after the talk, the people who felt underwater more often than not had noticed the words *sustainable* and *appropriate*. The groups that felt they hadn't yet reached the level of credibility with others they desired wanted to talk about the word *discipline*. Those who desired this credibility from partner development teams often wanted to dig into *engineering*. Groups coming off a series of outages couldn't get enough of *reliability*, and so on. I wouldn't say this approach is solidly diagnostic, but I have come to find it practically useful for helping me shape how I talk about the subject.

Why do I bring this up? For me it is a clear reminder that when we tell someone a story about SRE as part of our advocacy efforts, different people will hear different things in that story based on their background and their current needs. I know that "consider your audience" isn't remotely new advice, but it never hurts to have a reminder.

If you can (with authenticity and proficiency) speak using the terms and register of your audience, do so. If you speak the language of the finance people in your organization and you are talking to an audience of those people, by all means use finance terms in a nongratuitous fashion.

That being said, it is possible to take this too far. If, during your talk preparation, you get even a whiff of constructing a "buzzword bingo card," dial it back. Or maybe when you say certain things, they ring hollow to your ear. You get to decide what works for you. I've learned that there are certain business-speak words that set me on edge when I hear them, so they almost never pass my lips.[8] Ideally you can find the right intersection between the words you like to speak and the words the audience is accustomed to hearing.

---

7 I will be the first to admit I could be making this up; I'm not immune from the human trait of identifying patterns where they don't really exist.

8 I'm a little hesitant to reveal them publicly for fear of them showing up in some sort of torture scenario, but here's one: *learnings*. I can't stand the word *learnings*. Which are your sandpaper words?

Some Story Ideas

A moment ago, I gave an example of a story you can tell about SRE, namely the "What is it?" or definitional story. It's a good place to start, but there's a whole panoply of stories that can and should be told about SRE, depending on what you hope to accomplish in the telling. Here's a list of some other ideas off the top of my head:

Efficacy
> A story about how a partner group was suffering with reliability issues, SRE got involved and helped with X, Y, Z, and now they are in a better place, as shown by...

Reputation
> A story about how famous company X adopted SRE.[9]

Possibility
> A story about how comparable company X adopted SRE (how it went well, how it had issues but then overcame them, etc.). If they can do it, surely we can too...

Surprise
> A story about an outage and the surprising result or finding uncovered by SRE as part of their deftly run postincident review process.

Transformation
> This is what things used to be like for us, but now, *N* months later, we are in this better place.

Day in the life
> Here's what happened during a sample day/week, including a selection of the things we did to contribute to company-wide or partner team success.

Mystery/puzzle
> X was a situation that made no sense; here's how we solved the mystery step by step.

Expert at work
> Here's how an expert approached a problem, how they thought about it, steps they took, etc.

---

9 Full disclosure: this is my least favorite out of the bunch. Your company and famous company X are almost always going to be very different entities on the inside—what works for them may not work for your company (see the stories of people not becoming Google even though they followed everything in the SRE book). That being said, sometimes management wants to be reassured by SRE's bona fides based on a famous company they hope to emulate. Use with caution if you have to use this at all.

There are many other ideas for stories you can tell at work. If none of the listed ideas inspire you, perhaps look back over the years of videos of sessions at SREcon (see Appendix C) and I'm pretty sure you will find some compelling seeds for your own talks.

As a tip on this topic, I recommend you collect stories as you go. The life of an SRE is fortunately or unfortunately never dull. On a daily basis, we find ourselves in situations that make for good stories to tell others. Be it an outage, a meeting with an aha moment where someone has an interesting take on the subject, a tech problem where the answer to a question led to an even better question—all of these are great story fodder. I highly recommend you do this: keep notes on these things as they come up, either in a running file/online document or in a (gasp) paper notebook.

Other People's Stories

As an important part of teaching you how to collect stories, I want to mention that you must be sure to get explicit permission to retell these stories from both the people involved and the organization. Many organizations have explicit policies and processes around public presentations. If you plan to tell these stories publicly, be sure to get the proper clearance to do so.[10]

How to Ask for Permission

Asking for explicit permission is crucial, but it doesn't have to be hard. It can be as simple as asking, "This situation is a perfect example of how something we didn't expect to happen bit us. I'd love to tell this story, suitably anonymized, in a presentation in the future. Would you be OK with that?" When being asked, people want to make sure they personally won't look bad, that the story will be told in good faith for good reasons, and that nothing improper will be revealed. Be sure your ask for consent takes these concerns into account.

One variation related to other people's stories that is a little harder, but magnitudes of order more effective: don't just collect people's stories to retell, collect the people instead. It is great to tell someone else's story, but often, if you can have that person do

---

10 You didn't hear it from me, but it is in your best interest to build a good direct relationship with whomever clears materials for external publishing in your organization. If you gain a reputation for being extra careful around these rules and extra easy to work with, that will often smooth your path to future approvals.

---

the telling, it will be a kerjillion times more effective and impactful.[11] Even if they can't be a part of your presentation every time you give it, you might be able to record a video of them speaking—replay that.

Give Up Your Airtime

For me, there's another good reason to have others tell their story that may or may not apply to you. As an older white male who sees mostly other people who look like me being given the opportunity to speak in public forums or in front of management, I am not OK with the lack of underrepresented voices. I want to see this change in the SRE and larger tech communities. In order for this to get better, it is incumbent on me to give up some of the airtime I regularly receive as an established speaker to others so they can be seen "on stage" too and be models. If you are in a similar position, I encourage you to think about these questions as you plan your SRE advocacy.

If the importance of doing this from a social justice and equality perspective doesn't immediately ring true for you, I would suggest that there is an SRE-esque rationale at work here. Hearing from varied voices, with their different perspectives, is going to provide more "signal" (something SRE is very fond of) and provide a more thorough understanding of the subject.

Secondary Stories

Just a quick note about stories like the ones we've been discussing: all of them have room for an ulterior motive or two. Because stories can be such good carriers of information, there's bandwidth not only for the main purpose of the telling but also for secondary stories. I'll pick an idea from the previous story ideas at random to demonstrate.

Let's say you've been frustrated with the lackluster postincident reviews your organization has been doing lately. Maybe they have been a bit on the perfunctory side; perhaps it is clear to you that there's more to be learned in the process. One sign of this is that the last three have all been attributed to "human error" as the final conclusion.

---

11 I want to acknowledge that this path can be fraught with peril; for example, in cases where you are a much better speaker than your special guest. This then becomes a speaker preparation and coaching problem (or a video-editing problem), which in almost all cases can be overcome. I assert that hearing someone's experience firsthand is ultimately going to be more impactful, even if the speaker isn't a pro. I can coach someone to be a better speaker, but I can't coach someone into having the original experience.

Next time you get called upon to talk about a past outage to management, perhaps you could choose the "surprise" idea from the list. In that telling (and I know you see this coming), you could be sure to construct a cliffhanger midstory that includes something like "Originally, we were going to attribute this to human error, but something about that didn't sit right..." At the end of the story, you could posit the question, "What else could we learn if we didn't prematurely conclude our investigations and attribute failures to human error?" or make some other not-so-subtle statement.[12]

In a similar category of "a good device, but try not to be too heavy-handed," it can be useful to find a story from your own experience where you successfully modeled the behavior you would like to see the organization adopt. "Here's how I failed and leveled up based on that experience" can be popular because everyone loves a good failure story. It has the plus of coming across as authentic (perhaps the best story is your own story) without being too preachy if handled properly. One suggestion: have a colleague review your presentation before you give it. These kinds of stories can have a "devil *is* the details" trap. It can be hard to decide how detailed your recollection needs to be to get your point across. Other people are likely a better judge of this than you are, hence, the suggestion to have someone else review it first.

The Challenges the Stories Present

The stories we deal with in SRE advocacy are sometimes harder to tell than you might expect. Let's talk about a few challenges that get in the way:

Challenge 1: Difficult stories

One very specific challenge we have when constructing stories for SRE advocacy is that sometimes, we have to tell the story of the dog that didn't bark.[13] Often we have to describe situations where the value of our work is seen in what didn't happen—the systems that didn't go down, the outages we didn't have, the data loss that was prevented, and so on. Telling a compelling story of a negative or of things functioning the way they were designed to is almost always harder than describing some crisis that did happen.

So how do we handle this challenge? For me, the answer centers on contrast. That's the key element that lets us make sense of photographic negatives. Our task in this scenario is to bring into sharp relief an object (like your system and how it operates) against a background (the load, the behavior of your dependencies, the conditions

---

12 Want someone else's premade story with exactly this conclusion? Check out Nick Stenning's superb 2019 SREcon EMEA talk, "Building Resilience: How to Learn More from Incidents" (*https://oreil.ly/-f88V*).

13 Arthur Conan Doyle reference, although have you heard of the preparedness paradox (*https://oreil.ly/0fhMc*)? Might not want to read that Wikipedia article; it may make you sad.

that would have taken it down in the past, the sociotechnical context, etc.). Sometimes we can begin with a description of a related outage, stopping at the point in the story when the problem is no longer happening and explaining what you changed and its positive results.[14]

In the sidebar "Resilience Engineering Again?" on page 45, I note that we should be taking the opportunity to discuss questions like "What contributed to things going well? And how could things have gone worse?" Here's that opportunity.

Resilience Engineering Again?

The discipline of resilience engineering and my fondness for it appear in a number of places in this book. The discussion of telling stories around a negative reminds me yet again of resilience engineering talks I've heard that mentioned:[15]

- A useful train of inquiry about an outage is, "How could this have been worse? What prevented this outage from getting worse? What didn't happen and why?"

- Erik Hollnagel's work on Safety-II (and Nancy Leveson's further development of Safety-III) leads us to explore what would happen if we focused not just on the hour during which we had an outage but also on the vastly larger amount of time when things seemed to be going well (the rest of the time when we weren't experiencing a downtime). Instead of asking what the root cause was that led to the outage, it may be useful to ask the provocative question, "On the day before the outage, what was the root cause of things going well?"

Challenge 2: How the stories develop

Another challenge you are going to encounter sooner or later, especially if you are speaking to Western audiences,[16] is that reliability work is very seldom linear in nature. The dragon we slay once doesn't usually stay slayed. Don't expect your SRE stories to be linear, either. At some point, it will become abundantly clear to you that the shape of the work is a lot messier. Sometimes we have loops (recall the nurture feedback loops from Chapter 2), sometimes our reliability zigs and zags, maybe you had a bad month due to seasonal traffic, and so on.

---

14 Ironically, this is an example of counterfactual reasoning (i.e., using something that didn't happen to explain something that did), which I will warn about in Chapter 10.

15 Pretty sure at least one of these was a John Allspaw talk, so credit to him for giving such good talks that the questions stick in my head even past my precise memory of when I heard them.

16 Other cultures don't necessarily expect their stories to follow a linear structure.

We very seldom get a full picture that looks like a perfectly straight line from bad to better. If you were to zoom out from the complete graph, you would more likely get something that looked like a child's crayon picture. This complicates the story we want to tell. But that's OK—it's just the existential truth we have chosen to live with.

There are two ways I know to handle this concern: either elide the issue in your head and make peace with the gross simplification you are about to engage in (ideally, disclosing it to your audience) or be very clear that you are describing a select slice of or window into the larger picture. I believe the longer you are in the SRE realm, the more striking the nonlinearity of our basic reality becomes. My hope for you is that your skill at translating this reality for others to understand grows at the same rate as your awareness.

Challenge 3: Conveying the right lessons

Be very cautious about emphasizing "heroic effort" stories because they can have unintended negative consequences. It can be very tempting, especially in situations where you are craving external respect and recognition, to lean into narratives where a person on the team rappelled down the side of the building and then valiantly fought the blaze for 30 hours straight without food or sleep until it was vanquished.

All of that may have happened, but glorifying "hero culture" will lead you to construct a culture and organizational expectations that are unhealthy and unsustainable. When I hear "30 hours without food or sleep," I hear it as a failure in the organization's incident response procedures, not something to be celebrated. "Worked straight through the weekend/holiday/night," "woke up the entire team," and "80-hour work week" are similar red flags that should be approached as problems, not evidence of commitment or dedication. If you do need to say these things during a readout of an incident, be sure to emphasize fixing them in your postincident review along with the rest of the repair items you might have.

To understand this topic better, I highly recommend you watch one of the most powerful talks I've seen: "The Cult(Ure) of Strength" (*https://oreil.ly/JEUH_*) by Emily Gorcenski. It was one of two tech conference talks where I cried. In this session, Gorcenski did an excellent job of capturing the broken thinking that leads us into the "hero culture" trap.[17]

---

17 It's also the talk that stopped me from ever again using the term *war stories* to refer to an outage story.

Challenge 4: Picking the right main character

Another people-related tip: don't forget the people when telling stories for SRE advocacy. An SQL server is not the only important character in your outage story. Another existential truth when it comes to SRE is that all of our systems are sociotechnical. Large, complex systems do not run in isolation. They run in a context that includes people, so if your story consists entirely of things with blinking lights that go beep-boop, it is almost certainly incomplete.

One Last Tip

To end this chapter, let me offer one last tip that is true for all sorts of advocacy and public speaking, not just SRE advocacy. I've had the good fortune to be able to give many talks and presentations over the years. I have learned that my best talks are those that changed me during the preparation or presentation. I wish the same experience for you at some point. Get in touch; I'd love to hear that story from you.

PART II

Becoming SRE for the Individual

CHAPTER 5

Preparing to Become an SRE

There is no one singular path to SRE. I don't want to go even a single sentence into the topic of *So you wanna be an SRE?* before making that clear. In this chapter, I'll be discussing some potential "prerequisites" (quotes added because, well, there's no one singular path and this isn't going to be a mandatory list) that will get you squarely into a place where becoming an SRE is possible.[1] And to be extra clear, this chapter is not constructing a test that requires you to know everything I list or you don't pass and can't call yourself an SRE. It is an exploration of the elements that support an individual's pathfinding through the challenges of SRE. Chapter 6 will offer some more specific advice on how you can transition from an existing role to SRE, but first, we have to set the scene.

I'm going to do my best to provide suggestions on preparations[2] for SRE that are specific to SRE and not just something you would expect to need to know for any modern operations practice. Topics like *automation* will get a single mention (in this sentence, as a matter of fact) because they are table stakes for any operations-related job role at this point.

In *Fear of Cooking: The Absolutely Foolproof Cookbook for Beginners (And Everyone Else)*, a sadly out-of-print book about learning how to cook without a recipe,

---

1 To avoid any rising sense of panic, I want to state right up front that there is an aspirational aspect to this chapter. It is not a checklist that you have to complete before you can set foot in the SRE space. Worst-case scenario: it is good to know what you don't know.

2 It is worthwhile emphasizing that this chapter is focused more on what you need to know and how you can prepare versus who you are at the core or have to be to thrive in SRE. For those things, I'd redirect you back to Chapter 2 on the SRE mindset. Do a quick compatibility check with questions like "Are you a curious person?", "Do you like to solve problems, no matter where they take you?", "Is a life of service attractive to you?" and so on to see how your nature fits with what SRE asks of a person.

the author, Bob Scher,[3] suggests that he doesn't actually do any cooking; what he does is create and maintain the proper conditions for the food to cook. That's roughly how I feel about this subject too. I can provide my best information on what you need to set up the conditions to become an SRE, but I can't promise the dish will turn out exactly as you hope. With that framing in mind, let's jump into this topic.

Do You Need to Know How to Code?

Rather than burying this in a footnote in a chapter in a different book in a filing cabinet in the basement of your local planning office, let's talk about the single most asked question I get on this topic: "Do you need to know how to code to be an SRE?"

The short answer: yes, yes, you do.

For years, I resisted this answer. I resisted this answer in the face of information like the well-known Google policy of only hiring SREs that have the same coding competence as SWEs (their software engineers/developers[4]). I probably resisted this answer so hard because at no time in my own career did I identify as a developer or software engineer, despite having done a reasonable amount of coding in the operations space myself. I wanted to believe that there may be a path to SRE in which integration skills, where one assembled other people's components, could replace coding skills entirely.

I'm here from the future (well, technically my present and, therefore, your past) to tell you that I have now been entirely convinced that being able to code is a prerequisite for SRE.

Here's why:

- If you don't know how something is built, your ability to understand how it can fail is severely limited. The word *reliability* in SRE almost always refers to the reliability of software systems. You can see where I am going with this.

- Ideally, learning to code (at a certain depth of learning) includes learning about things like efficiency (of algorithms, storage, performance, effort, resource usage, etc.), error handling, abstraction, configuration, architecture, decomposition, integration, dependencies, documentation, and eloquence of expression, to name some overlays. You really need to be educated and challenged on all of these fronts before you can dance SRE. More on these things later.

---

3 Fun fact that will only impress the people who are as old as the hills like me: Bob Scher was a former DEC engineer.

4 And indeed, I am told that crossing between the two job ladders is relatively common as a result.

- Learning to code will help teach you how to debug or troubleshoot. See the sidebar "A Lesson Long Learned" for an example of a personal lesson I learned pre-SRE.

- Many of the tools and data formats in the coding world are now a crucial part of the day-to-day life of an SRE. The easiest example of this is source control, but there are many others we take for granted like the JSON and YAML data formats.

These are just some of the components of what I think is a pretty compelling case: you need to know how to code to be an SRE.

A Lesson Long Learned

Everyone I know has a story like this. I can still clearly recall the time in my first computer science class when I was trying, trying, trying to fix a bug in my code for an assignment I had due the next day. I would run the code, reproduce the bug, and then make a change to the source code to try and fix it. Run the program, work to reproduce the bug, attempt another fix. I did this over and over. Nothing I did seemed to help.

This went on for an embarrassingly long amount of time (definitely over an hour).

At some point, with a very audible yelp, I realized I had been making changes to a different source code file (different file entirely) than the one being used to run the program I was executing. Every change I had made over the last hour had absolutely no connection to the program I was running.

I learned some important lessons that day. You would be surprised how often those lessons come in handy decades later. Or maybe you wouldn't.

The very next questions I usually get when I lay this case out, usually accompanied by a little bit of fear in the eyes, are along the lines of "How much of a coder do I need to be? Does scripting count, or do I need to be able to write an operating system? Do I need to be a software engineer?"

These questions are a little harder to answer and are perhaps a little more situational than "Do you need to know how to code?" Later in this book, we'll be talking about how SRE fits into an organization. Besides a glib answer pointing out that SRE has *engineer* (as in *software engineer*) or *engineering* in the acronym (and all that implies), some of the responses turn on the question, "What kind of an SRE do you want, or does your organization want you to be?" I realize my people are inordinately fond of answering a question with a question, but I do believe that a prompt for a little soul-searching in this context is a reasonable response.

Let me explain in two different ways: earlier I gave a whole incomplete list of considerations/concepts that coding demands of you. Simple scripting can include these things—I've seen some awesome shell scripts in my time. But the engineering-esque considerations (efficiency, abstraction, architecture, decomposition, and so on…) are not as often expected of us as part of that activity.[5] If you don't have coding experience that has provided a reason to wrestle with these aspects of a system, it limits the level at which you will be able to engage with your systems as an SRE. That's explanation one.

Explanation two is organizational: later in the book we will discuss the integration of SRE into the larger structure of an organization. If your organization believes an SRE team should be able to improve the reliability of a system by proposing or making code-level changes to that system—well, best be able to code, friend. One metric of organizational cohesion is whether an SRE individual or team has write/commit-level access to the main source control repository. That's not something you will (or perhaps *should*) get without knowing your way around code.

So let me take this back to my original answer as a way of closing this section: coding experience may be a strong factor in what kind of SRE position is available to you or your organization.

Do You Need a Computer Science Degree?

Here's the short answer to this question: not necessarily, but if you don't have a CS degree, some employers will require you to have enough of a working knowledge of certain CS concepts to be able to fake it.

For example, I wouldn't be the least bit surprised if you were asked a Big O notation question in an SRE interview. Basically, they are looking to determine if you know enough about algorithmic analysis to determine how efficient a process might be, given a large amount of data to process. Will it be efficient enough to finish in a reasonable timeframe, or will it take until the heat death of the universe to complete?[6]

Now, will someone actually come up to you at work and ask you a Big O question? Your workplace will probably never get that exciting, but it is entirely possible that the scenario mentioned in the footnote could become real when you find that a service you care for is starting to melt down thanks to the current implementation, and you need to figure out what to do about it.

---

5 I'm not trying to demean or disparage scripting here. I wrote an entire 600+ page book with an otter on the cover about it back in the day. I am in no way suggesting that you can't or won't bring an engineering mindset to it—I really hope you do. My assertion is that for *simple* scripting, the considerations aren't usually a requirement or a priority, and hence, they're not often expected in that context.

6 So, for example, if a snippet of code has to repeatedly walk the entire data set one or more times ($O(n)$ or greater), that's not going to work when you are faced with a massive number of records. An SRE should be able to flag this at the very least as a scaling limitation and ideally come up with something more efficient.

The list of CS concepts you need to know is remarkably similar to the ones I mentioned in the section "Do You Need to Know How to Code?" on page 52. So either you learn about those topics through some rigorous coding experience, academically via computer science, or you learn about them through some other path. Your call.

Fundamentals

In the section "Do You Need to Know How to Code?" on page 52, I mentioned a healthy (albeit incomplete) list of fundamental topics, which I suggested you would ideally encounter if you made any serious foray into coding. It's an important list. Rather than repeat it here, let me just say that if you haven't already encountered all of those things through your coding experience or computer science studies, pretend I have written them in this section, too, because you are still on the hook for them. In this section, let's look at some fundamentals that we haven't discussed already.

Single/Basic Systems (and Their Failure Modes)

There's no skipping over the basics. SREs have to understand basic systems and how they work. You can't put together larger systems that scale without understanding basics like operating system concepts, networking, permissions, and protocols and how they fail. These are the same basics you would expect systems administrators to grasp for their work.[7]

Distributed Systems (and Their Failure Modes)

Once upon a time, when we were still shoveling coal into the computers in our machine rooms to keep them running, we could point to a rectangle and say, "This, this is my system." I don't say this to invoke any nostalgia but just to highlight that the days of dealing with nondistributed systems are, with rare exceptions, gone baby gone. In their place, often in response to scaling concerns, our lives are filled with distributed systems, whether they are explicitly labeled as such or not.[8] These days, your chance of caring for a microservice-based architecture or a geographically dispersed system as an SRE is pretty good. Your chance of working on a system with fault tolerance or primary/secondary components is extremely high.

---

7 I'd like to be very careful here. I am mentioning system administration as a shorthand for a collection of knowledge and expertise that I believe most people will recognize. I am not using it for comparison purposes or to assert any sort of hierarchy or evolutionary path relationship to SRE.

8 If you wanted to make the argument that distributed systems are just a subset of "complex systems" and SREs need to be able to reason about complex systems in general, I probably wouldn't put up much of a fight. Distributed systems have their own particular constellation of failure modes that I believe SREs need to understand, hence, this shout-out.

So given this, it is in your best interest to spend some time studying distributed systems and how they can fail. Let's go back to the idea of a fault-tolerant system with primary/secondary components I just mentioned because it is relatively familiar and starts to get more complex fast. You will need to know how to construct an architecture with redundant components in active/passive or primary/secondary configurations and the sort of things that can go wrong with them.

Next come those with active/active or multiple primary components. This might lead us into questions of where write operations will take place (for fault tolerance, performance, or spreading the load) and how decisions around this might be coordinated between those components.

And now, welcome to the world of latency, consensus algorithms, distributed timekeeping, and data consistency…

I can keep going; and so should you (be able to). At each step, the systems created can and will fail in particular ways that will be up to you to identify, debug, remediate, rebuild better, etc. For this example, I took just one aspect (data writes) and turned the complexity knob up a few clicks. As an SRE, you will be expected to be able to pick other aspects of systems and reason similarly about failures in a distributed context.

Statistics and Data Visualization

One thing I regret not studying in school, back in the days when my brain was spritely and full of neuroplasticity, is statistics. In several places in this book, I claim monitoring/observability is a bedrock activity/concern for an SRE or SRE's role in an organization. I have learned the hard way that fluency in statistics is required for anything beyond cursory work in that direction. I am not suggesting you need to become an actuary, but you need to have facility for concepts like percentiles, how standard statistical operations aggregate/compound, trending, and other nonsurface statistical topics. To this day, I still wish I was better at statistics.

There are a number of teaching resources for statistics for engineers or for people new to the topic. I would suggest you find one that explains it in a way that works for you. In addition to these resources, I'd recommend you seek out the lectures and whitepapers Heinrich Hartmann has written on the topic because they directly address the SRE crowd.

Statistics helps us understand and manipulate data, but there is also the adjacent skill of being able to represent data for visualization effectively. It doesn't get nearly enough airtime when we discuss skills an SRE needs to have to be effective on a daily basis. Here's why it matters: the ability to improve reliability in most situations is predicated on the capacity to have concrete conversations about objective data. Those conversations can either be greatly helped or greatly hampered by how well or poorly the data can be represented and understood by all parties in that conversation. There's a story in and about the data (more on this in a moment); get good at telling it.

There's some really good, published work on data visualization. A great place to start is with the books Edward Tufte writes and publishes.

One quick warning for you: once you start to pay attention to good data representation and you are able to spot issues with it, it will unfortunately be like suddenly acquiring perfect pitch—you will begin to notice out-of-tune pianos everywhere you go. This is an incredibly valuable outlook, though it also means you will become the person in the meeting who says, "No, it doesn't make sense to use a line chart here because there's no connection between these separate data sets, and showing one is misleading," while the others roll their eyes. Sorry.

Storytelling

This may seem like a strange inclusion in this fundamentals list,[9] but I bet I can convince you in one sentence that you need to pay attention to the art and skill of storytelling:

> A postincident review/postmortem is fundamentally a story, a story you will have to tell, and tell well, at some point.

Did that work? For further reinforcement, I could pan the camera a little forward in time and say, "Next time you are in the middle of an outage and you have to explain to a peer or a manager what's going on, that's a story." Or I could harken back to the earlier discussion of data visualization and the need to construct and relate a story with the data at hand.

Humans are wired to receive information through stories. Tufte's books will convince you that stories are one of our best mediums for transmitting, receiving, and comprehending complex, multivariate sets of information like those associated with

---

9 I was tempted to call this section just "Collaborative Communication" because your communication skills will make or break your ability to live up to the important goal that SRE be "relentlessly collaborative." So, um, work on that too.

reliability. It is in your best interest to become a better storyteller and story listener as a result.[10]

Be a Good Person

I realize it is unexpected to include a "be a good person" section, but hear me out. It is incumbent upon SREs to learn continuously and actively, personally improve, and be the best we can be around privacy, ethics, inclusion, and equality (and others in the constellation of values these represent).

Here's why:

- We are entrusted to run some of the largest and most important systems on the planet. The comic book cliché "with great power comes great responsibility" is still true.

- Often we are the person in the room who can notice an unintentional flaw in data handling, coverage/representation, responsibility, etc. We need to continuously educate ourselves so that we will be prepared to spot and address issues in this domain. Some larger organizations have privacy engineers—if yours doesn't, you may want to consider what it would take for you to gain a little expertise in that area.

- A system that is not accessible to our users is not reliable. A system that does not preserve a user's privacy is not reliable. A system that makes bad decisions because it relies on data that only represents a single demographic instead of a representative sample is not reliable. A system that incorrectly addresses a user with the wrong pronouns or name is not reliable. I can go on (and you should), but I think you get the idea.

- SREs think in systems. It would stand to reason that this puts us in a position to be able to identify systemic oppression. What happens at that point, I leave up to you, dear reader, to decide.[11]

Bonus Round

In this section, I'd like to mention some subjects, the absence of which won't preclude your entry into SRE but will likely come knocking on your door at some point.

---

10 If you are looking to sharpen your storytelling skills in a professional context, I highly recommend Nancy Duarte's books.

11 One possible path is described in Chapter 32, "Intersections Between Operations and Social Activism," in *Seeking SRE*.

Non-Abstract Large System Design (NALSD)

NALSD is the Google term for the process of designing and reasoning about large systems. If you aspire to work on systems, or if your organization requires systems that can seriously scale, draw an arrow so this section is placed in "Fundamentals" on page 55. If scaling is not an immediate concern, pencil in time very soon to explore this topic in depth because it will likely come looking for you, current concern or not.

Finding good information about this topic can be difficult. Chapter 12 in *The Site Reliability Workbook* deals with this. I've found it surprisingly helpful to review some of the "So You Want to Get an SRE Job at Google?" interview prep courses on the subject. The *highscalability.com* blog[12] is also really helpful for thoughtful descriptions of large-scale architectures. I recommend picking an example architecture and spending some time trying to answer as best you can *why is this component here?* and *what happens if* <random component> *fails/recovers?* This exercise can be fun to do in a small group of people.

Resilience Engineering

I will profess my love for this topic elsewhere in the book, but I thought it deserves a mention here too. *Resilience engineering* is the academic discipline that has been studying resilience as a concept in largely noncomputer domains and systems (like aviation and medicine) for quite a number of years. Relatively recently, the ideas and approaches of resilience engineering have really caught fire in the SRE community as we've recognized its capacity to help us explore some of the key aspects of resilience in our systems too. I highly recommend checking out Chapter 28, "SRE Cognitive Work," in *Seeking SRE*[13] and watching some of the talks given at SREcon on the subject. There are some great books, papers, and academic programs on the subject. Resilience engineering will challenge your thinking about resilience and reliability in all the right ways.

One small warning: just like my analogy in the data visualization section on perfect pitch, studying resilience engineering can cause you to go bananas in the same way when you hear most of the industry use the term *resilient* (when what they really mean is something like *fault tolerant, redundant,* or, at best, *robust*).[14] My head has never returned to its previous size after the talk I heard John Allspaw give in which he

---

12 As I write this, the blog is in transition, so I hope it continues to be the great and unique resource it has been under Todd Hoff. An adjacent set of resources that could be used for a similar purpose are Alex Xu's System Design Interview books (and course) (*https://oreil.ly/0bbVy*).

13 There are some fabulous resilience engineering articles posted at the Adaptive Capacity Labs blog (*https://oreil.ly/qhE-6*) that are worth checking out.

14 A John Allspaw talk, the same one I am about to mention, was the moment where I first learned about this suboptimal language usage.

said (my summary), "Resilience is not having a spare tire in your car when it breaks down; it is having an understanding and command of transportation such that you can still get to your destination."

Chaos Engineering and Performance Engineering

I've made it clear in past writings that I'm a fanboy for chaos engineering (the real stuff [i.e., the scientific exploration described at Principles of Chaos Engineering (*https://oreil.ly/TDHEz*)], not "breaking stuff in production"). I'm lumping it together with performance engineering for the first time here, for a very good reason. At some point, you are going to get sick of living a reactive life. As appreciative as you might and perhaps should be of what outages have been able to teach you about your systems, you are going to start to wonder if there might be a different way to learn how your systems will behave right at the edge of your understanding. That's where chaos engineering and portions of performance engineering (e.g., load testing) can offer you answers to questions you didn't even know you needed to ask. As long as you take care with your experiments and your expectations (you are still going to have outages), both can be tremendously useful tools.

Machine Learning and Artificial Intelligence

I suspect this is another one of those suggestions that appears to come out of left field and seems peripheral to SRE, but hear me out for a moment as I tell you a story I haven't shared with very many people. When I was putting together *Seeking SRE*, I went looking for multiple contributors who could write about the subject of SRE and ML. In that quest, I spent some time talking to the person responsible for the operational aspects of ML at a very large social media company (that shall remain nameless). In that conversation, in several different ways, that person explained to me that to them, ML workloads were no different than any other kind of workload from an operations perspective. Sure, you may have to treat the model generation/training, distribution, and evaluation differently (perhaps using differently sized resources), but beyond that, same job, different day.

For a number of years, this became my default understanding of the subject. And then one day, in a discussion with some brilliant software architects I know, I realized that this view of the space perhaps was leaving out a key consideration that deserved much more attention. In many (most?) ML situations, there is a component of the system that does not function in the fundamentally deterministic way we like to depend on when we design systems. Instead, the behavior of that system becomes tied to the data flowing into the system in a probabilistic manner. In the past, our components would behave in certain ways based on the logic we programmed into them. In an ML world, we now have components that change their behavior based on models that learn from the data being fed to them.[15] I've heard that shift in thinking described as "Software 2.0," and while you won't find me using such a grandiose term, I do believe this causes us to have to contemplate reliability from a very different vantage point. Similarly, with the widespread availability of large language model–based AI systems, we are in the midst of some seismic shifts in the field, taking place as this is written.[16]

As a result, I'd highly recommend you spend some time exploring even the basics of ML and AI so that you will have some building blocks for your thinking on the subject when it shows up on your SRE doorstep. One excellent step in this direction is the book *Reliable Machine Learning* by Cathy Chen, Niall Richard Murphy, Kranti Parisa, D. Sculley, and Todd Underwood (O'Reilly, 2022).

What Else?

One of the aspects of site reliability engineering I enjoy very much is its capacity to encourage us to investigate, articulate, and iterate on our understanding of reliability as new situations and technologies arise. I've offered my thoughts on some of the prerequisites which give us the ability to do this, but I suspect you might have others. Do get in touch if you have found something not in this chapter that was crucial to your connection to SRE.

---

15 Exposing how those models are functioning in a way that a human can comprehend is still very much an active topic of research and may never be solved. You might argue that we have already been moving to a world where the systems we are constructing are so complex, an understanding of them can't fit in a person's head. I wouldn't disagree, but I believe there is still a profound shift to be considered here.

16 A quick shout-out to our new robot overlords, who I guess I welcome?

CHAPTER 6

Getting to SRE from...

In Chapter 5, I provided some ideas on the preparations one might need to become an SRE. If you haven't read it, you may want to check it out before continuing with this one. One thing that chapter doesn't do, however, is assert that everybody has to start in the same place on their way to SRE.[1] In this chapter, I'll try to offer some tips for individuals who might want to enter SRE from some common jumping-off (or in) points. The word *common* is key here because I come from a "big tent" perspective—there isn't a set of preordained predecessor roles required for entry into the field. In this chapter, I will be focusing on the entry routes I get asked about the most.

Are You Already an SRE?

I know this is perhaps a strange question to start the chapter with, but I have to ask it. In my experience, in almost every organization I meet, there are at least one or two people who go beyond "SRE-curious" and are actually operating from an SRE mindset in their job without any formal recognition or training. They are already actively working toward collaboratively improving the reliability of everything they touch. They are asking the right questions in meetings, initiating postincident reviews, building the right tools, and so on. Sometimes they are doing this in a fairly public fashion, but often they are working quietly in their own corner of the sky.

If this is you, congratulations, you may already be an SRE on the inside. Your challenge will be getting others to recognize it and the organization to codify it so you can do the role full-time with the backing and support of the organization, instead of it being a side effect of how you think and operate. The chapters in Part III may be of help to you there. One last suggestion: start to establish your connection to the SRE

---

1 Now would be a good time to reread the Adrienne Rich poem excerpt at the opening of the Preface.

community. Watch past SREcon sessions and SRE-focused content from other conferences on YouTube, drop in on SRE-related Slack teams and subreddits (details in Appendix C), and attend SRE-focused conferences virtually or in person. Finding others who are already primed to have the sort of discussions you want to have can be tremendously supportive.

From Student to SRE

If you're a college student,[2] then my advice varies depending on your course of study. Before I get to that differentiated part, I do have some ideas for all college students:

- Look around for a job that gets you closer to working with infrastructure.[3] Centers, colleges, or departments with research computing can be good places to start. Compute-heavy departments like computer science or engineering (which likely also have research computing) are also good starting places. Your school almost certainly has some sort of centralized IT support—the jobs there *could* be an OK place to start too.[4]

- Back in my day of running a computer science department's computing and networking environment, I led a student volunteer systems group that my predecessor started (see the paper "Tenwen: The Reengineering of a Computing Environment" (*https://oreil.ly/eXn0-*) by Remy Evard for some fun ancient history). This volunteer group gave students the opportunity to work on systems projects that often became part of the infrastructure used by the college. Sometimes the students were even responsible for running those services. It was also common for us to hire students from this group to work for us in higher-responsibility roles. I bring this up because you may be lucky enough to attend a school with student activities like this (or other venues like hackathons) that are a good gateway to experience.[5] Seek them out.

---

2 If you are a high school student or a "lifelong learner," welcome! This section is largely directed at college students, but there is good advice here for you too. You have likely already figured out that college students have a number of opportunities you don't, but do persevere. The drive you have makes you some of my favorite pre-SRE people. The field needs you.

3 Infra jobs are useful for certain kinds of future SRE activities, but there are others. If you can imagine wanting to approach SRE from an application-level perspective, finding a developer job that would let you focus on building reliable software is a great idea as well. Those jobs also exist in these settings.

4 I'm hedging my statement here because the jobs in a central IT group may be more likely to be of a transactional sysadmin/help desk nature. My sense is that the quality of these jobs is actually diminishing over time, so this is becoming a less good place to start a career leading to SRE.

5 I say, with no small amount of pride (even though the credit goes to the students themselves), that many of the students in this group went on to work for an impressive list of employers.

- Part of the goal of these suggestions is to get you access to resources, mentorship, and community you wouldn't ordinarily get sitting in a dorm room or at home by yourself. I have separate tips for each of these:
  - All of the major cloud providers want to court students in the hopes they will turn into revenue streams later in life (cynical, but true). As a result, they all offer some sort of respectable "free credits/access for students" program. Find one or several and take advantage of them to build a sandbox on the cloud where you can spin up and play with whatever technology tickles your fancy.
  - You may be able to get a wee bit of mentorship and community via some of the social media/virtual community listed in Appendix C, but an even better idea is to seek out conferences (virtual or in person) aimed toward your SRE interests (SREcon is an obvious one). Almost all conferences have either special rates or full grants/scholarships that make it more affordable for students to attend. Schools often have some money set aside to further offset costs of conferences for their students, so you may be able to get a free ride if you ask nicely. Conferences are a tremendous opportunity to level up your thinking and can also be a great place to jump-start your job search.[6]

OK, now on to the advice per course of study. I'm of the opinion that you can become a good SRE independent of what you study (though some majors/concentrations have a leg up). Here's my noncomprehensive set of advice:

- *Computer science/computer science–adjacent students.* Pay attention in class. No, I'm not kidding (says the CS major). Seek out and pay close attention to classes that contribute to your understanding of scaling/performance, distributed computing, queuing theory, and architecture, even if those are your most boring theory classes. I am here from the future to tell you they will pay off.

- *Engineering students.* Become CS majors. Kidding, just kidding (don't hurt me)! But perhaps do take some CS classes not offered in your department or college if it doesn't have the ones you need to supplement your incredibly useful engineering education. Maybe teach those CS students an engineering thing or two when you do so.

---

6 One small meta tip about conferences: it can seem, especially if it is your first time, that everyone else already knows everyone there. This is never true (there are always new people); you are just seeing either repeat attendees or people who are arriving with a premade set of connections (like a group coming from the same company). See if there are "welcome" pre-events for students or newcomers you can attend, or, barring that, find someone with an organizer badge and ask them for suggestions for a first-timer. Chances are, you will come away from the experience with one or more introductions to other people. Just having a buddy or a known friendly face at the same event can improve your experience a whole bunch.

- *Sciences (all flavors).* Besides the tremendously useful training for how to approach problems scientifically, I think it is safe to say that there are very few corners of the scientific world that haven't been touched by computing, often large-scale computing. I'm thinking of things like computational biology/ bioinformatics, network research, experimental physics, etc.[7] There's your in. Figure out what you need to do to do that type of computing "right," taking courses or (perhaps self-led) training toward that end, and you could easily be on SRE's doorstep.

- *"Humanities" students.* I am not trying to give short shrift to the musicians, artists, language majors, architects, gender studies students, ethicists, etc., by lumping them all together here. I firmly believe every one of you is learning valuable skills and approaches that will drive and enrich your work as SREs. Find the things in your field of study that will contribute to SRE[8] and learn/practice the heck out of them. For example, in Chapter 5, I suggested that having well-developed storytelling skills would be beneficial to an SRE. I can think of several humanities domains of study that produce expert storytellers.

- And in addition to mastering your field of study, get yourself to a keyboard and do what is necessary to backfill your technical knowledge with the stuff we talked about in Chapter 5. Classes like the free, online Introduction to Computer Science class from Harvard (CS50x) (*https://oreil.ly/K8HZm*) could be helpful with this. I say "go backfill your knowledge" perhaps a bit too glibly or casually, so let me acknowledge that it's going to be a bunch of hard work for you. But persevere. SRE needs you.

From Dev/SWE to SRE

Given the discussion in the last chapter around the coding and software engineering requirements for SRE, you might think that SWE is just a hop, skip, and jump away from SRE. In some organizations (notably Google), it is. But I don't think it is for most of us. The incentives present in the dev world don't necessarily lead people to focus on the places where the two professions could intersect. If you would like to make the switch with less difficulty, it means you will need to be intentional in shifting your focus to these areas as a first step onto the bridge.

---

7 Jess Males, a crack reviewer of this book, points out that in a research environment run by grad students in their spare time (which happens more often than you might think), it is not common to get exposure to "enterprise" or even many operations best practices. Software licenses or support contracts may be scarce too. Don't let this keep you from taking these jobs; just go into them understanding the deal.

8 If for some reason you can't identify what they are, get in touch with me. I have yet to find a field of study that is totally irrelevant to SRE, and I would be glad to help.

Which areas? Start here:

Behavior in production
How does your code really function when in production? This includes questions around behavior when the conditions aren't perfect (what happens if your connection to the database is 30% slower than it was in your dev environment or the network passes every other packet?). How will the code handle partial upgrades when different versions could be running at the same time? How about scaling and security; how will it behave when the internet can throw any input at it? What about split-brain situations (if the network becomes partitioned)? Does daylight saving time do anything interesting to its behavior? How does the code react to failures in dependencies? And so on (I'm just getting started).

Failure modes
As an important subset of the previous item, do you have a good sense of how your code could fail? How much load can it take before it falls over? When that happens, how can you tell that it is about to fail?

Instrumentation for operability/observability
At some point, someone else is going to have to figure out whether your code is running well and perhaps debug it if something goes awry. What have you built into the code to make this easy or at least possible?

Release-engineering considerations
How easy have you made it to handle upgrades? Schema changes? Rollbacks? Is that version of the software tightly coupled to other components? How are you handling dependencies?

Documentation
Have you already written good documentation for an SRE audience (assuming you know what constitutes "good" in this case—you may have to ask and iterate)? Chapter 19, "Do Docs Better: Integrating Documentation into the Engineering Workflow" in *Seeking SRE* has some guidance on this question.

If a number of these things seem to boil down to questions like "How much do you think about running your systems in addition to building them?" or "How much do you think about the operating environment that supports the code you write?" then that would be a reasonable summary. But besides just sitting down to have a good think, my strong suggestion is to shadow some of the operations professionals in your org if they are amenable. Just spending a little time with them (especially if you get to see systems under stress, perhaps an outage or two) will begin the alignment process in your brain. If your company offers the opportunity to do a rotation with an internal SRE or at least an operations group (and more should), jump at it.

Now, if all of this leaves you complaining, "But I waaant to coooode!" then there is good news here. I have yet to meet an SRE group that didn't need some coding work done, at the very least, on the periphery of the systems they are running. There are always tools that need to be built that either no one has had the time to build yet or that need help with "infracode" (coding in config languages used by provisioning tools). If you can offer your services, even if it is to assist with performance or reliability optimizations, it will create a connection that will be beneficial to everyone involved. Going from Dev to SRE can be relatively easy if you are willing to start thinking and stepping in the SRE direction.

From Sysadmin/IT to SRE

This is the most personal section for me because it is the road I actually walked. I will make every attempt to describe this path without implying that SRE is some sort of evolutionary step (up?) from systems administrator,[9] but there is a shift, and perhaps an expansion of thinking, required to make this transition—so prepare yourself for that.

Before I get into what is different between the sysadmin and SRE roles, I'd like to start with what is the same. Let's first look at some of your strengths that will help you if this is a transition you hope to make. Some of the sysadmins I respect the most got into the business and stayed there because they wanted to help people. While we love to build things and mess with the blinking boxes, ultimately, sysadmins live to serve, to bridge the gap between the technology and the people that have to use it.[10] SRE comes from a similar place. Sysadmins and SREs draw on the same desire to serve.

Another commonality between these two operations professions is a well-exercised skill for troubleshooting and debugging. You can't do either job without it because the laws of physics (or better, the complexity) around "it just works" are equally true for both. You can intentionally hone this skill through debugging challenges. Code debugging challenges on the web are relatively easy to find, but there are also intentionally broken virtual machines (VMs) and containers available to challenge

---

9 In fact, when I first started to talk to people about SRE, I would show them the human evolution illustration in Rudolph Zallinger's *March of Progress* and say, "The relationship is *not* this," to attempt to drive this point home.

10 I just want to acknowledge that I know (oh boy, do I know) that being in the middle can be a difficult place. I once attended a lecture by Edward Tufte, mentioned in Chapter 5, where he said, as an offhand comment, "Graphic design would be so great if it weren't for the clients." I have a considerably warmer view of our users, but I do understand where he was coming from.

your infrastructure skills, like those found at SadServers (*https://oreil.ly/7tc9t*).[11] If you can't find one you like, pair up with a colleague and have them make one for you. It should also be noted that challenges like this are very common for interviews and some certifications, so there are a number of incentives to pursue this route.

Those are two similarities that I think are particularly important. There are a bunch more, including (ideally) the importance of documentation, understanding of large swaths of technology and tooling, a security and privacy-centric mindset, strong professional ethics, and so on. Practicing and improving in all of these areas as a sysadmin will support your transition to SRE.

Given the similarities I've listed so far, it might be tempting to think, "OK, so I just need a title flip and I'm good to go." Alas, it is not that simple.

Title Flips; Don't Do It (Except in One Case)

This point was so important, I had to pull it out of the main text to be sure it came across loud and clear. I've seen this title-flip strategy, where a sysadmin or DevOps team all receive new SRE titles or team names, implemented a depressingly large number of times in the industry.

Let me be crystal clear: *it does not work*. A change of title may be easy, and you will indeed get a team of people called SREs, but you are not going to reap the benefits of site reliability engineering. If titles change without any change of focus, skills, mission, priorities, goals, etc., it will almost certainly be a disappointment.

Sometimes companies make title changes in an effort to attract more or different candidates for recruitment purposes. In my experience, this goes one of two ways if the job ads say "SRE" but nothing else has changed in the org: either (1) people with SRE experience will suss this out within five minutes of the first interview (or earlier) and bounce, or (2) people who don't know better will apply and get hired, so you will get more of the same.

But what about aspirational title changes, those changes where there is a real desire to transform an existing position to become more SRE? I have a bit of a softer stance on such changes when made in good faith. However, the rules are pretty much the same. If the change is made in isolation without the commensurate cultural, strategic, and organizational changes mentioned before—we are back on the same road to nowhere. The maxim you'll see in all O'Reilly SRE books, "Hope is not a strategy," is repeated for good reason.

---

11 A related story: one of my colleagues used to be in charge of building the workstations used by teams in a capture-the-flag contest. In the process of preparing those machines, he would place a hidden VM on them (that he wouldn't tell the teams about), which would lay dormant for the first part of the competition. Then, on day 2, it would suddenly wake up and start attacking the team "from inside the house." Fun, fun!

The softer stance comes into play when an organization is early in its adoption of SRE or SRE principles. In cases where titles have changed as part of a larger process to adopt SRE but things just aren't there yet, I'm standing here holding pom-poms, ready to cheer you on. My best advice in this case (which you will hear echoed in other places in this book) is to give yourself (singular or collective) plenty of time and compassion to reach this aspiration. I feel pretty safe in saying that changes of this sort always take longer than you expect to yield results.[12] But keep on keeping on.

The first step here has to be an internal one. You want to get to a place where your brain is reflexively thinking like an SRE's. If you haven't already read Chapter 2 on the SRE Mindset, do that now. If you have read it, maybe go skim it one more time because that is your destination.

This is going to be a change in focus for you. This is going to be a mindset change from "monitor all the things" to "measure reliability from the customer perspective, not the component perspective," from a default of "keep everything up 24-7-365" to "the appropriate level of reliability," and from "transactional system administration"[13] to "nurture feedback loops in your organization."

I know that the last paragraph sounds, at best, wildly aspirational and, at worst, like unobtainium to a large number of people reading. I know you are reading this as a break from staring at your endless ticket queue that got longer by two tickets since you started this sentence. I also know that you just received two useless email messages from your monitoring system ("You've got mail!"). I'm not saying this to freak you out or cause you to keep glancing over your shoulder in fear. I've just been there.

So how are you going to be able to take a step from your current context toward the SRE mindset? If only you had some source of data that would show you where to focus to improve reliability in your org. If only you had an easy way to know the delta between what you want to monitor and what you are monitoring…

The good news is that just such a data source exists, and it is right in front of you. Your ticket queue represents not just a bunch of transactional work but also a really good signal of the contributing factors that lead to both reliable operations and outages.

---

12 One reason I feel so safe is that data from places like DevOps Research and Assessment (DORA) bears this out. See the discussion in Chapter 11 for more details.

13 Hat tip to Tom Limoncelli for the term (or at least where I first heard it).

That ticket queue is potentially (though it probably wasn't intended as such) a rich source of data on reliability in your organization—if you take a moment to analyze it through the right lens. Similarly, those email messages from your monitoring system are cries for help from it. If you can determine the delta between those messages and the messages that would let you understand the reliability of your system from a customer's perspective, you have taken a major step in the right direction.

I mention the ticket queue and the monitoring emails because they are examples of somewhat less obvious resources for changing your mindset.[14] The basic idea here is that SRE seeks to improve the reliability of systems in a collaborative manner, using objective data. You may have more of those sources of data right at your fingertips without even realizing it. If you are a fish, you have both a really nuanced understanding of water and a tendency to not pay close attention to it.

More obvious resources to you (since we talk so much about it in SRE literature) are the outages in your environment. In many sysadmin environments, there is nothing resembling a postincident review conducted after an outage. At best, after a major outage, there might be a somber or sullen meeting that management calls with the team to "discuss" what happened. But that's not all that has to happen as a result of the outage. You could (ideally, with your colleagues) do a separate, deeper analysis of the situation and discuss it in an informal manner.

I want to be very clear that I am not advocating that you stand up in your usual blamey meeting with management and attempt to school them on what a real postincident review is and how they are doing it all wrong. Attempting to commandeer those meetings to make them something they are not will not go as well as you imagine in a daydream. The informal analysis and discussion I am suggesting could be a step toward improving them if you play it cool. Do this a few times and you might start accumulating material and expertise that could lead to an alternative way to handle postincident discussions (as we discuss in Chapter 10) that would be attractive to management. And even if you are not successful in assisting your management in approaching your outages in a more useful way, you will have at least started training yourself and changing your internal focus—and that's what this chapter is all about. Baby steps.

One other related small step you can take is to pay close attention to the language you use around outages and other reliability-related discussions. I'm the child of a sociologist, so I learned roughly around age seven that language constructs reality. As a simple example, using terms like *contributing factors* instead of *root cause* can

---

14 Niall Murphy, a reviewer for this book, suggests I should make sure I am not overpromising with this ticket queue idea. Ticket queues aren't always useful or even truthful sources of data, so your mileage may vary. The key takeaway here should be that a shift toward SRE involves looking around your environment for sources of signal.

change both your internal and external framing of a situation and what you can learn from it.[15] It makes a surprising amount of difference. (See Chapter 10 for more on this.)

Best Seats in the House

There is a good discussion to be had (as prompted by Kurt Andersen, a reviewer) about which roles or even which categories of people have the most distinct gap between where they are and where they need to be to be SRE. For example, students and SWEs (devs) may have a smaller gap from where they are to SRE than a preprofessional who is not technical entering the space. That discussion could lead to a different way of thinking about the role-X-to-SRE paths. The more specific taxonomy I settled on in this chapter works for me, but there is definitely merit in a more generic framing as well.

That discussion led me to realize that the people like sysadmins who currently have a direct connection to production outages and (ideally) operations-oriented situational awareness from ticket queues have some of the best seats in the house (even if the theater stage is on fire) to observe reliability.

This further suggests that others who don't currently have this clear of a view (be they SWEs, students, preprofessionals, etc.), who are sitting farther back or are in obstructed seating, should take it upon themselves to get closer to the action.

As a final piece of advice for a sysadmin who wants to enter SRE, I just want to point out that you don't have to do this in isolation. In Chapter 5 and earlier in this chapter, I've suggested a number of activities you can do with a colleague or a group of people. These include things like reviewing the architecture of large-scale services, close reading of other people's postincident review blog posts, analyzing your ticket queue, etc. Sometimes you are, to quote a friend, the "standalone sysadmin," so you have to walk this path by yourself. But sometimes you are lucky enough to work with other people who are game. If that's the case, ask them. It can be a lot of fun to change your mindset (and potentially your team culture) together with others.

---

15 Pretty please, don't treat this suggestion like some kind of drinking game where you get points for how many times you can slip the term *SLI/SLO* into polite conversation at work. Yelling "Bingo!" at a blamey meeting with management is also highly discouraged. I say these things in jest, but I am deadly serious about the benefits you will reap simply by paying attention to the language you and others are using when discussing reliability-related topics.

Generic Advice

To conclude this chapter, I want to offer some generic advice to everybody else not mentioned by role or expertise in this chapter, since an exhaustive list isn't possible or desirable. The question from Jess Males, one of the book reviewers, is, "What do we tell people who are, for example, currently network operations center (NOC) staff, desktop support, Windows server specialists, UA/testing staff, and so on?" My slightly more generic answer follows.

Technical Role X to SRE

For you folks, I'd like to mention that every one of the roles mentioned in the question cares deeply about reliability, even if they aren't currently viewing what they do through that lens. While I believe that there could be technical roles that have no connection to reliability, I'm a bit hard-pressed to name them as I write this. So that's the first piece of advice: find your connection to reliability and figure out how to swim in that direction. If it isn't immediately apparent how to do this, my corollary would be to notice which of the practices or even ideas in this book piqued your interest as you read it. What got you excited? Start there.

Nontechnical Role X to SRE

Kurt Andersen rightly points out that the advice in this chapter is almost entirely directed at people looking to enter SRE from another technical role. Guilty as charged, since that's the first place I see companies drawing their SRE hiring pool from—but it is not the only source. There are definitely nontraditional paths for people with a keen interest in reliability to be trained (or self-trained) into this role. I encourage those folks to find a single toehold and start climbing in the directions mentioned elsewhere in this chapter. For example, if you have a sales background, you (ideally) have an eye for seeing customer problems. Use that skill as a starting point for engaging with reliability.

Track Your Progress to Keep On Keeping On

Finally, and this applies to everyone I explicitly addressed in this chapter and everyone I didn't, Virginia Wilson, my fabulous editor, points out that it is really important to track your progress as you go along so that you can feel a sense of forward momentum. That sense can help propel you even when you feel mired, when the job interviews aren't panning out, when the existing organization is indifferent to your ideas, and so on. The things you write in a journal or say to yourself when in the pit of despair don't have to be any bigger than "read another chapter of the *SRE book*" or "attended my first SRE conference"; they all matter, and they are all signs of progress.

CHAPTER 7

Hints for Getting Hired as an SRE

This chapter is entirely written for the SRE job seeker, not the employer. I suppose you could reverse engineer the advice here to get some valuable tips as an employer, but the lovely Chapter 2 by Andrew Fong in *Seeking SRE* about hiring may be a more direct route. In this chapter, we will talk about how to evaluate job postings, and then I will give you advice on preparing for and then nailing your interview.

Roles That Are Out of Scope

There is a large alligator pit we need to cross before we can talk about how to get a job as an SRE. I will attempt to do so as delicately as possible. Scattered throughout this book, like raindrops from a gentle summer sun-shower, are less-than-subtle hints that not every SRE job/implementation is the same as every other one. This heads us into the identity and self-definitional aspect of the SRE field. Which jobs are SRE and which are less so?

I've tried very hard to avoid suggesting that there is only one true definition of SRE or what an SRE job is. I will continue to hold that line. That being said, SRE job "creation" through activities like title flipping pushes my relativism past the breaking point. I'm not going to judge anyone who is in a job like that; it just scores low on my internal game of "Is it SRE or not?" and hence, title-flip positions are largely going to be out of scope for this chapter. There is an entire Chapter 23 in *Seeking SRE* on SRE antipatterns if you would like to go into depth about different configurations of roles titled SRE that likely aren't.

If you are looking to land one of those positions (and more power to you), I would suggest making sure you are caught up on the latest thinking in the sysadmin/DevOps/IT service management/help desk support realms. A great place to start in this regard would be Jennifer Davis' book *Modern System Administration* (O'Reilly, 2022), followed by "the classics" in the DevOps field like Jez Humble and David Farley's *Continuous Delivery: Reliable Software Releases through Build, Test, and Deployment Automation* (Addison-Wesley Professional, 2010).

Scrutinizing the Job Posting

It wouldn't be fair for me to indicate that some jobs are more SRE-like than others without saying a little bit on how to spot the difference from the get-go. First, let's take a look at how to evaluate a posting for an SRE job. I'm not going to be giving you general advice on how to evaluate job ads[1]; there's lots of job-hunting resources that can help with that. When I scan an SRE job posting, I'm looking for both what they have included and what is absent from the text.

In the text, I might scan for (in no particular order):

The tech mentioned
All of the following is "first impression" fodder and should not necessarily screen a job in or out, depending on what you are looking for.

What I look for	What I learn from it
Modernity of the technology mentioned	Where are they on the adoption curve for various tech stacks?
How the items hang together	How cohesive is the environment? For example, Kubernetes and Prometheus experience required makes sense as a pair, while Kubernetes and Nagios experience required gives a hint that the environment is likely more "split brain," with a more modern infrastructure sitting next to a more "well-loved" (but still active) infrastructure.
Mention of "proficiency with a ticketing system"	How transactional is the environment? How quickly will things move in that environment if it is ticket-based?
Specific versions of software ("SuperCoolDB version 2.4")	They need a very specific thing done now. What happens next (upgrades, etc.) may or may not be important.
Mixture of on-prem and cloud product and feature names, mixture of vendors, mixture of commercial and open source	Are they all in one environment or the other? Do they have a monoculture? Need variety or stability in your life?

---

1 OK, I can't help myself. If the job ad mentions "ninjas" or "rock stars" or appears to have a little too much testosterone ("We work hard and play hard!"), I would be inclined to run in the opposite direction. This is basically, "Tell me your workplace has a toxic culture without telling me it has a toxic culture."

What I look for	What I learn from it
Mention of programming/scripting language(s)	Coding has at least some importance to them. Early in the book, I made the case that SREs will need to know how to code for a number of reasons.
Mention of traditional IT technologies (e.g., "printers" and "print servers")	The job has a traditional IT component or even focus.
Heavily skewed toward CI/CD and environment provisioning tools	May have previously been a DevOps position. Differentiation from the past role and transformation to an SRE mindset is likely going to be required.
Presence or absence of a monitoring technology	What connection, if any, would monitoring have to this role? (Hint: it should have one.)
Services that are consumed (third-party or otherwise)	More of a "what am I getting into" from a dependencies perspective. If you previously have had a terrible time with vendor X, you may want to avoid an environment built on X.

The human connections

Here you are looking for an indication, any indication, of collaborators and stakeholders. This is likely more of a "Have they left this out of the job ad?" factor, but with a little less scrutiny. This whole subject often gets left out of job descriptions and relegated to interview conversation.

Scale or accomplishments

Organizations with large environments, big customer bases, sizable revenue streams, exceptional traffic loads, etc., often brag about them in their job ads. I find myself being a bit torn about this aspect of an ad. If scale is your jam, this could be useful information. If bragging like this is a turnoff and you'd prefer to see a more "help people" mission or a clear indication of who they serve, then this is also information you can take into account. I've been clear in other places in this book where I believe SRE centers on these ideas of service to others. If you share that understanding and value, look for an indication in the ad that the organization recognizes this.

Diversity and inclusion

I've made the argument that diversity and inclusion is crucial to a healthy SRE culture in multiple places in this book. I personally want to see an indication that an employer recognizes this and is willing to put their money where their mouth is. As with human connections, this sometimes gets left out of the ad; I freely admit I am biased in favor of ads that address this in a nonperfunctory manner.[2]

---

2 …and kindness, connection, respect, and general humanity. But that's just me and not specific to SRE. Lest you think diversity and inclusion is a box every employer ticks these days, I have the experience of being in a job interview where the CEO looked at me like I had multiple heads when I mentioned I wasn't interested in working on a team entirely consisting of people who looked like me (white, cis-male). I have a very clear memory of her saying, "Wait, this really matters to you?" We ended the interview shortly after that…

There's a boatload of other contextual aspects to scrutinizing a job ad, many of which are not specific to SRE. What have you heard about the company or organization (and, if lucky, specifically about their SRE jobs)? Can you detect a title flip (e.g., last week the job was posted with a different title but the same description)? How long has the job been posted? Do you see SREs from the company participating in the larger community (perhaps giving talks at SREcon)?

Do They Publish Good Public Postincident Reviews?

I'm putting this question in its own sidebar because it is dynamite (both in how great it is and how volatile it can be, so one has to be careful). One way to evaluate a job posting is to look for postincident reviews that the company has publicly published. There is a tremendous amount of information that can be gleaned from a good review (not to mention adverse inferences you can make from bad reviews). You can often directly ascertain some details of their tech stack and the architecture of their systems, including how they have engineered their fault tolerance. Indirectly, you can get a sense of their troubleshooting, internal communication, and other processes.

The reason I say this information is volatile and needs to be handled with care is that they may still be feeling a bit raw about their incidents. If you bring the subject up in the interview as an attempt to show you really have done your homework, there are lots of ways your commentary might be misconstrued. Given this, my most conservative advice is, "Definitely go look at their postincident reviews for context, but don't bring it up in the interview yourself."

Answers to these questions can help bias you in favor of or against applying for a position. Rather than dwell on those, let's actually move on to the interview process.

Sometimes You Don't Have to Tick Every Box

A tip from Jess Males, one of this book's crack reviewers: don't think you have to meet every bullet. Overly specific and extensive lists of "required" technologies often have people self-selecting out of applying in the first place. While there's much to be done with the practice of crafting job descriptions, we also have the opportunity to challenge interviewers on whether overly long "requirements" really are absolutely required.

Preparing for an SRE Interview

How you prepare for an interview can be heavily dependent on the position and the organization. Preparing to interview for an SRE job that shares the same requirements of an SWE position may require you to bone up on your coding skills and computer science knowledge.

Preparing to interview for an SRE job that is heavily skewed toward release engineering might necessitate spending some quality time with a test environment and some CI/CD tools. Given this, is it possible to make any general recommendations? Regardless of the peculiarities of the position, there are four fairly universal topics you should be prepared to talk about in any SRE interview. I cover them here and include resources for each.

There's some significant overlap between this topic and what we just discussed in Chapters 5 and 6. All of the advice there for subjects to explore for becoming an SRE is useful to know for interviewing as well. As a result, I'm going to be brief here and redirect you to that chapter as appropriate.

NALSD (non-abstract large system design)
> If you plan to apply for SRE positions that involve scale in any way (which is quite frankly going to be most of them, I believe), you could do no better than to bone up on the subject area Google coined as NALSD. You should do this even if you never intend to apply to Google because it will stretch your skills and thinking in all the right ways.[3]
>
> *Resources.* *The Site Reliability Workbook* has a lovely chapter on the topic. There are a number of good talks on the subject (*https://oreil.ly/M4iqj*) given at SREcon (freely available on YouTube). I also recommend Google's public SRE Classroom (*https://oreil.ly/QNFhn*) materials and sessions, some of which have been delivered at SREcon. There is at least one course on prepping for an SRE interview, which costs money and is a decent intro to NALSD.[4]

---

3 Tip 1: find a large whiteboard and spend some quality time with it. In addition to it being helpful for practice, you will almost certainly be standing, in person or virtually, at a whiteboard as part of any interview that includes NALSD. Tip 2: during the NALSD-esque part of your interview, always take the time to clarify, confirm, and reconfirm that you understand the parameters of the system you are being asked to design.

4 One course is "Grokking Modern System Design Interview for Engineers & Managers" (*https://oreil.ly/5NrjJ*). A second one I like very much is the "System Design Interview" course (*https://oreil.ly/0bbVy*) by Alex Xu. His books on the subject are also well worth seeking out.

Monitoring/observability

Much has been said about the importance of this topic to SRE all throughout the book, so I will uncharacteristically avoid belaboring the point here and simply suggest you be on top of it before you go to your interview for all of the reasons we've discussed. I'm also going to add "statistics for engineers" to this bucket because this is the context where that most often appears.

Resources. Practical Monitoring by Mike Julian (O'Reilly, 2017) and the *Observability Engineering* books by Charity Majors et al. (all from O'Reilly) are great places to start. If you expect to discuss SLIs/SLOs, be sure to review Alex Hidalgo's book *Implementing Service Level Objectives* (O'Reilly, 2020). There have also been some great talks given at the Monitorama conference over the years that are available online for free on YouTube (*https://oreil.ly/4yAyg*) and provide practical guidance.

It could also be helpful to you to stand up one or two of the open source monitoring tools that are the current darlings of the SRE space (Grafana and Prometheus come to mind as of this writing) and/or gain access to some commercial offerings (cloud provider or third party) and play with them all. Ideally, you would set them up to mimic a configuration that would be used to monitor a production environment. While building this out, I'd encourage you to pay attention to how the various offerings you are playing with are similar and how they are different. If you are refreshing your basic statistics knowledge, there are many noncomputing-centric online courses on the topic. I also recommend the Statistics for Engineers workshops given by Heinrich Hartmann, which can be found in a number of places online, including YouTube and his website (*https://oreil.ly/fqhLB*).

Computing Fundamentals with a practical bent

By *computing fundamentals*, I am casting a wide net for topics that include computer science, computer architecture/operating systems, distributed computing, networking, and coding fundamentals mentioned in Chapter 6. By *practical bent*, I mean "as applied in the real world." As an example, when looking at computer architecture/operating systems, it would be very beneficial to spend time understanding how Linux and the Linux kernel works at the operating system level. For networking, while learning about something like the OSI model is good, studying and playing with real networking protocols in a home lab would be even better.

Resources. See Chapter 6 for a bunch of resources, like the online CS50x class (*https://oreil.ly/K8HZm*), to find the best ones for you and your current level of knowledge.

Troubleshooting/debugging

Prepare to demonstrate that you can troubleshoot an outage and have done so before. The likelihood that you will be given a scenario during an interview and be asked to role-play how you would react is really high.

Resources. There are lots of resources on the internet for learning to be a better troubleshooter; reviewing some of those could be useful. Chances are you have already started to build these skills, either explicitly at work or just from day-to-day exposure (it is hard to be in the tech world or interact with the tech world and escape the experience), so reviewing those examples is a good idea.

What to Ask at the SRE Interview

Congratulations, you've passed whatever was required for preliminary screening(s) and you have made it to the main interview round. You've been answering all of their interview questions handily (thanks to your prep from the previous section), and now you've come to the point where you are supposed to ask them things. This is your chance to probe to determine if the position and the organization is a good fit for you. What do you ask?

Be Prepared for Broken Interview Situations

Before we get too deep into what happens in the interview itself, I just want to sound one bell of warning. You should be prepared for job interviews in the middle of which you learn that the job you thought you were applying for isn't the one they are actually hiring for.

There are lots of reasons, some more savory than others, why the job posting doesn't match the reality on the ground. If you spot what looks like a red flag flapping in the wind during your interview, it probably is one. I'd also remind you that the "cockroach" principle (if you see a single cockroach, there is almost always not just one cockroach) applies here as well. What you do at that moment of realization is up to you, but I recommend you tread carefully with clear eyes.

I note that there is a ton of decent advice available for the generic job seeker, which you should definitely consult. I'm going to limit what I have to say to SRE-specific questions.

Here are a few suggestions for conversation topics. Note: there are far too many questions here to be able to ask in the ten or fifteen minutes you might get within a single interview session. Be strategic. Pick the ones that most directly address the things you are most concerned about and/or spread them out over the different sessions of your interview loop.

Tell me about your monitoring system.

Earlier in this book, I mentioned asking this in my own interviews and the surprising answers I received. I still think this is a great question for exposing all sorts of information on the role of observability, organizational structure/collaboration/ownership, how decisions are made based on data, how early monitoring/reliability is considered in their process, and loads of other things. I encourage you to pay attention to both what is said and what is omitted when you ask about monitoring.

Subquestions:

- Who owns monitoring in your organization?
- How many monitoring systems are there in active use?
- Who (which apps/services and teams) sends data to those systems, and who can (or does) access the monitoring systems to look at the data?
- How easy is it to onboard a new application/service to your monitoring?
- What decisions are made using the data in this system?
- Are there alerts generated from this system? (How do they work and—importantly—do people hate them? Are they actionable?)
- What makes you happy and unhappy with your current system?

Tell me about your postincident review process.

Here you are trying to get a sense of how intentional and effective they are at learning from failure. This will also often give you a good sense of group and organizational dynamics at play (and sometimes the bureaucracy involved). As discussed before, this can be a key component for tending toward greater reliability, so you can often get a sense of how much of a priority reliability is all up in the organization.

Subquestions:

- Do you hold postincident reviews after your outages (and what are they like)?
- What is their purpose?
- Who is "in the room" for them?
- How do you document your outages? Do you ever go back and look at these documents?
- Can you tell me (at whatever level of detail you are comfortable) about a recent outage?

- How are outages coordinated when they happen? (Is there a tool, does everyone hop on a bridge/chat? Is there a single chat space for all incidents?)
- Do you have a sense of the most common classes of outage you have seen in the last N months? (For example, are they config-involved failures, cascading failures, overload/resource-deprivation failures, code bugs...?)

Tell me about your on-call setup.

I don't find this topic nearly as important as the others, but I wanted to sneak this in because it has the potential to materially affect both your general experience and your work/life balance. It can also offer some insight into how humane the organization is in general.

Subquestions:

- Is there an on-call component to this position and how is it scheduled? How is it compensated? Do people get time off after incidents?
- Who in the organization participates in an on-call rotation? (Just SREs? Are there devs on call too? How about managers?)
- When was the last time you personally were "paged" as part of on call. If never, what about someone else who was on call? Is that answer measured in days, weeks, months, or minutes?
- Do people get paged equally often between work and off-work hours?

What problem or problems does SRE exist to address (or is SRE currently addressing) in your organization?

It would be good to hear a good, crisp answer to this question, if possible, but don't hold your breath. In my experience, people seldom offer a direct answer to this question. They very rarely provide a problem statement when asked. I almost always have to dig deeper by asking something like "I definitely agree that is an important aspect, but I didn't quite catch the problem you are trying to solve in your reply. Can you tell me the problem(s) SRE is attempting to address?"

It is possible they may not have a good answer to this question, which is useful information in and of itself for you about the position. See the sidebar "I'll Ask the Questions Here" on page 84 for an important warning. If that happens, you could back down to a question like "What are some 'recent wins' by SRE in the past 6 to 12 months?" If they can't answer even that or begin to articulate any successes in that time period, this may not be the position for you.

Can SREs check in code to major repositories in your organization?

Here you are probing just how direct an impact SREs are allowed to have on the reliability of applications and services. It also gives you a sense of trust and collaboration between SREs and devs/service owners. You will learn about the coding expectations for the job and the parity between SWE and SRE roles there.

I'll Ask the Questions Here

I think it is important to warn you about a potential response to these questions you should be prepared to handle. Sometimes you will hear, "We want the person we hire for this position to create the answers to these questions you are asking." Then you'll have a good sense of the maturity of their SRE efforts and your role in building it.

Assuming that this is something you want to do (and this is not a straightforward assumption—you may be looking to join an already established team), you should then switch your line of inquiry to determine the feasibility of the idea in their particular context. You'll want to understand clearly, at least:

- The history that led them to this point.
- The amount of organizational, institutional, people, and financial support available for SRE.
- Past attempts at running at this hill. (Have there been previous attempts at SRE practices?)
- Their expectations around time. What would they expect to be accomplished and by when?
- How they will measure the success of an effort like this.
- Where in the organizational chart would this effort sit? Often, there has to be a negotiation between feature work/priorities and reliability work/priorities. If the people behind (planned) SRE efforts and the people doing the feature work are too far apart on the org chart (for example, if you have to climb up the organizational tree three levels before you get to the person capable of calling balls and strikes), that negotiation could turn into a lot of work. Is that something you'll enjoy doing?

All of that is actually not the tricky part about the "the person we hire will be responsible for figuring those things out"[5] response you might get in an interview situation.

---

5 Kurt Andersen, a reviewer of this book, points out that this situation is far more likely to come up for manager or director candidates. I'd like to think that the info in this chapter can be helpful for candidates for those roles as well. Several eons ago, I was interviewing for a job and was asked about how I saw myself advancing over time. Young and naive me gave an answer about not wanting to go into management because it meant I would have to take my hands off a keyboard and cease building things. Even though this was many years ago, I still remember the interviewer responding, "At some point you start building things out of people."

The tricky part is that it may be followed up with the question, "So, how would you answer these questions?" Essentially, you have now set yourself up to have to answer your own hard questions. Be prepared to do so. Have at least some rough answers in your head so you can say, "Without knowing a bit more about your specific environment, I can't give a definitive answer, but in many environments, they do (roughly) X and I would start with…"

Win!

Congratulations, you got the job! or

Boo, you didn't get the job!

If it is the latter, I'd highly recommend (after the sting has started to go down) that you engage your SRE mindset and treat this like any other outage where some system didn't meet expectations. As funny as it may sound, it wouldn't be a bad idea to write up your own postincident review of the hiring process for this particular job. Not only would this be good practice, but it may help you to cast a dispassionate eye over what happened and see what you can learn from the experience.[6]

Good luck. I believe in you!

---

6 If you'd like to see an example of this, check out Michael Kehoe's SREcon talk, "A Postmortem of SRE Interviewing" (*https://oreil.ly/QdmYa*). It offers some spot-on advice for people doing the hiring, and it might also give you some insights into the process as well.

CHAPTER 8

A Day in the Life of an SRE

When people ask what a day in the life of an SRE looks like, they are mostly asking the question, "I get what SRE is all about, *but what do you actually do?*" While I could go all Phoenix Project[1] on this question and write a semifictional narrative about a semifictional SRE character, instead I will attempt to directly answer that question.

To get there, let me first mention the adjacent question: What does an average day look like for an SRE? I'm pretty skeptical that there is such a thing as an average day. I don't ever recall coming home at night and thinking, "Gosh, that was an extra average day." Different SRE jobs can be significantly different from one another. But even with taking that out of the equation, I'm not sure you could average the highest high days on the job with the lowest lows to produce anything like an average day.

Modes of an SRE's Day

Instead of trying to come up with some mythical composite day, let's instead look at some of the "modes" of the job that are in play on a daily basis. Just to be clear, these modes are meant to be descriptive, not exclusive. You can be in several at once or switching rapidly and seamlessly between them. If it helps, you can think of them as "hats we are wearing at any one moment."

---

1 Gene Kim et al., *The Phoenix Project: A Novel About IT, DevOps, and Helping Your Business Win* (IT Revolution Press, 2013).

Incident/Outage Mode

There are some days[2] on the job when you will be involved in an incident for most or all of the hours of that day. Those days feel qualitatively different from the days when you are not working an outage.[3] There is a particular blend of emotions associated with most outages (fear, anxiety, and sometimes anger, happiness, or relief upon resolution) and a fight-or-flight response that I think it is safe to predict you will feel to some extent. The depth and volume of this emotional response is often tied to the severity of the outage, the maturity of your incident response process, and the people who are working on the outage with you.

If you are on call, the probability of this being your primary mode for the length of your on-call rotation is pretty high. When you are in this mode, your experience is almost entirely reactive as the outage in front of you, not your internal planning, dictates what you will be working on.

Postincident Learning Mode

I put this mode here somewhat aspirationally because, ideally, after some recovery time (see the section "Recovery and Self-Care Mode" on page 93), you have the opportunity to begin engaging in the collection of activities and entering into the headspace necessary to successfully review the memories of an outage to learn from it. There is an investigative period where you attempt, in retrospect, to discover in detail and in totality what happened during an outage. You are responsible for documenting it in a way that others can understand without having been there. This investigation likely includes a combination of technological inquiries (like looking for data in your monitoring systems) and human inquiries (talking to colleagues to discover what they knew/understood and when). There may be a presentation aspect where you run or participate in a postincident learning meeting on the subject.

Why Postincident Learning Mode May Be Aspirational

I just want to acknowledge that there can be several reasons why this mode would be aspirational for you.

You may find yourself working in an organization with a less well-developed or even perfunctory approach to postincident reviews. Sometimes, you personally can level up your org's postincident review process; other times, you are not in a position to improve the situation.

---

2 Unfortunately, sometimes the notion of "day" gets stretched beyond 24 hours when you have a multiday outage. Remember to take care of yourself and your colleagues when this happens.

3 Though this section is calling out the impact that outages have on our mental state, I want to note that SREs can and should be having a positive impact on how others are experiencing the outage as well.

If it is the latter, and this makes sense for your situation, see Chapter 7, the chapter on getting hired as an SRE, and start updating your resume. If that is a little too extreme, I will say that just having awareness of what could be better about your learning from failure can often have a positive impact. You may be able to gain some ideas for how to improve things from Chapter 10, which is about learning from failure.

Builder/Project/Learn Mode

Yup, sometimes we sit down and build or build out things. Sometimes we spend time learning things. There's a whole spectrum of possibilities, including:

- Coding a custom application or service to perform SRE tasks or offer self-service interfaces to your users
- Provisioning new environments or infrastructure (in many cases, via some infrastructure-as-code tool such as Terraform)
- Improving your monitoring/observability/alerting universe
- Deprecating some service
- Removing toil from the operation or use of a service
- Improving some aspect of your release-engineering process (perhaps writing a test to catch something you learned about in an incident)
- Fixing the code of some part of a service that failed last week (similar to the previous item)
- Running chaos-engineering experiments
- Writing documentation
- Learning a new technology in anticipation of using it some day

That's just a very incomplete list of things I can think of off the top of my head, but it is a start. Your personal list may look similar or very different, depending on your organization and job role.

When I review that list, I realize I listed a bunch of largely fun things. In the interest of full disclosure, I do want to mention that the job isn't always happy bunnies hopping through meadows. There will definitely be times when you will be doing drudge work or the equivalent of cleaning out the Augean stables. Here's one place where the "removing toil" aspiration of SRE definitely comes into play. Here's hoping you can add that to your list.

Architecture Mode

This is a mode I wish happened more often in the world, so if it turns out to be largely aspirational for you in your current position, I totally understand. Ideally, an SRE can bring their expertise and experience to bear at the planning stages of a project, not just when someone wants to toss something at production or when it is failing there. Here, an SRE is showing up to design and planning meetings where they are acting as a representative of and an advocate for "reliability." Ideally this is happening in the same fashion in which you would invite a security person to those conversations early on in the process to make sure someone is keeping an eye on the security of a system that is being built.

In organizations where SRE is new and an unknown quantity or is thought of as "the people who respond to pages," this participation at early stages in the process is rarer, hence, my wish that it happened more. If this is the case for you, sometimes it is possible to parlay your postincident review work into a seat at the table. I want to offer a very strong warning to tread carefully and politically when doing this. No one wants to hear "This outage would never have happened if you had had an SRE in the room when it was being designed" (no matter how true you believe this to be).

If you are currently in a position where this notion causes you to sigh deeply because having access early in the process feels so very distant to you, I want to encourage you to keep pushing in whatever way you can.[4] Architecture mode offers so much potential for improving reliability. Beyond the basics of spotting single points of failure (SPOFs) before they manifest in the world, there's lots more you can do. For example, if you are hoping to create best practices, standard infrastructure building blocks, good monitoring from the start, and so on, this is often the best place to inject those into the development process. There's some further discussion of this idea in Chapter 16.

Management Mode

I leave this here to acknowledge that SREs are not always individual contributors (ICs). Sometimes we manage people or have larger managerial or supervisory roles, such as tech lead. There was a paper published at a LISA conference in 1995 that I found comforting when I first got into management.

---

4 Here's a secret about SRE and reliability: in the real world, the challenges around it are not always technical. Sometimes they are highly political. As much as you might be loath to go there, it will likely be in your best interest to hone your political chops at the same time you improve technically. Political problems have political solutions, so attempts to solve them with technical solutions almost never work. Know the difference and proceed accordingly.

In "Something to Nothing (and Back)" (*https://oreil.ly/O7TSX*), author Gretchen Phillips says:

> My daughters visited the office with me last fall and when we went home at the end of the day, they said "Mom, all you do is talk all day. What's your job?" I tried to explain to them that I go to meetings, I talk to people, and I read (and sometimes answer) my mail. But after saying this, I realized that I too felt like I didn't really "do" anything anymore…I was feeling quite dissatisfied about the amount of work that I would get done in any day; sadly, I had become a manager.
>
> Persisting in this depression much longer than anyone would like, I finally snapped out and realized that not only do I do something; I go to meetings, I talk to people, and I read (and sometimes answer) my mail; but that what I do is important and clearly some of the techniques that I'm using are valuable. This revelation occurred after returning to work after being sick (and I couldn't work from home) and finding a huge pile of things that needed attention on my desk and in my mailbox. And not one of my technicians (system administrators) had attended to these matters. In fact, several projects were waiting for me to help them along to the next step.

So, as an SRE manager, maybe the answer to the question, "What does your day look like?" is "I go to meetings," and that is very much OK.

Planning Mode

As an SRE, some portion of your hypothetical day will be spent on planning.[5] There's lots of planning to do, including:

- Implementation plans associated with architecture mode or builder/project mode
- Capacity planning
- Self-definitional work (what should we do as a team, what's the purpose of SRE in this organization, where do we want to go with it, etc.)

This is all pretty standard stuff, so I'm going to move on to the more interesting collaboration mode.

Collaboration Mode

Throughout this book, I've asserted repeatedly that SRE is "relentlessly collaborative," but what does that look like in real life? There are many, many possible facets to this answer, because collaboration is a many-splendored thing. Let me offer three examples (beyond those already mentioned in this chapter, for example in architecture mode) which I think are illustrative.

---

5 At least I hope it will. If not (remember that "hope is not a strategy"), see the discussion about proactive versus reactive and the need to strike a balance later in this chapter.

First off, the SRE practices of SLI/SLO definition and implementation (and the related work for the monitoring/observability to support them), emphatically *require* (in *almost* all cases[6]) collaboration. Working with your colleagues—developers, product/project managers, stakeholders, businesspeople, etc.—to understand the system well enough to be able to reason about its reliability and create SLIs/SLOs is deeply collaborative.

A second example is a review process that goes by different names in different organizations. I've heard roughly the same idea called "production readiness review," "application readiness review," "prelaunch review," and other similar names. While there is some variation in when these take place in a service or product's life cycle and what the actual review entails, the basic idea is the same. SRE gets involved sometime prior to a new or newly revised service being deployed to production to help determine what is necessary for it to run reliably in production and how close it is to that standard. This is often a checklist- or form-based activity. An SRE will use a standard checklist or form as the basis of a number of discussions with a product team. Together, they will look at various operational aspects of the planned service prior to it moving forward to launch.

Production Readiness Review/Application Readiness Review (PRR/ARR) Is in This Section for a Reason

I want to bring out something implicit but important about the PRR/ARR example. This example is intentionally in the "Collaboration Mode" section and not in some nonexistent section called "Gatekeeping Mode." It is crucial that you and the people who are going to engage with you in these practices view this work as a collaboration as much as possible. It is very easy for these activities to slip into the "requirements we dread or at best tolerate through gritted teeth" category and for the SREs associated with it to take on a gatekeeper role.[7]

This tends to happen when the process is perceived as onerous, persnickety, or idiosyncratic and/or the value of reliability in production is unequally shared. Call me naive, but I believe deep in my heart that the people who build things truly want their code to run as intended in production, even if the incentives in the situation don't always support that. Tap into this shared desire. It is incumbent on the SRE to communicate and act with empathy to strengthen collaboration.

---

6 Because you are going to ask about the word *almost*: sometimes SLIs/SLOs are created for entirely internal services that you or perhaps your team own and consume, and you never have to talk to anyone else. Those cases are rare and probably less interesting, but they exist. If your SLI/SLO work does not fit into this really narrow edge case and you are not collaborating with others, I'm prepared to argue that you should take a good, hard look at how you are going about this work.

7 More on this in Chapter 16.

My last example of collaboration mode shows up elsewhere in this book, but it is grounded in a truth that deserves repeating. SREs work to support services and systems for other people to use. We are constantly trying to meet and understand the expectations of our customers (external or internal) as a prime directive. This means we are (or should be) spending part of the hypothetical day collaborating with our customers. So how does this work in practice?

It's a little hard to answer this question in a fashion that addresses all of the possible service/product scenarios, so I'm going to fall back to something basic and state that it starts with listening to the customer. Questions beget questions, so how does an SRE listen to their customers? An equally basic answer to this is: through our monitoring work. Our monitoring often offers a strong source of signal if we use it to ask the right questions. I should also note that SLIs/SLOs have at their heart an ongoing collaboration with the customer.

Recovery and Self-Care Mode

This is at the end of the list of modes because it should accompany every other mode, not because it is less important than others. SRE is a compelling and potentially all-consuming career. It offers a particularly potent brew of exciting and interesting work, combined with a sense of responsibility and self-worth that can lead very easily to overextending yourself. This, plus the general cultural milieu around hero worship and romantic appreciation of courageous "smokejumping" or "rappelling down the side of the building to save the day," makes it very easy for SREs to fall into an unhealthy and unsustainable work life. Don't do this.

Take care of yourself (and others).

Burned-out humans don't build or participate effectively in reliable systems.[8] When I hear that someone is regularly working 60–75 hours per week (even when said with pride), I no longer hear that as something to be celebrated or appreciated. Instead, now I hear that as a failure in the system that should be fixed.

The type of work we do requires that we take time for recovery and self-care. Despite the cultural messages we have received around this, this is a perfectly valid mode to be in, so don't skip it. If you are in a management position, make sure this is part of your culture and that your employees feel comfortable in taking the time they need for recovery and self-care. Besides just being the right thing to do, it will ultimately lead to better reliability in your world.

---

8 Most of the systems we build become sociotechnical systems. Resilience engineering has lots to say on this topic.

Balance

I feel I would be strongly remiss if I simply said, "Hey, so SREs do a bunch of things, and they move in and out of a bunch of modes" (which is true) without saying something about the ways these can combine to form a more or less effective result.

There are a number of diametrically opposed aspects that come into play on a daily basis for an SRE, a good number of which I have already mentioned in this chapter. Here are a few:

- Toil versus work that has lasting value[9]
- Reactive versus proactive work (sometimes discussed as reactive versus project work; are you firefighting versus fixing the code in a service to improve its reliability?)
- Interruptive versus "flow state"
- Solo versus collaborative work
- Crisis versus noncrisis

It's pretty easy to keep going with a list like this thanks to the nature of the job, but I want to stop and talk a bit about some of the existential truths that make discussing balance in this context a little more complex. While it would be swell to be able to be Pollyanna and just say to you, "Strive for balance in all things," followed by some equivalent of a mic drop you do with a keyboard, it's not so easy.

People really like to quote a version of "every SRE needs to spend at least 50% of their time on engineering work"[10] or some version of the "50% project work" dictum, but they usually leave out the rest of the quote. In this case the quote continues "...when averaged over a few quarters or a year. Toil tends to be spiky, so a steady 50% of time spent on engineering may not be realistic for some SRE teams, and they may dip below that target in some quarters." That quote is specifically about toil, but similar statements exist around reactive versus project work as well.

The key thing to note here is that while striving for balance is a great idea, there are often situational factors that complicate that effort. For example, one factor that I have seen come up again and again is the difference between the "early service" and "mature service" experience. New services almost always are noisier, require more

---

9 And all of the other attributes of the word *toil* as we use it in an SRE context, see Chapter 6, "Eliminating Toil" in *The Site Reliability Workbook* for details.

10 Also from Chapter 6 in *The Site Reliability Workbook*.

reactive work, and provide more toil to be stripped away.[11] I bring this up because SREs can get stressed by the meta-situation of spending less than 50% of their time on their desired kind of work, through no fault of their own. Sometimes you just have a new service you have to roll with. Sometimes you will be asked to step in to deal with a more mature service that is on fire, and—guess what—you may be doing more firefighting than proactive work. To my way of thinking, these situational factors are like weather patterns for services. I know sometimes it is going to rain hard for a period of time, and so, I am mentally prepared for that eventuality.

Ideally things will level out. If they don't actually level out, that's where the striving for balance (or the quitting to find it in another position) comes into play. Sometimes the lack of balance is situational in a less fun way because the organization or the context around your role has issues or deficits that don't offer a light at the end of a tunnel.

I don't want to sugarcoat this for you. There are bad jobs in SRE. If you have one and you have the economic flexibility to leave it, I support you doing so. You deserve to be happy in SRE.

Let's not leave this chapter with such a sad trombone; instead, let's reframe the previous doom and gloom. One of the things I value strongly about SRE is that it brings up this subject at all and offers a clear opinion on it. As I mentioned early in this book, SRE attempts to be a sustainable operations practice. Balance is an important part of this. I hope you can find it in your SRE practice.

Make a Day in the Life a Good Day

To bring us back to where we started as a way of getting off this ride and ending this chapter, I want to say something about exercising choice. In this chapter, I've tried to fill out your understanding of what you may encounter in an SRE's day. I've also tried to emphasize aspects or qualities that can (and I think should) be present—like balance. It is my experience that those qualities and positive experiences don't necessarily manifest in the way or amount we would like if we are not mindful and intentional toward them. I would encourage you to choose that path.

---

11 The degree of which can also depend on how mature the organization is, how many times they have launched something with this profile in production, how experienced the people working on the project are, etc.

CHAPTER 9

Establishing a Relationship to Toil

Given how often the subject of toil comes up in the SRE context, it is remarkable how murky the topic remains, how imprecise we are in our writing and conversations on the topic, and how disconnected it is from our development and operations practices. Some of the best writing on the subject can be found in Vivek Rau's Chapter 5, "Eliminating Toil," in *Site Reliability Engineering*, and in Chapter 6 of *The Site Reliability Workbook* (O'Reilly, 2018) by a larger cast of authors. If you have not read both of those chapters yet (both are free online for all to access), I strongly encourage you to do so before proceeding with this one.

In this chapter, we are going to avoid the rehash of those chapters that most articles on toil undertake and instead focus on ways SREs can establish a nuanced and healthy relationship to toil once they have read those fundamentals. To do that, I'll quickly quote the definition and then use it as a springboard to start our exploration.

The first step in this process is increasing the precision of how we describe toil when discussing it. There's a good reason why some cultures have a substantial vocabulary around the weather patterns we file under the heading of *snow*. Different manifestations of snow can necessitate different responses or at least produce different experiences for people. Being able to speak about toil in a nuanced way gives us more options for how to respond to it.

Defining Toil with More Precision

The first trap we need to avoid is getting mired in the colloquial understanding of *toil* (stuff we hate to do). Vivek Rau's expression of the "Google definition" of the word in the *SRE book* is helpful for this. He lists the following as characteristics of toil in his definition:

- Manual
- Repetitive
- Automatable
- Tactical
- No enduring value
- O(n) with service growth[1]

Rau is quick to point out that it isn't necessary for an effort to check off all of these boxes to be identified as toil, but the more each bullet point is true and the more characteristics match, the more likely it's toil.

Though Rau does not connect the dots this way in his chapter, if you start to observe some of the negative side effects of toil he mentions,[2] that can also confirm your identification of toil. I would just caution you that using this method relies on trailing indicators. By the time you spot any of these indicators, damage is already done (similar to identifying which mushrooms are poisonous by tasting them).

Are Incidents/Outages Toil? Are Tickets Toil?

The *SRE book* leads the section "Calculating Toil" (Chapter 5, "Eliminating Toil") with the amount of time Google's teams spend doing on-call work and lists on call as the second-greatest source of toil (with interrupts being the first). This might lead you to conclude that on call is strictly a toil engine. Let's explore this by asking a basic question: "Are incidents/outages toil?" and the corollary of "Are tickets toil?"

---

1 Quick explanation for our noncomputer-science major readers: this characteristic describes work that scales linearly with the growth of the service. For example, if it takes an hour to do the work by hand to add 100 users to the service, 10 hours to add 1,000 users, and a little over 4 days to add 10K users, it is scaling linearly. In general, SREs are keen on being able to scale our services without having to grow the team (at least at this rate) whenever possible.

2 Just a reminder that in Chapter 5, "Eliminating Toil," of the SRE book, it is suggested that toil can have the impact of "career stagnation, low morale, creates confusion, slows progress, sets precedent, promotes attrition, causes breach of faith." There are real consequences at stake here.

I say "it depends" if I'm being charitable. If I am being less charitable, I would say that both are toil "more often than not." The type of work that comes in via tickets is usually just straight-up toil that closely hews to Rau's formulation. Incidents where the situation is a repeat of a previous incident are pretty clearly toil as well.[3] But those are not the interesting cases.

A more interesting case is a novel incident where the situation leading to a loss of service has never been seen before. Others have made the argument that on-call experience is valuable because it offers an education about systems and production environments that cannot be obtained elsewhere. Presumably they are referring to on-call experiences of novel incidents. Novel tickets could conceivably be a low-intensity version of the same idea. This leads us to the peculiar conclusion that sometimes, things aren't toil until they are.

The magic element that makes this alchemy possible is whether we are able to learn from it—this provides the enduring value that bounces the experience out of the toil bucket.[4] This emphasis on learning/learning from failure is one place where SRE is internally consistent.

Whose Toil Are We Talking About?

When defining toil, there's a very simple question we shouldn't omit even if there is a common assumption around the answer, namely, "Whose toil is it?" We are almost always referring to *our* toil in this context, that is, operational toil as experienced by the operators of the system, not the customers.

That answer is a little unusual given how many other places in the book I exhort you to consider things from the customer's point of view; for example, I urge you to monitor systems from the customer perspective, reliability as a measure of satisfying customers' expectations, and so on. Relieving customer toil is usually relegated to the purview of product management or the people shaping the development of a product. There's an interesting exception to this rule we will discuss later in the section "Dealing with Toil" on page 103.

---

3 And you can make the argument that the repetition is a potentially good indication of insufficient project work effort. It also helps broaden the definition of *toil reduction*.

4 At this point, you may be thinking, "Hmm, so what can I do to make a larger percentage of incidents (and tickets) novel/learning experiences?" Yup, that is indeed the question.

Customer Toil, a New Frontier for SREs?

I want to make two forward-looking asides before we move on from customer toil. First off, just as SREs are often advocates for customers on subjects that are not strictly reliability concerns—for example, security and privacy—I think we have a similar potential to be a force for good in meetings and in planning processes around reducing toil for customers.[5] We are really good at spotting toil, so if you see something, say something.

Second, my instinct says there is an interesting connection between operational toil and customer toil but that there has been insufficient research to explore it to date.

Like what sort of connection? Well, for instance, operational toil is sometimes exposed to the customer and transformed into customer toil in the form of multiple steps they have to perform to submit a provisioning request. Customers might have to make three separate requests (computer, storage, and networking), which is a reflection of the operational toil involved. (Latency between initial request to final fulfillment is also really high in a multistep process like this, but that's just another side effect.). This isn't Conway's law per se, but it certainly feels like a resonant frequency.

There is an entire frontier on this subject to investigate. If you have thoughts on this matter, please get in touch to share them.

Why Do SREs Care About Toil?

Two more fundamental questions we need to ask are why are SREs in a relationship with toil at all, and what is the nature of that relationship?

Given that SRE is an engineering discipline overflowing with paeans (or perhaps elegies) to reliability, you might think that the rationale for SREs to engage so heavily in a battle against toil would be strongly rooted in some sort of impact on the reliability of a system. This may be a bit controversial, but I am here to tell you that it is not true.

Most articles on the subject have tried to make the case that ameliorating toil requires automation, automation reduces mistakes, and a reduction in mistakes leads to greater reliability (or some variation of this argument). Toil has a real connection to SRE, but I don't believe reliability through automation is that driver. Anyone who has

---

5 Fair warning: not all customers will perceive the value of toil reduction the way you might. They might view the cost/benefit trade-off differently than you do. Also, as Niall Murphy, a tech reviewer of this book, points out, sometimes when a team is "better at cranking through manual stuff and worse at coding, it might actually make sense as a trade-off."

seen automation as the unintentional bad actor in a recent outage or who has a more nuanced view of automation and how it can fail can spot just how shaky this case actually is. Usually these articles give examples of theoretical cases where automation is the silver bullet, but on the whole, I don't buy it. Let me offer three other ideas, the second of which is the one you should probably tell your management:

Aesthetics

This is the connection I believe in the most. SREs work to eliminate toil because it offends their aesthetic sensibilities. In plain terms, they find toil inelegant, inefficient, unnecessary, suboptimal, and just plain yucky. This is a reflection of how our brains are wired, somewhat similar to having perfect pitch and the daily challenges that brings (i.e., every time you attend a concert and the piano is out of tune, which is basically most of the time).

Money

There is probably a gentler way to say this, but people cost money. Recruiting and paying highly trained technical people like SREs (and SWEs) costs lots of money. Organizations have many reasons to want their expensive people to be doing work that moves the world and the revenue forward, meaning work that is the antithesis of toil. They have a significant financial interest in avoiding the last bullet point from Rau's toil characteristics list ("O(n) with service growth") since their balance sheet would prefer they hire as few people as possible to operate as many services as possible.

Use of time/job satisfaction

This is arguably a subtopic of the previous point because, ultimately, it is about money, but it is important enough to highlight separately. There are second-order effects of toil at play here too. For example, most technical people would prefer to avoid spending their entire day toiling versus building, so team happiness and hence retention can be strongly impacted. Excessive toil also adversely impacts the amount of cycles available to do other (preferred) work. The references I mention in this chapter and other writing found on the internet will convince you that toil can quickly go from being a mild irritant to a real menace if left unchecked.

These three drivers dovetail nicely. An SRE's constitutional makeup leads them to want to address toil, and the organization's financial interests lead it to be happy (and the people reducing the toil to be happy) to incentivize this work even if it is not directly related to the primary reliability-focused aspects of the job description.

The Dynamics of Toil: Early Versus Established

Now that we have a better definition of toil and an unvarnished understanding of why we care about it in the first place, we can move on to a more nuanced understanding of it as a system in and of itself. Let's talk about a couple of distinct kinds of toil and how and when they manifest.

One thing I have noticed that can get in the way of establishing a healthy relationship to toil is the somewhat crude way we talk about how it comes and goes, manifests and changes. Usually the entirety of the story people tell is, "There is some toil and we worked to reduce it." The nuance that is missing here is the dynamics of the situation. One such dynamic is the connection between service maturity and toil.[6]

In the vast majority of cases, new services have more toil associated with them. Why?

- New services are still in the process of tuning their monitoring and alerting. They are, as a result, "noisier."

- The processes required to operate a system are almost always classified as "nonfunctional requirements," meaning they aren't part of the set of core features that must be built as the raison d'être of the service. That service/product/project is being built to do something or provide something to customers; the thing you have to do to run the service is very seldom one of those core features. Though it would be swell if those operational levers were well considered during the design phases, it is probably appropriate that most of the attention was paid to the core functionality.[7] Often the required automation to reduce toil isn't coded until much later in the process (if at all). This, by the way, is one of the strongest arguments for the assertion elsewhere in this book that it is important for SREs to be in the room during the early stages of a development effort.

- As much as we would like to believe in our own omniscience when it comes to running services, often the environmental or contextual aspects of how a system will function in production only become clear when we get into production and hidden assumptions and limitations bite us ("Oh, you mean a single endpoint can handle just 100 different forwarding routes; that's just swell!"). We are then in a position of bailing out the boat a bucket at a time (toil) while we hopefully find the source of the leak or build a better boat.

---

6 A Google blog post (*https://oreil.ly/Ichv5*) also describes a relationship between service maturity and reliability.

7 While I understand that the focus on functional requirements can also be responsible for other omissions, I tend to be a little less forgiving when scaling concerns are left out of the planning process. Security too.

- Another less probable but "happens more than you would expect" variation on the previous item is that the customers of the service start using the newly built service in unexpected ways. As a slightly contrived but true-to-life example, imagine what happens when people start using the new email system as their document-archiving system or their large-file transfer system. You may find yourself having to deal with a whole bunch of storage allocation or management toil that was never expected.

So why does this "new services have greater toil" dynamic matter? First off, it allows us to set our expectations around toil in a realistic manner. We can mentally prepare for (and build into our team commitments) a period of time with greater toil and toil reduction work. It is the difference between being caught in the rain and knowing it is going to be a rainy day because we understand something about the weather formations in the area. If you can rely on future effort to reduce the toil of a new service,[8] then you can think of the toil you are initially stuck with as finite, which makes it much easier to bear.

A second reason this dynamic matters is that it suggests we can distinguish between *early toil* (the toil that is associated with the early days of a service) and *established toil*. Early toil will, in theory, diminish as part of the engineering work performed to mature the service, as we discussed earlier. Established toil is much trickier. Established toil can be either toil that was never cleaned up during the creation of a new service that just continues to hang over the team or (worse) toil that is somehow integral to the service. Identifying the source of the established toil allows us to understand the potential amount of effort that will be required to excise it, up to and including a total rewrite.

A related observation that will be important in the next section is to note that *early* versus *established* starts to get us talking about toil as it manifests in and against the dimension of time. A nuanced approach to the subject will pretty much always require we place toil into a chronological framing.

Dealing with Toil

This is the last section on establishing a relationship with toil. Now that we have a wider and more nuanced understanding of toil and how it behaves, what are we going to do about it?

---

8 As in, you work in an organization that is committed to toil reduction in their engineering planning and resource allocation. If you know that your organization is the opposite of this, that's a much less pleasant story.

Much of the (largely non-Google) writing on eliminating toil seems to suggest that the story goes like this: Identify toil in your environment. Eliminate it through some sort of automation or self-service mechanism.[9] Done. Easy, right?

I'm not yet ready to claim this is an original law, but I believe the evidence is strong enough to declare the following pretty solid postulate: I assert in a Newtonian fashion that toil cannot be created or (most importantly for the purposes of this discussion) destroyed—at best, it can be transformed. Call this "conservation of toil" if you'd like.[10]

Let's look at what this means and why it matters.

In the tale we tell ourselves where automation is a deus ex machina solution to toil, we usually elide the inconvenient truth that the toil hasn't been eliminated, it has been transformed.

Transformed into what? Complexity.

Now that we have a new layer of code running to "eliminate the toil," we have a new challenge. You will need to manage, take into account during planning, and discover/respond to that code's failure modes. Don't get me wrong, I believe that in the overwhelming majority of cases, this is a wise bargain to strike with the universe, as long as you go into it eyes wide open and are consciously accepting the trade-offs.

In the tale we tell ourselves where self-service mechanisms we create are the grand liberator from toil (well, at least *our* toil—see the previous section "Whose Toil Are We Talking About?" on page 99) we usually elide the inconvenient truth that the toil hasn't been removed; it has just been shifted from the operations staff and spread as finely as possible over the users of the system, who are now collectively shouldering the burden. So where's the trade-off inherent in this transformation of toil? This moves us to a maximally distributed/decentralized system where every user now has their own individual dixie cup of toil,[11] which offers its own challenges (complexity again). As before, this is usually the right call to make, as long as you are prepared to live with those challenges.

---

9 Which, in many cases, they are happy to sell you.

10 In a strongly worded comment on the text during its review, Niall Murphy pointed out a corollary, or perhaps an exception, that I left out since he disagrees with my assertion that toil can't be eliminated. Design can directly change toil requirements. So, perhaps I would rephrase my original statement as "created or destroyed except by fundamental design choices and changes." That's not often an option (and I might be tempted to claim that after a fundamental design change, it is no longer the same system…).

11 When I discuss a tiny amount of toil, I refer largely to self-service provisioning scenarios where a dev can use an internal process/website/tool to request something and get it without having to ask another group for that resource. For scenarios of larger scope, for example, full-on "you write it, you run it," book reviewer Kurt Andersen rightly points out that "the main problem with pushing responsibility/ownership of systems onto the teams who create them is enabling them to manage the complexity of doing more than writing code."

In the broader sense all of this matters because in order to have a healthy relationship with toil, it is important to have a clear-eyed understanding of what really happens when we "eliminate toil."[12]

Exploring Conservation of Toil

I know that there is a sizable subset of readers (because I'm one of them) who will want to dig into this idea in a bit more depth, so here is the director's cut sidebar addressing two further questions. Please feel free to skip if this sort of noodling is not your jam.

Question 1: How can toil not be created? Didn't you say that early services bring with them new toil?

Super good question. I believe when we make certain architectural decisions in the construction of a service, we are tapping into the toil inherent in that pattern (that has always been part of that pattern; we are not creating it). For example, if we decide our service is going to involve separate identities for "users" or "accounts," the door to the room where the universe keeps its toil has been opened.

Question 2: Let's imagine that I rewrite my service to no longer have users; haven't I just removed/destroyed that toil?

To address this question, I'd probably first ask the magician how they did this trick without incurring a complexity hit (or pushing that complexity someplace else). I'd also be inclined to be curious about whether the rewrite has produced a system that is accurately described as the same service (which admittedly dodges the original question by dismantling it).[13]

I believe there are lots more questions to explore about this conjecture. My fond hope is that the SRE community will explore the theoretical side of toil more.

Intermediate to Advanced Toil Reduction

Most of the discussion of toil reduction focuses on single system examples. The story is usually something like "There was a system that required X manual steps to operate it. We automated away that step. Yay us," or "We spent a significant amount of time vetting and approving requests for X, so we created a self-serve system that didn't

---

12 After pondering this question for some time, I find myself starting to wonder whether the term *eliminating toil* is problematic in and of itself. I also wonder whether thinking about toil from a harm reduction perspective would be a useful replacement for eliminating toil.

13 For some reason, I'm reminded of the saying, "If my grandmother had wheels, she'd be a streetcar," used to show how hypotheticals of this ilk fall apart.

require us to do that. Yay us."[14] These are all good stories and every one should be celebrated. And in fact, you may need to amass an entire series of these stories before you have accumulated enough reputational capital to convince people to allocate the engineering resources required to level up your toil reduction work.

The next step up from those single-system victories is mounting efforts to identify and eliminate whole classes of toil from the environment. For example, if onboarding a new service to the central monitoring system has traditionally been a laborious one-at-a-time task, a project that makes it trivial for a new service owner to build in telemetry that flows to your monitoring is a dual win. Not only does it make "the right thing" the easy thing, but it hops over an entire class of toil around monitoring in your environment. The usual onboarding contribution to "early toil" could then be absent on launch of a new service if your project is a success.[15]

A further expansion from single-system toil efforts was hinted at previously when I mentioned the value of talking about toil within a chronological context. Engineering capacity is (to be pragmatic[16]) a woefully finite thing. If you consider time when thinking about toil, it naturally leads you to start asking the important question, "Do I allocate my finite capacity to address past toil (established), current toil (early), or future toil?" More advanced toil reduction efforts usually aim to reduce the toil you are going to have. It is common (and perhaps advisable) to have some combination of temporal directions in play at once.

There is one last intermediate-to-advanced step up from smaller-scope toil reduction work worth mentioning. It can be good to conduct research designed to identify and often quantify toil (usually in terms of cost to the organization[17]) in the environment. This can take it beyond the "I'll know it when I see it" place we all start at to a standard/practice and a currency figure the business knows how to reason about. These efforts are usually undertaken in one of two ways: ask the humans or ask the computers. Surveys, interviews, and work shadowing fall into the first category. Analysis of ticket system data, postincident review taxonomies, and "manual" tool usage stats are examples of "ask the computer" data collection.

---

14 This is an example of taking the toil off a central entity and spreading it out amongst all the users with all the complexity it entails.

15 Though I am going to assert that there will still be some *tuning*-related toil headed your way.

16 As opposed to viewing it theoretically with magical thinking like "We can always hire more people" or "We can always move people around to take care of that if it happens."

17 Chapter 5 of *The Site Reliability Workbook* has a lovely section on ways to quantify toil and its current impact that will be highly persuasive to people controlling budgets. There is a further good discussion about budget conversations in Chapter 13 of this book.

In my experience, as much as we would like to gather our data and analyze it without having to resort to talking to people or collecting self-reported data from humans, both approaches are required. Presuming you are asking the right questions; surveys are more likely to help you identify the gaps in your machine data or spot toil-related human decision-making processes.[18] They can help you uncover things like "sometimes, the automated deployment system is not used because it doesn't handle a particular use case" or is "too onerous to configure."[19]

What Are *You* Going to Do About It?

To end this chapter, I just want to point out that we all need to form a relationship with toil (the SRE kind), both as individuals and as organizations. That relationship can and will change over time, but it will always be either intentional or unintentional. Your call.

---

18 We all want to get our work done. People are more often than not willing to take a toil hit on a daily basis "invisibly" if it means getting the job done. Asking people about how they do their work will uncover this toil, but you are going to have to ask first.

19 To be clear here, you might be able to spot the behavior in cases like this from your logs, but identifying the rationale is a whole other thing.

CHAPTER 10

Learning from Failure

There are lots of SRE practices in this book, but this is the only one that is getting its own chapter. Learning from failure is at the nexus of an active SRE practice that seeks to lead us to the appropriate level of reliability we desire. To best explain, let's look at the roads that meet at this crossroads.

First off, you have monitoring/observability—previously described as the most crucial things to get solidly in place as you start your reliability work. That data gives us clarity on the current state of our systems, the *what is*.

Second, you have work planning processes like SLIs/SLOs, which allow us to specify with a reasonable degree of clarity our intentions and objectives for *what should be*.

And finally, you have incidents/outages (with the accompanying response practices). They provide (whether we like it or not) data on how *what is* can diverge or has diverged from *what should be*.

The practices around learning from failure sit at this crossroads. They allow us to create and nurture the feedback loops that will help us iterate from where we are to where we want to be, using the information we have from how we have diverged. But that only happens if we are intentional, hence, this chapter.

Talking About Failure

Before we get to the specific activities associated with learning from failure, I believe it is important to discuss a few overarching ideas that will inform them. One idea that is very clearly articulated in the resilience engineering literature (which we will talk about toward the end of this chapter) is that how we talk about failures dramatically affects how we approach and think about them. On the surface, it might seem like a failure is a specific fact pattern that won't change because we use different words to describe, conceptualize, or frame it; however, in practice, small changes in language do have a significant impact.

In our field, I find the best example of this is the use of the term *root cause*. For many years, after an incident we would launch into a spirited investigation to determine the root cause of the failure, which we would then proudly write up in a root cause analysis (RCA). I feel pretty confident that a significant percentage of people reading this section either work for or have worked for an employer who still to this day hunts for "the root cause" so it can publish an RCA.

What's the problem with this term? Well, over the years, with the gentle prodding of the resilience engineering community (which had broadened its view beyond aviation and other physical high-stakes environments to include software), it became clear that most nontrivial incidents just didn't work that way. In most nontrivial incidents, there wasn't a single root cause with a single causal relationship we could point to. Complex systems fail, not surprisingly, in complex ways.[1] We've come to realize (and speak accordingly) about "contributing factors" instead of a "root cause" as an acknowledgment of this complexity.[2]

It might not be immediately obvious why this shift in terms is so significant. With a shift in terms, we can get a shift in perspective and framing. If you default to speaking of incidents as having a root cause, this will often drive behavior that seeks to find that single, unitary root cause. This leads to unfortunate practices like "The Five Whys" (see the following sidebar).

"The Five Whys" (and Why You Shouldn't Ask *Why* Unless You've First Asked *What*)

If you have never been exposed to this idea before, let me quickly clue you in to it so you have the opportunity to run screaming should it come up. *"The Five Whys"* is a practice or instruction that says we should be asking *why* over and over again (kind of like a three-year-old) until we come to the root cause of an incident. The internal monologue might go something like this:

> The system was down.
>
> *Why?*
>
> Because the server stopped running.
>
> *Why?*

---

1 Yup, this footnote is yet another exhortation to go read Dr. Richard Cook's paper "How Complex Systems Fail" (*https://oreil.ly/F2sX3*). It is barely five pages long, and you will thank me afterward.

2 It is not uncommon these days for companies to publish "root cause analysis" documents that suggest an incident happened due to *this, this,* and *this other* contributing factor. I find this amusing because, well, which is it, a root cause or contributing factors?

Because the disk filled up.

Why?

Because a log file got too big.

Why?

Because the log file trimmer stopped running.

Why?

Because it got left out of a config file.

Aha! The root cause is that the log trimmer got left out of a config file. Let's make sure we have the log trimmer in all of our config files. (*Pats self on back.*)

I bet you can spot at least one problem with this admittedly contrived but still realistic example.[3] When we spend effort chasing a single causal chain, we invariably shed entire swaths of important information that are crucial to understanding (and then later learning from) an incident.

It is OK to attempt to go deep into a single thing you have observed, but not at the expense of ignoring the rest of the contributing factors in a situation. Sometimes you have to make sure you have answered all of the *what* (as in, *what happened?*) questions before you put *why* on repeat.

"The Five Whys" is a particularly overt example of how focusing on a single root cause can be detrimental to learning from failure; others can be more subtle. Use of this term encourages us (even subliminally) to stop looking deeply at an incident once we think we have identified a single clear causal chain, and that's an antipattern. How we talk about incidents and failure matters.

Postincident Reviews

Postincident reviews are in many ways the primary actual work associated with learning from failure, so we are going to spend a good long time in this section. We'll explore what they are (and what they are not), some common traps people fall into in the process (and how to avoid them), and a few ideas for leveling them up even further.

---

3 For example, we seem to have completely skipped over the question, "What on the system was sending enough log data to fill a disk?" Could potentially be important, no?

> ## A Quick Note About Nomenclature
>
> Let's get some quick clarity on nomenclature. Postincident reviews are called different things by different people. Once upon a time, it was common to call them *postmortems* (and it still is).[4] Some people who want to lean even more strongly into the subject of the chapter call them *postincident learning reviews*. And finally, I have also heard them called *retrospectives*[5] or *retrospective reviews*. These terms are largely interchangeable, so I am going to stick to *postincident review* (PiR sometimes) in this chapter. Feel free to swap in your favorite term as you read.

Postincident Reviews: The Basics

To set the scene, let's talk about the very basics of what a postincident review looks like.

You have an incident and/or an outage (sorry). You and/or your team mitigate the issue. Now it is time for a postincident review.[6]

A postincident review is a process that involves investigating, documenting, and discussing an incident and the circumstances surrounding it with the intention of constructing a shared understanding of the situation and learning as much as possible from the experience. It is not uncommon after the review to determine repair actions that should be undertaken to reduce the likelihood of a similar incident happening in the future.

There's a tremendous amount of nuance to be found in the previous paragraph, so let's start to take it apart piece by piece by answering some questions.

Q: *When do you start a postincident review process?*
   A: Ideally as soon as possible after the incident is resolved, not later than 24–36 hours afterward, because human memories fade. This isn't always as easy as it might sound, because after a particularly nasty or prolonged incident, all the team wants to do is sleep; so do the best you can.

---

4 This term has fallen a little out of fashion as of late, likely because (ideally) there are no deaths involved in the incident.

5 Which I don't use because then you have to fight the Agile people for the term.

6 …or not, we'll get to that decision a little later in the chapter.

Q: Do you kick off a postincident review after every outage?

A: There is some difference of opinion on this subject (some organizations include this as part of their operational excellence rigor), but the broad consensus is you should do one after every significant incident (however you define that word). I would add to this answer by suggesting that another criteria could be if it offers the opportunity for you to learn something useful. If you have a nonnovel repeat incident that is indistinguishable from one you have already probed in the past, it may be more productive to spend the time to actually act on what you learned from the previous postincident review (which possibly is why you are back in the situation) than it is to repeat the review.[7]

What a Postincident Review Is *Not*

For increased clarity in the midst of describing what a postincident review is, I'd like to mention a few things it is *not* since I see people demonstrate confusion about this on a regular basis:

It is not a list of action/repair items or an action/repair item–generating process.

Later in this chapter we'll talk more about people's rush to skip to the "What are we going to do about it?" stage. But here, let's just say that while a postincident review can generate action items after an incident has been thoroughly analyzed, it is primarily meant to be a learning process.

It is not a document or report.

Yes, it is a best practice to write down what you have learned so others can share in the knowledge (perhaps in the future), but don't mistake the finger for the moon.[8] Sometimes these reports are published publicly (perhaps as part of a public apology), so it is in your best interest to demonstrate that you actually learned something in them. Here's another pro tip: standardized templates for documenting postincident reviews can make it easier to conduct further meta-analyses of your collective experiences in the future.

---

7 Note that there is some nuance worthy of discussion here too. For instance, if this is a publicly visible repeat of a previous publicly visible incident, it is likely that you will need to perform and publish a second review to your customers. And well, good luck 'splaining…

8 From the Buddhist Shurangama Sutra (*https://oreil.ly/CHbn7*): "It is like when someone points his finger at the moon to show it to someone else. Guided by the finger, that person should see the moon. If he looks at the finger instead and mistakes it for the moon, he loses not only the moon but the finger also. Why? He mistakes the pointing finger for the bright moon."

We are not attempting to write a detective story or solve a murder mystery by establishing the definitive causal chain responsible for an incident. As mentioned before, incidents are more complex than that. Plus, the process of seeking a unary root cause to the exclusion of all else sheds surprising amounts of potential learning.

It is not an attempt to assign blame.

There's a whole other sidebar coming up on just this list item, so I will defer the elaboration for just a moment.

Postincident Reviews: The Process

Let's get down to the brass tacks of how the review process works. The first and arguably most important step is to construct a detailed chronology of the event, including its predecessors and successors (what happened before, during, and after the incident). The goal here is to document what happened in enough detail such that it will be possible—as much as possible—to come to a detailed shared understanding of what happened. Ideally after reading your documentation of the incident, someone who was not there at the time will gain an accurate understanding of what went on. Let's talk a bit about shared chronologies, real-time reviews, and how you might schedule your postincident review process meetings.

Creating a shared chronology in a document

The shared chronology needs to have enough detail so that not only will the reader understand *when* things happened (both in time and in relation to other things) but also:

- What decisions were made (and what ideas were rejected)
- What information the people involved had at the time for context (monitoring/observability data, etc.)
- Who was involved and who was not involved that one might expect (i.e., "Pat, the subject matter expert, was on vacation.")
- What resources (documentation, people, etc.) were consulted[9]

Ideally when documenting all of this, you are able to include direct supporting information. For example, if the people involved in the incident were looking at three

---

9 Notice I didn't say, "and what resources were not consulted" or "what people should have done." That would lead us right into one of the traps for postincident reviews that we will be discussing shortly. Hold on to this thought, it will be important later.

graphs in the monitoring system, then including screenshots of those graphs at the time of the incident is tremendously helpful to those who would look at the situation after the fact to ascertain why certain decisions were made. If key statements were made in a shared communications channel during the incident, include them. You get the basic idea.

This may sound like a considerable amount of work, and indeed it is.[10] A good postincident review chronology can take heaps of effort to put together. In addition to a single individual writing down their experience, it may be necessary to have a facilitator interview multiple people to get the data needed. But one thing most people who have prepared an extensive postincident review will tell you is that sometimes the most surprising insights come out of the investigative process when least expected ("Wait, what? I didn't notice that data point before. Oh, that's really interesting, that means that…but if that is true, then how can?…Oh, I see. And that started two months ago?").

Reviewing the chronology/incident in real time

Once you have the written draft finished and ready for discussion, it is time to review the incident in real time with your colleagues. Everyone involved in the incident (at the bare minimum) piles into a real or virtual room and walks through the documented chronology,[11] adding or correcting information and perspectives as you go. I strongly recommend having an experienced, neutral facilitator[12] present to guide the discussion.

SRE as Facilitator

Providing experienced, neutral facilitation of postincident reviews is an excellent role for SRE to take on in an organization.

It takes a certain kind of personality—hence, a certain kind of SRE—to be a good facilitator of any discussion. When present, a combination of strong people skills plus the SRE mindset can be magic in these contexts.

---

10 Some organizations have internal templates or guides for creating postincident reviews that try to make this a little easier or at least a little more structured. The *SRE book* has a pretty bare-bones example of a postmortem doc in Appendix D. There are more detailed examples available if you do a web search.

11 I realize "as documented" is a naive statement because these meetings can and do go off the rails, especially if the facilitation is weak or the personalities in the room are overstrong. This is one reason why I encourage you to interview multiple people. If your meeting dynamics are "suboptimal," one helpful technique to make sure everyone's voice is heard is to conduct separate interviews ahead of the meeting instead of relying on people to speak up there.

12 *Neutral* in the sense that they personally did not participate in the incident or have a direct connection to it.

We will get to some ways these discussions can go wrong (and right) in just a moment, but before we do, remember: how we talk about an incident, even down to the specific question words we use, can have a profound impact on how much we learn. Asking *how* (something) or *what* happened encourages us to stay in an investigative place and to learn more about what just happened during the incident. Asking *why* has the opposite effect of moving us past discovery right to diagnosis and future steps. Holding off on asking *why* in the meeting until the end dovetails with the next step in the process.

Meeting again the next day

I realize what I am about to suggest doesn't happen in most organizations and will frustrate the people who want to get to the "just fix it" part, but hear me out.

Many (most?) organizations move right from discussing the shared chronology in the meeting to a planning conversation designed to collect action items for fixing the situation. Many organizations rush through the chronology review to get to this part, centering it in the process as the most important thing. I am going to highlight how problematic this is (dare I say, gold emboss it) in the traps sections coming up to convince you that rushing to create action items kinda misses the main point.

Instead, I recommend that the first meeting be devoted to *what happened* and a separate (perhaps smaller) meeting be convened the next day to answer the question, "What are we going to do about it?" This next-day meeting removes the rush to create action items and also gives the key people a little time to mull over what they just heard and make better recommendations for repair items.[13]

Blameless Postincident Reviews

Every SRE book has at least one mention of *blameless postmortems*.[14] Here's mine.

I'd like to think that the goal of conducting postincident reviews as learning exercises (not shame-and-blame processes) has widely permeated the operations collective consciousness by now. But I still hear stories where a team has not followed this conventional wisdom; hence, I want to say just a few things on the subject.

You can't fire your way to reliable.

---

13 The next-day meeting is most important for significant/novel incidents. If people complain that they don't have time for two meetings, the question arises, "Surely learning more, so we can make more effective corrections and better systemic changes to avoid repeats, is worth the time?" Saying something slightly more political than that in a meeting is probably in order, but you get the idea.

14 To muddy the water a little bit, I have to admit that I am sympathetic to J. Paul Reed's assertion that because humans are wired to assign blame, at best we can be blame-aware instead. See this article (*https://oreil.ly/0-fLg*) on blame for more details on this idea.

Firing the person who made a mistake that led to an outage doesn't improve the reliability of a system; it just reduces the size of the team by one (probably important) person. I still hear of environments where this is the common practice. In those cases, there definitely is learning from failure, just learning all the wrong things.

The organizations that celebrate people for failing and presenting what they learned from that failure so others benefit are better positioned to actually learn as a whole.

Postincident Reviews: Common Traps

When you get into a room with a bunch of people to talk about an incident, various things can go wrong[15]—or at least suboptimally—that are specific to the review process beyond the usual "people in groups" issues. I have been in reviews where every one of these traps comes up (thankfully, not at the same time).

I feel compelled to warn you that this is another one of those "perfect pitch" situations where someone with perfect pitch notices the instruments that are out of tune (almost all of them) whenever they go to see live music. You, too, will notice these traps over and over again in the wild, and it will rankle you. I would feel bad about this if I didn't think spotting these things and taking gentle and politic action wasn't so helpful for improving learning from failure in these moments. Of all the sections in this chapter, this might be the most important one. For each trap, I am going to describe what to look out for, why it is a problem, and a way to course correct and improve on the situation.

Trap 1: Attributing the issue to "human error"

Problem. While it may be undeniably true that a human made a mistake in the situation, that's not the problem with attributing something to human error or "pilot error." The problem occurs when people are content to apply the label *human error* and move on without going any deeper.

How to do better. There is tremendous value in identifying the personal, systemic, or organizational context that led to this mistake being made. We have to assume that person thought they were making the right decision at the time. At that crucial moment, the action we are calling *human error* made sense to them. Given this, now we have better questions to ask: What didn't the person know at the time? What was missing from the error message/monitoring dashboard/documentation/etc.? How did our tools and processes fall short at that moment? I think you can see the potential here for much greater learning if we don't stop at human error in our postincident review process.

---

15 A tip of the hat to Nick Stenning, who introduced me to this material, and to Jessica DeVita, who inspired/contributed to it.

Trap 2: Could have…, Should have…, Would have…, Failed to…, Did not… (counterfactual reasoning)

Problem. I guarantee that you will hear people using these phrases all the time in their postincident reviews: "The person on call could have switched to the backup servers." "The dev should have reverted the config." "When the SRE failed to reboot the load balancer…"

The problem here is that these are all statements that describe events that didn't happen. Telling a story about something that did not happen to understand something that did is counterfactual reasoning. Postincident reviews are meant to investigate what really happened—fleshing out a story about what should have happened is at best a distraction from that purpose and at worst a method of berating the people who were involved in the incident.

How to do better. Focus on what happened, not what you wish had happened. If you find yourself drifting into counterfactual reasoning, call it out if you can, and instead try to steer the conversation back to what actually happened during the incident.

Trap 3: Judging decisions made during incidents based on outcomes (using normative language)

Problem. If you find people are starting to use "judgy" adverbs like *hastily*, *carelessly*, or *inadequately*, you probably have drifted into normative language in describing your incident—a cousin of trap 2, because we are once again judging the situation and people for something they didn't do or have.

When we talk like that, we are assuming the people already knew what was going to happen when they did the "wrong" thing, and they did it anyway. But that knowledge, the knowledge of the outcome of an action, is only something we enjoy in hindsight. The people who were in the thick of things didn't and couldn't definitively know the outcome of their actions at the time they took those actions. Judging them based on the one thing they couldn't know at the moment is unfair and unhelpful.

How to do better. Same remedy as for trap 2: focus on what happened, not what you wish had happened (if you had perfect or prescient knowledge). Try to figure out what the people knew at the time and exactly what personal, systemic, or organizational contextual support was lacking such that the decision was suboptimal.

Trap 4: Assuming machine infallibility (mechanistic reasoning)

Problem. This is peripherally related to trap 1, in which we were content to blame a single individual and the mistake they made. Sometimes people talk about an incident as if humans in general always make mistakes and their humanity is the source of a problem. Jessica DeVita likes to call this the Scooby Doo fallacy: "The system would have worked fine if it weren't for those meddling kids." It's very common to hear people talk as if the machines would still be humming along fine if it weren't for that bone-headed mistake made by a person. They pushed the wrong config, turned the wrong knob, disconnected the wrong wire, etc. Here the human is portrayed as the chaos agent who thwarts the mechanistic perfection of our systems. The problem here is that's actually not how things work in the real world. Finding that humans are faulty does not lead to finding the real faults in a system.

One way I like to demonstrate this when talking to an audience is to ask people to raise their hand if they are responsible for a system that is in production. I then ask them to keep their hands up if that system would still be running successfully if they didn't touch it at all[16] at least once a day <pause>…once a week <pause>…once every two weeks <pause>…once a month…" Virtually no one lowers their hands at the once-a-day mark, but there are very few (if any) hands still up as I get to longer and longer time periods.

That's because, when speaking of the services we run, we are actually referring to a sociotechnical construct that consists of both the machine and the humans that interact with it. In reality, humans aren't usually the villains; they are often the source of adaptive capacity (paging resilience engineering!) that allows the systems to continue to function when there is a required change or unexpected problem.

How to do better. If you find yourself in a situation where the human is being set up to take the blame, ask what can be done to support the people in this position instead of vilifying them, and move on. Consider them as part of a system that needs improvement. How are the processes and resources in the system itself deficient? This leads to more holistic learning from failure.

Trap 5: Ignoring the positive (missed opportunities)

Problem. There are questions we seldom ask in postincident reviews that would open whole new neighborhoods of learning. In postincident reviews, we are so focused on all of the ways things went wrong that we don't realize there is considerable learning to be found also in what went (or usually goes) right.

---

16 If we ever get the chance to talk in person, ask me about the day I lost root access on every one of my hundreds of machines at once. Good times.

In Chapter 4, I mentioned Erik Hollnagel's work on Safety-II and Nancy Leveson's work on Safety-III, which suggests that there is great benefit to focusing on not the short swath of time we are having an outage but the rest of the time when things are going as expected. If we can learn what is allowing things to work well and bolster those parts of the system, it could have a profound impact on preventing incidents in the first place. The idea that we could learn about failure by learning from success still blows my mind. Highly recommend that you do a web search for their research; it will forever alter your perspective.

How to do better. If we ask questions like "How does this usually work?" or even "What stopped this incident from being even worse than it was?" we often discover some of the aspects of the environment that already act in a positive way to improve fault tolerance and reliability. If a postincident review can identify mechanisms like these, it could provide pointers to approaches that would be even more impactful if given just a little more support.

Learning from Failure Through Resilience Engineering

In Chapter 5, I mentioned that resilience engineering would come up in several places in this book, and well, here we are again. I know of no other discipline that is as focused on or adept at learning from failure in a way that is applicable to SRE. Much of what I cover on the topic in this book is either influenced by or drawn from that discipline and its related body of work, so I wanted to point you to the same well should you want to go deeper into learning from failure.

One hook that might capture your attention is the definition of *resilience engineering*. David Woods defines it in "Resilience Is a Verb" (*https://oreil.ly/PIBl1*) (well worth reading) as:

> Resilience concerns the capabilities a system needs to respond to inevitable surprises. Adaptive capacity is the potential for adjusting patterns of activities to handle future changes in the kinds of events, opportunities, and disruptions experienced. Therefore, adaptive capacities exist before changes and disruptions call upon those capacities. Systems possess varieties of adaptive capacity, and Resilience Engineering seeks to understand how these are built, sustained, degraded, and lost.[17]

---

17 David D. Woods, "Resilience Is a Verb," in *IRGC Resource Guide on Resilience (Vol. 2): Domains of Resilience for Complex Interconnected Systems*, eds. B. D. Trump et al. EPFL International Risk Governance Center, 2018.

For me, this offers a way to begin to think about resilience at a deeper level than the colloquial use of the term (often as a synonym for *fault tolerance*), which I find really attractive. I encourage you to explore the literature of this field if this also piques your interest.

What We Mean (and What We Could Mean) When We Say *Resilience*

In Chapter 5, I mentioned that resilience engineering familiarity will give you a greater sensitivity to how the term *resilience* is used in common parlance. I want to cement that experience for you with another selection from David Woods. I believe the following taxonomy offers a peek at a deeper way of conceiving of and practicing SRE.

As summarized in Cook and Long,[18] David Woods proposes[19] the following four senses of the term *resiliency*:

Term	Describes how a system...
1. rebound	...rebounds from disrupting or traumatic events and returns to previous or normal activities
2. robustness	...is able to manage increasing complexity, stressors, and challenge
3. graceful extensibility	...extends performance, or brings extra adaptive capacity to bear, when surprise events challenge its boundaries
4. sustained adaptability	...is able to adapt to future surprises as conditions continue to evolve

I think most SREs work in the space somewhere around *rebound* and perhaps *robustness*, but there is no reason why we have to stop there in our thinking. If you find this intriguing, I encourage you to look into the work of the folks at Adaptive Capacity Labs and resilience engineering in general.

Learning from Failure via Chaos Engineering

Another field that can really enhance our efforts to learn from failure is chaos engineering. Chaos engineering has always delighted me because the idea that creating failures could be desirable (for our learning) was highly counterintuitive to sysadmin me when I first heard about it many years ago. There are whole books on the subject,[20] so this will only be a quick introduction.

---

18 Richard I. Cook and Beth Adele Long, "Building and Revising Adaptive Capacity Sharing for Technical Incident Response: A Case of Resilience Engineering," *Applied Ergonomics* 90 (January 2021).

19 David D. Woods, "Four Concepts for Resilience and the Implications for the Future of Resilience Engineering," *Reliability Engineering & System Safety* 141 (September 2015), 5-9.

20 In fact, I recommend you read the book *Chaos Engineering* by Casey Rosenthal and Nora Jones (O'Reilly, 2020).

At this point, I'd dare to say that most operations professionals have heard about chaos engineering. Unfortunately most people have a very rudimentary understanding of this field as just "break stuff in production using chaos monkey." When I talk to people about the subject, I much prefer to start with this definition from "Principles of Chaos Engineering" (*https://oreil.ly/5qcJa*):

> Chaos Engineering is the discipline of experimenting on a system in order to build confidence in the system's capability to withstand turbulent conditions in production.

The keywords I like to emphasize are *discipline* and *experimenting* to make it clear that chaos engineering consists of intentional, scientific-method (hypotheses leading to experiments) explorations designed to increase our understanding of a system. We just happen to be using failure as a primary ingredient in these experiments.

Chaos engineering experiments aren't riddles; rather, they ask questions we don't know the answers to in order to help us understand how the system will behave under adverse conditions. So for example, "How will the system fail when it starts to run out of memory?" is a question we might explore. If we already know that an application will go boom when we turn off the backend database, "Let's see what happens when we turn off the database" is not a chaos engineering experiment.[21]

"Principles of Chaos Engineering" suggests that experiments follow this form:

- Start by defining "steady state" as some measurable output of a system that indicates normal behavior.
- Hypothesize that this steady state will continue in both the control group and the experimental group.
- Introduce variables that reflect real-world events like servers that crash, hard drives that malfunction, network connections that are severed, etc.
- Try to disprove the hypothesis by looking for a difference in steady state between the control group and the experimental group.

The famous Netflix Simian Army (*https://oreil.ly/LyRfn*) (chaos monkey, chaos gorilla, etc.) were some of the first and most public steps in the direction of tools for chaos engineering. Later work on fault injection (building a way to precisely induce failures into specific components of a system at will via an API) and testing harnesses took the idea even further. If you are interested in this subject, I recommend taking a look at the state of the chaos engineering world today.

---

21 Though something like "How quickly will the service fall over when the database fails?" could be a valid question if you don't already know the answer.

Would You Like to Play a Game? (Simulations)

There is a whole swath of chaos engineering efforts that lean more on the *socio* side of sociotechnical systems. This allows us to explore how people understand and respond in certain unforeseen circumstances. The discussion in the main text focused on experiments with machines to learn more about a system, but these are in some ways experiments with people.

There are a number of variations on the idea of running simulations of disasters to learn from this aspect of responses to failure. Examples of this sort of chaos engineering are Amazon's GameDays (*https://oreil.ly/Hg1_-*), Google's Disaster Recovery Testing (DiRT) (*https://oreil.ly/xmmF-*) and tabletop simulations like Laura Nolan's card game described in Chapter 20 of *Seeking SRE*.

Learning from Failure: Next Steps

As a way of bringing this chapter to a close, I want to suggest a few next steps for what to do after your postincident reviews or chaos engineering experiments have been completed. The key theme for all of these is making sure we do something with what we learned instead of just leaving a document somewhere to gather dust:

"Book clubs"/"graduate seminars"
> As suggested previously, it can be tremendously helpful (and really fun) to get a group of people together on a regular basis to review past postincident reviews either from internal or external sources. It's a great way to keep lessons learned alive and build culture in an organization.

Engineering surprises mini-newsletter
> There is probably a better name for this, but if every once in a while, you send out a brief "Check out this cool unexpected thing we found in a chaos engineering experiment" or "Top 3 things we learned from the last load balancer outage" email, it has a way of engaging people, distributing what you learned, and getting people interested in learning more from failure.

Reviewing production readiness, application readiness, and design documents
> Ideally, you would drive some of what you learned back into the software development process so the failures you now understand don't repeat themselves in the future. Engineering reviews and meetings like this are good places to bring the knowledge back. Even creating reference documents based on this information that people want to read ("Top 10 Ways Not to Use Our Caching Layer") can make it more likely that the organization can learn from these failures.

Meta-analysis and ML

Once you have a corpus of documents about your incidents, you'll need to decide what to do with it as a whole. Sometimes more advanced organizations will spend time to mine the information found there (for example, to determine the top cause categories of incidents for the org as found in Appendix D, "Results of Postmortem Analysis," in *The Site Reliability Workbook*).[22] There is also considerable work being done in the field to use ML to leverage the information found in this sort of corpus.

There's a tremendous amount of interesting work to be done in the realm of learning from failure. I hope you will join me in this endeavor.

---

22 If you are into this sort of analysis, the Verica Open Incident Database (VOID) (*https://oreil.ly/QCmVA*) is a public corpus of incident reports that you might want to explore.

PART III

Becoming SRE for the Organization

CHAPTER 11

Organizational Factors for Success

In Chapter 5, we discussed a set of factors that would make it more likely for an individual who wanted to enter SRE to succeed. This is the twin chapter, which explores some of the factors that can help organizations successfully adopt SRE. It would be swell if I could just tell you to collect a group of people who embodied the individual factors detailed in Chapter 5 together and you'd get an instant, fully functional SRE team that works in your organization, but I'm afraid it is a little more complicated than that (though that wouldn't be a terrible idea either).

Let's get right into some factors that can impact the success of SRE in your organization.

Contributing Factor 1: What's the Problem?

This may appear obvious, but organizations skip or elide over the following question far more often than you might expect:

Do you have a problem that SRE could possibly address?

Once upon a time, I received some professional product manager (PM) training, and that has been both a blessing and a curse. It has taught me to ask the question, "What's the pervasive problem in the marketplace people are willing to spend money on that this product is designed to solve?" which has brought clarity to so many situations (a blessing). It's also taught me to recognize when the initial answer or answers to that question do not actually constitute a problem and hence require asking again or reframing (a curse). For example, if you ask, "What problem does your product solve?" you may get an answer like "This product offers a way to monitor your infrastructure in different cloud providers."

But that is not a problem statement, it is a feature statement. So we are back to the beginning: "Now tell me the problem the product solves?" (rinse and repeat). When I get into one of these conversations, I usually don't stop asking the question until I hear a real problem articulated.[1]

I bring this experience up because I have encountered precisely the same dynamic when asking, "What is the problem you have that SRE could address?" "Not enough SREs," "We need people to run our infrastructure," or even "We are going to expand to a global footprint" are not problem statements.

Here are some statements that are much closer to identifying problems you could hand to SREs and expect results:

- We are spending too much time dealing with outages.
- We are worried that our global expansion will fail because our existing systems will fail.
- We don't really know how reliable our systems are now so we can't tell if it is OK to make changes.
- Our people spend too much time running the system (i.e., on toil).

Spend time to get a good, crisp understanding and articulation of your problems and see how well they match SRE's strengths (and weaknesses) before proceeding.

Contributing Factor 2: What Is the Org Willing to Do to Get There?

I stopped asking people, "Is reliability important to your organization?" so long ago I can't actually remember the last time that question passed my lips. I realized that everyone, absolutely everyone I talked with nodded vigorously and professed their love for reliability in response to that question. It turns out this is the wrong question.

The right question is, "What is the org willing to do to get there?"

To make that clear, here are some questions I could ask as part of a friendly grilling to get a sense of the viability of a new SRE effort or a nascent effort in progress:

---

1 If you, too, are going to probe like this to get a real problem statement, it will start to get frustrating. Be gentle but persistent until the person you are talking with finds their way (ideally) to an answer and, sometimes in the process, a change of mindset.

- Are they willing to devote engineering time to it?

- Are they willing to add work specifically intended to improve reliability to the roadmap?

- Are they willing to pull people off of feature work to focus on reliability issues when the need arises (which is to say always, but definitely after certain outages)?

- Are they willing to gate new releases based on missed service level objectives?

- Are they willing to actively work toward making sure postincident reviews are not perfunctory?

- Is their on-call schedule humane such that the work is sustainable?

- Are SREs in the right meetings early in the development process?

- Do SREs have direct access to resources like source code repositories, which would allow them to make changes to improve reliability?

I can keep going like this, but you get the idea. Quick observation: none of these questions are fundamentally technical in nature.

When I talk to organizations that are brand new to SRE, I discuss SLIs and SLOs, but I seldom go into detail about error budgets. I make this choice because "real" error-budget implementations have policies attached to them—policies that specify what the organization will do when the budget is exceeded or, more importantly, when it is depleted. This policy has to be agreed upon before they get to this point (and actually held to when they are there) because that's one of the clearest places where the reliability rubber meets the reliability road.

Contributing Factor 3: Does the Org Have the Requisite Patience?

As reported in Accelerate's *State of DevOps Report 2023* from DevOps Research and Assessment (DORA), it takes time for reliability work to show its biggest benefits. You can, and I recommend you do, get some quick wins, but the curve is generally shaped like the letter "J" (see page 33 in the report). Steve McGhee from DORA said to me in an email (quoted with permission), "These curves tell us simply that the outcomes (actual reliability) doesn't really happen until the capabilities (what new thing can we do now?) have really built up. We sometimes call it 'cumulative.'"

The amount of time before you hit the ascending part of that curve is likely going to be greater than you think. Is your organization prepared to wait until things really take off?

The best advice I can offer is:

- Set expectations appropriately at every opportunity.

- Communicate clearly about your plans (the use of the terms *phase* and *interim* are helpful to indicate incremental progress).

- Be sure to communicate your incremental success as it happens (this helps people with the waiting).

Contributing Factor 4: Can We Collaborate?

SRE is relentlessly collaborative. This is not just because we are delightful and friendly people, but because there is no other way to effectively improve reliability. Shaking your fist at the cloud, the dev org, and the business stakeholders only gets you so far. You need to work with all of those entities to iterate toward your reliability goals constantly. That may sound obvious, but I hear tales of organizational friction (for example, siloing) and lack of mutual trust and respect all the time.

There are a number of ways to determine the answer to the "Can we collaborate?" question, including some that overlap with the last couple of bullets in "Contributing Factor 2: What Is the Org Willing to Do to Get There?" on page 128. A few more questions to ask are:

- Does SRE collaborate on hiring criteria/interview questions for the larger organization (thus making it possible that people who are hired could do reliability-related work)?

- Has the organization ever set up "rotations" (or would it), whereby dev team members spend some time working in the SRE org and the SRE team members spend time working in other parts of the organization?

- How hard is it to get an invitation to another group's online collaboration tool channel or team?

- Who makes the tooling (including monitoring and observability) decisions in the organization?

Contributing Factor 5: Does the Org Make Decisions Based on Data?

There are echoes of the "What is the org willing to do?" question here as well, but this is important enough to warrant teasing out and exploring in more detail. Many of the best practices of SRE are predicated on the notion that we will carefully and intentionally set up the collection of reliability-related data and then make decisions based on it. While I guarantee that your finance people already have experience taking action based on what numbers tell them, not all parts of your organization may be similarly experienced or inclined.

The error-budget point I made previously is applicable here as well, because it is an example of making decisions with data, but even before we get there, it would be good to back up and confirm that your organization is passionate about data collection (read: monitoring and observability) in the first place. If the answer to your question of "Should we be monitoring X?" is "Why bother, we already know it is really reliable" or "That's another team's responsibility" or "We have more important things to work on," that bodes poorly for SRE adoption.

The initial questions I find that are most helpful when sussing out this prerequisite are all part of the conversation that begins with "So, tell me about your monitoring...?"[2] From here we branch out to the standard journalism questions: *What* do you monitor? *Where* do you monitor it from? *How* do you monitor it? *Who* does this? And (perhaps most important) *Why* do you monitor that?

Once you can get the lay of the land, then it is possible to dig deeper into "What do you do with this information?" Be prepared for a blank stare at that moment. Often the initial answer is, "We look at it to make sure nothing is wrong, of course!" This is the "eyes on glass" network operations center (NOC) approach to monitoring that is still quite prevalent and perhaps the first thing people think of when it comes to their monitoring system.

Don't be discouraged if this is the first answer. Follow-up questions about any analysis they have done on types of outages or effectiveness of the current monitoring setup may yield answers closer to the idea of data-driven actions. Your task at that moment is to ascertain how much of an appetite the organization has for further work in this direction.

Contributing Factor 6: Can the Org Learn and Act on What It Learns?

I talk quite a bit in this book about learning from failure. It's a key aspect of the SRE mindset. How (or perhaps *if*) it manifests itself on a daily basis is a strong determinant of whether SRE will succeed in an organization. The problem is that not every organization knows how or chooses to do it. I realize this sounds a little strange—of course every organization learns or at least attempts to learn from its experiences, right?[3] I

---

2 And if you can't have that conversation, that's a pretty clear negative indicator.

3 Note that I didn't say "learns from its mistakes" here even though this is the colloquial idiom. Are unplanned outages *mistakes* per se? Looking through an SRE lens (given what I said about our relationship to errors in Chapter 2 and what we know about complex systems), there's a pretty deep philosophical discussion to be had here.

guarantee that almost everyone who has been in the operations field for a substantial period has at least one story to tell you about their current or past employer not learning from failure.

Here are some suggested diagnostic questions for this section:

- Where and when does the org *intentionally* try to learn from failure? Do they do postincident reviews/postmortems/retrospectives?

- When the org does this activity, how perfunctory are the postincident reviews? Do people look forward to the process or is it seen as a necessary chore akin to filing taxes?

- Who in the organization participates in this process? How localized is that participation?

- Who is in the room when an outage is discussed (if it is ever discussed)? What is the tenor of that discussion (e.g., if it feels like learning or blaming is in the air)? Do people leave those meetings feeling better or worse?

- Does the info for one of these activities get written down? Has anyone ever looked back at prior write-ups? (Bonus: has anyone ever done any analysis of that corpus?)

- If it is written down, who in the organization gets to see it? Is it shared with leadership (and do they read it)?

- Is it shared with the public afterward? Sensitive question: how perfunctory is the public version? Is there a large delta between the internal and external version? How can the public tell that you have learned from the experience?

- Can you name any of the things that were changed (and ideally improved) from the process?

- Can you name any of the things that were changed/improved by teams or groups *outside* of the circle of people who experience an outage directly? Did another team modify what they were doing as a result of something learned?[4]

You may have noticed that there is a step-wise hierarchy of questions here that goes from "Do they do it at all?" to "How do they do it?" to "Do they do it well?" to "Did it work?" If your organization has not even stepped on this escalator, that's a red flag that should give you pause before contemplating bringing SRE into the organization.

---

4 This is a varsity-level question that requires a certain level of org integration not always reached, so I am going to put it in a footnote: if new best practices are put in place as part of this learning, do they cite the outage write-up so others can see where they came from and perhaps also derive some inspiration?

Contributing Factor 7: Can You Make a Difference?

I was originally going to name this section "Are You in Control?" but that question belies both the sociotechnical reality of complex systems[5] and the notion that one has to be in charge to make a difference. The conceit here is deceptively simple: if there is an action an SRE in your org identifies as conducive to improving reliability—be it a code change, an infrastructure change, an architecture change, a billing change, etc.—can they make it happen?

SRE is about careful, considered, constrained, and controlled change toward better reliability.[6] Without the capacity to make that change, SRE is just a lot of talking. I've had enough conversations with other SREs about how difficult it is in their org to do X due to organizational structure, silos, lack of trust relationships, policies, and a whole host of other reasons to not take this question for granted any more.

Ask yourself how hard it would be for an SRE[7] in your organization to make a change to:

- Documentation (team, organization, product)
- Code in a product or a production service
- Development, testing, and production infrastructure
- Tools being used for monitoring, deployment, etc.
- Their ratio of reactive to project time
- Hiring practices for developer and operations personnel (e.g., interview questions)

This is an incomplete list that may require some speculation on your part.[8] Not all of these are equally important in different contexts, but if you have slid all of the sliders over to "impossible," then it is likely that SRE will be a poor match for your environment.

---

5 I've said it elsewhere in this book, but I'll say it again: If you haven't already read Dr. Richard Cook's paper "How Complex Systems Fail" (*https://oreil.ly/lgJL5*), consider doing so pronto.

6 We're also kind of big on alliteration, but don't tell anyone.

7 And by *SRE* I mean an individual contributor, SRE manager, SRE director, and so on…

8 For a good deep dive into this question, see the blog post "What SRE Is Not" (*https://blog.relyabilit.ie/what-sre-is-not*) by Niall Murphy, one of the tech reviewers of this book.

Contributing Factor 8: Can You See (and Address) the Friction in the System?

Of all the contributing factors we will discuss, this one feels less pernicious to me because often, just asking the right question about friction in your organization can turn a light bulb on that stays on. For example, you might ask something like "How long does it take to file and route/escalate a ticket about an outage with this service to an SRE team?" followed by "What's your objective for the availability of this service?"[9] When the answer turns out to be something like "a total of two hours for the ticket to be escalated" but your objective is "the service can be down for no more than 10 minutes," everyone gets the problem.

---

9 Be sure to have one of those charts that shows just how much total downtime each "nines" permits (*https://oreil.ly/-ab-2*) on the table when you do so. You want four nines? No problem; you get ~52 minutes *a year* of downtime. Did it take an hour just to process the ticket? (*taps the chart*) Oops.

Once you start looking for systemic or organizational friction, it's usually easy to spot. Doing a modicum of analysis of roughly where the time in an outage was spent is another easy pointer to friction.

Outside of the outage context, for example, when determining how hard it is to iterate toward reliability, questions that begin with phrases like the following can expose friction:

- What does it take to…?
- How many steps are required to…?
- Who is allowed to…? or What approval is needed to…?
- How often do you (deploy, change, etc.)…?

Asking these questions gets you halfway to understanding the situation, but the killer question then becomes, "And how willing are the people involved to change this in any way?"

Past performance is no guarantee of future results, but it is a good sign if people in the organization can offer examples of ways they have reduced friction in the past.

SRE in Regulated Environments

Time for another counterpoint sidebar. The main text of this section has a very obvious bent toward "friction = bad"—the idea that friction will impede or perhaps even suffocate SRE efforts, and an organization will need to be willing to work toward friction reduction to have SRE be successful. But sometimes the friction in the process is not just intentional but also mandated by an outside force and can't change. So does this mean that our friends in regulated industries are left out in the cold from SRE?

All of the successful work by SRE teams in regulated industries would seem to suggest otherwise. I've spoken to and seen many talks by folks in the financial and fintech world, and they seem to be getting along just fine. The twist that makes this possible is a dedication to constantly asking which of their constrained practices are mandated and which are largely historical. As an example, a particular process may be required to enforce a "separation of concerns" where two roles need to give approval for a change before it can be applied. In that situation SRE might get involved not to eliminate this step in the process, but instead to remove as much toil as possible to complete it while still hewing to the requirement.

If you are in one of these industries, I encourage you to watch some of the SREcon talks from your cohort to watch how they have squared this circle.

The Fine Print

Chapters like this beg for a caveat statement, so here it is: even if you work diligently to provide or create as many of these factors in your org as is humanly possible, I can't guarantee your SRE efforts will succeed (certainly not the first attempt). There are many ways to tank an SRE adoption (in fact, there is a whole chapter of them coming up next). This is especially true at the organizational level. Good SRE efforts at companies fail all the time through no fault of their SRE teams, like when the "wrong" VP wins a VP turf war.

Throughout this book (without being explicit about it), I've suggested some ideas that can protect some against these organizational "acts of nature." For example, regular reporting up the chain and outward to the whole org about SRE wins/value can help build credibility and "stickiness" in an org. This in itself won't shield you from catching a lightning bolt in the face coming down from Mount Olympus, but it may make you less of an easy target if you are seen as a key partner in saving the business money.[10]

It's All About Organizational Values

As a way of wrapping up this chapter, I'd like to end by encouraging you to watch Narayan Desai's 2017 talk at SREcon EMEA on "Care and Feeding of SRE" (*https://oreil.ly/AfNls*), which was formative to my way of thinking about organizational fit with SRE. In this talk, he tried to capture some of the elements that made SRE so successful (or even possible) at Google. Though I have cautioned in both *Seeking SRE* and this book about comparing your organization to Google, the key message of "an organization's values are the key to SRE success" should come across loud and clear from his analysis.[11] Without saying it explicitly, the questions in each Contributing Factor section throughout this chapter are all designed to help you get some clarity on the values in your organization that might intersect with reliability and your SRE ambitions. I'd encourage you to take another pass through them with this in mind.[12]

---

10 To expand on this a little bit, SRE can help with cost containment, efficient resource usage, reducing staff costs via automation and toil reduction, outage expenses, improving development velocity, and so on. Be sure to tell other people when you are doing any of these things (and if you are not doing any of these things, best to start).

11 After Desai's talk, an audience member mentioned that in his organization, one sacred tenet they had was, "If we announce that we are going to do a release on X date, we always do that release on that date." This immediately conflicts with a common error-budget policy of gating releases if a service hasn't met its service level objectives. See how organizational-values conversations get really fun really fast?

12 If this subject interests you, I recommend you look at the body of work of sociologist Ron Westrum, specifically the Westrum Typologies (*https://oreil.ly/Nd-L0*).

CHAPTER 12

How SRE Can Fail

In a book that repeatedly emphasizes the value of learning from failure, we can't pass up the chance to apply the same idea to SRE itself. Specifically, we are going to look at how SRE efforts fail at the organizational level in real life, with an eye toward applying the lessons failure has graciously offered us. The material for this chapter is drawn from a number of sources, including Chapter 23, "SRE Antipatterns," by Blake Bisset in *Seeking SRE* and stories from real life.

Let's talk about what I mean by *fail* in this context. Though I am quite fond of how well the opening line of Tolstoy's *Anna Karenina* ("Happy families are all alike; every unhappy family is unhappy in its own way.") applies here, I can broadly overgeneralize to say that failure in this context looks like one of two things: (1) the organization has some sort of immune response and rejects an SRE effort entirely after a time, or, perhaps more tragic, and (2) it just doesn't receive anything near to the benefits or value SRE has to offer and SREs live a life of quiet desperation.[1]

OK, on to the contributing factors to SRE implementation failure…

Contributing Factor 1: Title Flipping to Create SREs

Let's get an easy one out of the way. It's also one I harp on in other places in this book, so I will try to be succinct. It is not uncommon to create an SRE team or an SRE role by just renaming existing roles or open positions with *SRE*. Sometimes this is done to make those positions more attractive from a hiring perspective or to attempt to raise the stature of the team in the org, because *SRE* sounds cooler/fresher/shinier than *Systems Administrator* or *Tier 2 Support Engineer*. In a small percentage of cases, the

---

1 Gosh, I hope this is hyperbole for most people, but I have talked to enough people to know that sometimes it can be this sad.

change of title is aspirational.[2] The organization legitimately wants to create an SRE function, and so it is attempting to mint it like currency. What an organization does after the title change determines if it tips to success.

If the organization does not make the substantial effort past this point to backfill the roles with real work on values/priorities, training, resources, communication, and culture (to name a few), at *best* you will create a stunted and marginally useful SRE effort. At worst (and quite frankly, this is the most likely outcome), you will continue to do business as usual with a fresh layer of cynicism shellacked on top that will make the existing team even less effective.

Contributing Factor 2: Converting Tier 3 Support to SRE

One variation of title flipping I see far too often is the attempted conversion of a tier 3 (or some other) support team into an SRE team. The organization takes an existing group of senior or advanced people who would ordinarily handle escalations of more difficult or substantial support requests passed on by tier 1 or 2 of the organization and calls them "the SRE team." This happens with no actual change to the function or mission of that team.

That last sentence is the key to the failure mode here. The issue isn't the experience level of the people, their level of access to the infrastructure, exposure to a broad swath of org-wide problems, or even their (ideally) well-honed troubleshooting skills. Those are all lovely ingredients that could be part of an SRE team. The issue here is what they live in service of. A tier 3 team has a great deal of value for an organization, but they are not there to create and nurture the feedback loops that tend to lead an organization toward greater reliability.[3]

Beware of Two-Legged Stools

A quick note about a latent failure mode: so far in this chapter, we've talked about the perils of converting an existing set of people in the organization to SRE. Even though I have used discouraging language around this idea because shallow attempts are doomed to failure, I have tried to leave the door open a crack—if performed with care and effort, such conversions to SRE are theoretically possible.

---

2 I wish I knew what percentage, but I am unaware of any actual research in this area. This statement is unfortunately based on anecdotal evidence I have collected over the years, not real data.

3 This is also true of security. A tier 3 support team might fix security issues as it encounters them, but you would not expect to rest your hopes and dreams for improving the security of the organization on them just because you give them a snazzy security-related title change.

But that leads us to another potential pitfall of converting an existing team I want to warn you about: ignoring whatever necessary function that team is currently performing. Substance abuse counselors and other professionals in the field will tell you it is unwise to simply try to excise an abused substance from someone's life without addressing what purpose it is actually serving for them. If someone is addicted to heroin, it almost always serves some purpose for them in their life (in addition to bringing all of the negative repercussions). Completely cutting it out of their life without taking this into account is like removing a leg of a stool.

Similarly, if you successfully retool an existing team to take on an SRE role, be mindful that the previous function probably existed for a reason—a reason the org has to be prepared to cover. I know this makes a successful transformation more complicated. Sorry to be the bearer of this (more complicated) news, but who would you rather hear this from, me or your disgruntled colleagues?

Contributing Factor 3: On Call and That's All

There's great potential for contradictory advice here, so I want to thread this needle very carefully. In Chapter 3, I suggested that it would be possible, with a sufficiently worked example, to build SRE culture starting with incidents and incident handling. The exact quote was "[John] Reese suggests that if you want to build an organizational structure that is a factory for building SRE culture, you could do no better than focus intently and intentionally on your incident handling and review."

This advice might lead you to rush into every SRE engagement and attempt to take over the on-call role in that partnership. I would like to temper this enthusiasm with a cautionary tale.[4] This is another example of "the shallow is the enemy of the good." I have seen a number of cases where this approach has backfired because the engineering leaders associated with the effort have misinterpreted the purpose of that work. In Chapters 2 and 3, I have been very clear that the primary purpose of on-call engagements is to learn more about the system and to use that knowledge to improve the reliability of the system.

Sometimes this gets lost. Sometimes the engineering leader views the primary purpose of the SRE on-call work as a hedge against developer pain or expense. I have personally had people ask about using SRE to handle on call as a cheaper source for exception handling "so the expensive developers could focus on developing features instead of…" I know of other engagements where all the SRE team did was "carry the pager," divorced from learning from failure or being empowered to make changes to the system to improve its reliability. Both of these constitute a failure in my book.

---

4 If you would really like a bucket of cold water dumped on your head with a counterargument, I encourage you to read Niall Murphy's Chapter 30, "Against On-Call: A Polemic," in *Seeking SRE*.

But whose failure? The failure of the engineering leader in this story could be willful ("I know about all that and I just don't care; I need someone besides us to hold the pager."), but it is even more likely that the SREs in the picture have done an inadequate job of educating people and building consensus around a shared understanding of the value of SRE.

I wrote this introductory book to SRE for a reason—a deeper understanding of SRE isn't easy to come by. It may be useful to you to bring chunks of this book into your discussions with engineering leaders. Don't take on an "on call and that's all" situation if you can help it. SRE can and should be much more than that. Co-define the rules of engagement in such a way that it will serve everybody involved and let you trend reliability in the right direction for your organization.

Contributing Factor 4: Wrong Org Chart

I am aware that addressing this situation may be beyond your capabilities because of organizational structure. Especially in larger orgs, those structures may be decided mysteriously by a distant leadership team "way above your pay grade." In those cases, take this as a helpful warning that you will have more friction in your daily activities than you might prefer.

The contributing factor goes like this: more often than not, an organization will conceive of engineering effort as a zero-sum game, treating engineering decisions as "either/or." In our case, the decision will be between effort expended by developers to add new features to software and effort expended on nonfunctional improvements around reliability. These decisions come up all the time. For example: "What are we going to work on for the next release, this shiny new feature or refactoring the code so it can better emit metrics while it is running in production?" The contributing factor I'm addressing here is not actually this endless set of decisions, it is *who* is making these decisions and where they sit in the org chart.

While writing *Seeking SRE*, I had the pleasure of interviewing Pedro Canahuati, who at the time was the head of Production Engineering at Facebook.[5] I remember very clearly him saying that one of the key factors of his and Production Engineering's success was that he reported to the same engineering leader as the person running the teams that added the features to their products. This meant that you did not have to go very far up the org chart to find the person who would be "calling balls and strikes" around which work the engineering org would be taking on.[6]

---

5 Be sure to check out his Chapter 13 in *Seeking SRE*; it is a good one.

6 That person is ideally also acting as a hedge against misaligned incentives. In the list of complaints I hear when discussing how SRE isn't going well in an organization, "features are always prioritized ahead of reliability" never drops out of the top three.

Those decisions (roadmap, response to issues/crisis, resource allocation, staffing, etc.) all require a healthy amount of discussion. The more people involved and the more hops up the chain you have to go (with info getting lost at each hop), the harder the decisions can be. This is what I meant by "friction in your daily activities." You may not be in a role in your organization that allows you to have any input into the organizational structure, but if you see a pattern where every decision has to travel "up the chain," it may be in your best interest to see if you can make changes that would bring convergence quicker at your level of the org chart.

Contributing Factor 5: SRE by Rote

If you currently work for Google, please skip ahead to the next section. For the rest of us, a warning: it is very easy, and I see it all the time, for an organization to get ahold of the excellent SRE books written by Googlers and ex-Googlers and try to implement everything in them just as described. Miles Davis used to say, "If you understood everything I said, you would be me." Similarly, if you could implement everything the way Google did, you would be Google (but I am pretty sure you are not). Google and Google SRE have a very special engineering culture and history that I feel confident saying your organization doesn't have.

I mentioned this in Chapter 11, but a quick repeat because it is useful in this context as well: it is worthwhile watching Narayan Desai's SREcon talk "Care and Feeding of SRE" (*https://oreil.ly/fsNel*) for further elaboration on the role of organizational values in SRE implementations. While the talk is ostensibly about how SRE succeeds in Google, there are some really important observations in it, including "SRE is a reflection of a particular set of values."

I believe it is possible to take inspiration from the Google books and adopt some of the practices in them, but attempting to replicate everything in those books is not possible. This is why whenever I mention the books on SRE, I am careful to advise people to read them with a critical eye. SRE grows differently in different soil; you need to find the SRE practices that work for you without measuring yourself by how many book chapters you can implement.

Contributing Factor 6: Gatekeeping

This topic is discussed in Chapter 16, but it is important to discuss in the context of SRE failure as well. It is remarkably easy for SRE in an organization to fall into a gatekeeping posture. The rationale is there (protecting the reliability of production); the practices are there (production/application readiness reviews, some potential error budget policies, limited access to production); the incentives are there (SRE is a scarce resource—it is easier to say "no" than "yes, and…" or "yes, but…"); historical precedents are there (change boards, compliance requirements, operations seen as a hurdle to get past), and so on.

Unless you actively defend against this possibility, the chance of you waking up and being surprised at what you see in the mirror is high. Once you are established as the gatekeeper, the ways SRE can fail in this situation are myriad. Besides setting up an oppositional structure rife with potential conflicts, it is simply a fact that wherever necessary, people will "route around damage" to get things done. When this happens it is very difficult to reap the rewards of SRE.

Contributing Factor 7: Death Through Success

Once established in an organization, it is easy to immediately overload an SRE organization. If you hand over all of production (especially including all on-call responsibilities) to SRE,[7] that can consume all cycles of the team. Burnout is a predictable outcome in these situations.

Scaling an SRE team or function is hard, in part because it can be difficult to find the right people to hire. It's important not to depend on this to prevent overload.

Stephen Thorne, in his talk "Getting Started with SRE" (*https://oreil.ly/3tj9f*), notes that it is critical for an SRE group to be able to regulate its workload and be able to push back as needed. A reliable mechanism to do so is seldom included in SRE adoption plans.

Contributing Factor 8: A Collection of Smaller Factors

This is the "death by a thousand papercuts" or "pecked to death by ducks" section. While the small items in this section probably won't kill your SRE adoption on their own, they are likely to wound it.

Let's get into the lightning round:

Invisible work.
> If an SRE team does not adequately communicate what it is working on and the successes it is having to the larger organization, it will often be undervalued. Operations (and other service) professionals have known for decades about the weird dynamic where the better things are going, the more invisible they become even when they are responsible for the increased reliability. People don't tend to think about how great their mechanic's work (or the work of the people who

---

7 Kurt Andersen, a reviewer for this book, notes: "This in itself is a warning sign. Abdication of responsibility turns eventually into an insulation from responsibility—and irresponsible behavior flows forth."

---

build vehicles) was when the car is running great. I put this in the "good problem to have" category, but that still makes it a problem if not addressed.

The "Too Much Reliability" Trap

There's a hidden trap in the invisible work problem. If you take my advice around communicating success with the rest of the org, you will find that there is considerable pressure to report greater and greater success over time. Everyone wants to show graphs that continue to move up and to the right month over month. Everyone wants to show that things are getting better and better. Often this gets conveyed as reaching for the next nine of reliability.

This can put us in conflict with the foundational idea discussed right at the beginning of the book about working toward the *appropriate* level of reliability. If your desire to show upward progress in your monthly reports is driving you to push a service beyond the appropriate level of reliability, this is a problem.

How big of a problem? *"How can it be bad for a service to be more reliable than planned?"* you might be asking. There are a few ways this can get you into trouble. Leaving aside the potentially unnecessary resources/staffing required to maintain that upgraded standard you will require but didn't anticipate, the bigger problem is around expectations. Even if you don't explicitly announce a commitment to this greater level of reliability, people are going to notice it and begin to depend on you as if you had done so. They will build services or practices that will depend on you maintaining that standard for their own reliability and functioning. When there is a week during which, for whatever reason, you don't deliver to that implicit standard (perhaps you released a new major version), the rest of the organization will be in big trouble. Even though you successfully delivered at the level you have been promising all along, that's not going to be enough. Your dependencies won't have built in the necessary mechanisms for handling your (reasonable) downtime because they didn't think they had to, and well, everyone will be in a world of pain.

The canonical example of this trap is the experience mentioned in Chapter 4, "Service Level Objectives," of the *SRE book* with Chubby, Google's distributed lock system:

> As it turns out, true global Chubby outages are so infrequent that service owners began to add dependencies to Chubby, assuming that it would never go down. Its high reliability provided a false sense of security because the services could not function appropriately when Chubby was unavailable, however rarely that occurred.
>
> The solution to this Chubby scenario is interesting: SRE makes sure that global Chubby meets, but does not significantly exceed, its service level objective. In any given quarter, if a true failure has not dropped availability below the target, a controlled outage will be synthesized by intentionally taking down the system. In this way, we are able to flush out unreasonable dependencies on Chubby shortly after they are added. Doing so forces service owners to reckon with the reality of distributed systems sooner rather than later.

I'm here to save the kingdom (strike the superhero pose).

It's worthwhile watching Richard Clawson's SREcon talk "The Why, What, and How of Starting an SRE Engagement" (*https://oreil.ly/a-soS*) because it discusses a number of ways SRE can fail by entering the engagement while giving off the wrong vibes. For this context, I recommend you pay careful attention to his story on how an SRE engagement failed because they went into the experience with an attitude of, "We're SRE, and we are here to save the kingdom." It is an easy trap to fall into that weakens our capacity to be relentlessly collaborative.

Lack of….

If you find you have a lack of introspection (learning from failure), balance (reactive versus project work, toil versus nontoil, etc.), a culture of curiosity, or the proscriptive items mentioned here and in the rest of the book, that deficiency is likely to bite you at some point.

Forgetting the customer.[8]

This can show up in all sorts of insidious places. It is very easy for us to spend huge amounts of time investigating performance numbers for resources that make up our services without ever asking, "So what does the customer see when they try to use this?" We often set up monitoring focused on components, not customers. SLIs/SLOs can be put in place that are completely orthogonal to user expectations of the system. When this happens, it is done with the best of intentions, and it makes sense to the person at the time, so I don't want to sound too harsh while pointing this out. I would just like to encourage you to constantly be asking yourself and others about how something will either reflect the customer perspective or how it will impact them. Do this until it becomes a deeply ingrained habit. If you or your team get the reputation for being the people who are always asking about the customer expectations and experience, that's not a bad rep to have.

Forgetting to have fun.

I realize that "fun" is not always in the corporate gestalt, but I believe it supports a crucial part of the SRE definition mentioned in Chapter 1. It is part of what makes an operations practice *sustainable*. I don't mean to suggest that an SRE engagement or adoption process is a nonstop party or even that the SRE life is always fun. But I do think if you and/or your team can't recall the last time your job was fun, you should pay attention to that signal—it is important. Is an SRE engagement without fun a failure? Probably not. If all of your SRE engagements are without fun, is that a failure? I would argue that it is.

---

8 In my experience, these last two items happen in such small ways and in such small scopes that they aren't usually visible as full-on organizational failures; they more show up as tiny micro-failures (™). That being said, if they happen enough, an SRE organization can definitely lose its way, so be wary.

How to "SRE" Your SRE Failure

As a way of concluding this chapter, I want to address what to do when any of the contributing factors we've discussed in this chapter actually wind up on your doorstep.[9] For me, the first question to ask is, "Are we in a scenario where SRE has already failed or is just in the process of falling?" For both of these possibilities, the fundamental idea is to apply your SRE mindset and skills as best you can (appropriate to the moment). For example, if you are in the midst of an SRE situation that is actively failing, that's perhaps not so different from being in the midst of an outage where the system is running in a degraded state. Incident response is all about a coordinated response that requires you to bring the right people together to triage and mitigate as necessary. Now, this may be a slower-burning failure than most incidents you encounter (and it probably isn't a technical failure), but you likely can still engage with it in a similarly intentional way.

If you find yourself at the place of "has failed" (and I am sorry to hear it), I suspect you have already guessed the analog I have in mind (an outage has happened) and what an SRE does in that case (the postincident review). If you are lucky, you will get another run at this hill and can apply the lessons uncovered in that review to your next SRE engagement. If not, you may have to wait until the conditions are right, in this job or your next, to try again.

---

9 The following suggestion is presented in very broad brushstrokes to provide the basic idea. I'm eliding a metric ton of details, including the need for institutional support to get the engine turning over again, the different roles an individual contributor versus a manager or director will need to play, and so on. A single postincident review-esque meeting is not going to fix the problem, but applying the SRE practices and mindset, even as an analogue, might help quite a bit.

CHAPTER 13

SRE from a Business Perspective

SREs love to talk about the practical aspects of site reliability engineering. I'd like to think you are holding an entire book of practical advice on how to implement SRE, both as an individual and within an organizational context. But strangely enough, there is almost a complete absence of information in the literature or the discourse at conferences on the connection between SRE and the business. This is even stranger because, at some point, everyone in SRE is going to need to talk to someone on the business side of the house about what they do and how to fund it. Let's start to fill this void right now. I tracked down two experts on the topic and asked them the questions I think you would want to ask.

Here are the people in this discussion:

- *Ben Lutch*, former head of SRE for all of Google for 10 years
- *Dave Rensin*, creator and former director of the Google Customer Reliability Engineering team (the team composed of SREs responsible for helping Google Cloud customers adopt SRE practices)

Communicating About SRE

Talking to the Business About Reliability

Dave: My first thing is always how do you think about the reliability of the service you're offering your users? Reliability is your most important feature. If you don't believe that (or I can't convince you), then there's no point in having this conversation. The conversation might go like this:

- Do you care about reliability? "Yes, of course I care."
- Is it a feature of your service? "Yes."
- Is it as important a feature as whatever other features you have in the service? If the answer is no, then we can just stop. You're not ready for this (and then maybe we have to teach you that you're wrong, and that's okay).

But let's say the answer is yes. Then we continue the conversation:

- How do you think about it? "What do you mean?"
- How do you measure it? For most people the answer is "That all depends on who's yelling at me today."

That's fine, but there is a more rigorous way to measure it. You probably have to have a short conversation about why *perfect* is the wrong goal and, therefore, you have to have an error budget.

If you can philosophically get to this place, then you are in great shape. The rest is details.

You have two choices here:

- You can decide that you're going to build those skills amongst your feature developers, and that's fine. That's a completely viable model, but here's what it will mean for them: you're going to go on call, etc.
- Or you can decide, just like you have frontend engineers versus backend engineers, you're also going to have production engineers, people who really understand what it means to operate something at scale. The skills to build something that can scale are very different from the skills needed to operate something at scale. They just are. This is a philosophical choice you have to make.

If you agree that reliability is a feature, you have to decide that either:

- Your devs have to learn how to do it and do it really well, and that means taking pagers.
- Or you have to hire specialty software engineers to go engineer and maintain those things in your system.

Which one you choose is up to you, but you can't have the first without doing the engineering mentioned in the second. Tell me which one you want. And if you choose the second option, the specialty engineer path, well, okay, now you're doing SRE. I like to think of it as SREs are feature devs focused on the feature of reliability.

Start by talking to the head of product. If you try talking to engineering first, you are going to be asking them to do work without product support.

Selling SRE

Ben: We're careful not to really sell SRE. We generally say having an SRE team is going to cause you some pain. It's going to be a different pain than you have now. We're going to make you do things in a way that you might not be inclined to do otherwise, in service of the health of the system and thinking about our customers. We're going to cause you some discomfort. And you've got to be OK with that. So there's a little bit of selling in that you want them to understand what they're getting, but there's a little bit of, "We're going to have really strong opinions, and we're going to force you to do stuff a certain way." You have to make sure everyone's on board with that.

At a high level, this is like eating healthy food or exercising. They've got to want it for themselves. You can't force your customer, that is, the product group, you're working with. They've got to have some of the religion already. And so the first thing you need to do is make sure the business folks (or the interface you're talking to) has a little bit of the religion of what you get and why this is a rare, important capability that opens up doors that would otherwise be closed. Because, if you're not reliable and people therefore don't depend on and trust the service, there are a lot of doors that will never open for you. And that reliability doesn't just mean that the service is there when you click a button; it means that your data is there, that it's handled responsibly and reliably. When there's an outage, you'll be communicated to in a forthright and rapid way.

If you feel like you have to force SRE on anyone, then either you're not doing a good enough job or it's not being rolled out to the right group. You want to be able to transmit the value so that the person you're talking to about SRE is excited. They're excited because they're like, "I can build more stuff and it's going to be more reliable and people are gonna love it. Even in the face of competition, I can add features, widgets; I can integrate with other stuff. These people are going to allow me to fulfill the vision I have, whether it's revenue or user happiness." You've got to understand the purpose of the people you're talking to, and if and how SRE fits into them achieving that goal. If you scare anyone into making a choice, your team will be miserable down the road. You can't scare people into making a choice.

Dave: I'm a big believer in preserving people's choice, preserving their agency. So if I'm going to talk to whatever finance person or whoever controls the headcount, someone who doesn't care about the technology, my conversation is always, "You have a choice between a few outcomes. If you don't fund this, this is what we think happens. Here's why we think that is the case. If you fund it to this level, this is what we think happens and why we think it. If you funded this other level, etc." If they want more users or more usage in the system, then here are the scaling points in the system. If we don't address it when we get to about this usage mark, you're going to hit downtime. Make a business choice. We'll happily live with the consequences of whatever choice you make, but our responsibility is to make sure you're making an informed and clear-eyed choice.

It has to be as close to objectively true as possible. You can't scaremonger them. It has to be, "You could probably get by with this, but you know, you will risk team attrition later, so this is our recommendation, and here's why." And as Ben would say, you absolutely have to quantify it in the terms that the person you're talking to really cares about. If you're talking to a product manager, it has to be feature velocity or user acquisition. If you're talking to a finance person, it probably is user acquisition or revenue growth associated with user acquisition. If you can't easily get to something like revenue metrics, then you haven't thought hard enough about it; you haven't done the work to have this conversation yet.

Successful teams are "Yes, if..." teams. It's your job to describe the conditions under which the request is possible. "Yes, we can redesign this system to handle 10x the users in two weeks *if* we can immediately reassign 20 developers already familiar with the code to the problem today. Is that possible? Oh. It isn't? OK. What *is* possible?"

You're not there to be the adults in the room and temper everyone's enthusiasm—that isn't your job. It is easy for SRE to be looked at as the wet blanket. That's not your job. Your job is to tell them what are the conditions that have to be true for their dreams to come true. And then discuss whether those are conditions we can make true, because sometimes in the conversation, you'll find yourself thinking, "If we suspend the third law of thermodynamics, we can absolutely do the thing you want to do." In those cases, you have to say, "So…that might not be possible just this moment."

When pitching SRE, the vague arguments people make for SRE around cost-avoidance, that is, "Outages cost a lot of money," are basically insurance arguments. They are weaker arguments trying to assert some unmaterialized, prospective risk. Everyone starts by selling it this way. It is far better to make an engineering argument about how much engineering we need to do by gathering real data.

For example, pick a single incident, pick a single feature sprint that was used to remediate the issue. What is the scope of the work so it doesn't happen again and then x number of events that look like it? This is a far better starting place.

Communicating Success Back to the Business

Ben: Essentially, you look at the parameters that are important to the business. How is the service scaling (whether it's in size, number of users, or amount of information stored per user)? There are things that the product team cares about that are important to the service's growth and success. You want to be able to demonstrate that the cost of the SREs versus the stuff the business cares about, that number gets smaller all the time. You put five SREs there and the service gets a thousand times bigger and doesn't fall over. Those are the kinds of metrics that allow you to say this is an investment. This is consistent with the thesis that the SRE team is good at scaling and brings in expertise from other places. This isn't reinventing how to scale all the time. In fact, we have teams at Google that have gotten a thousand times more traffic, their footprint is a thousand times bigger, and they've gone from 14 to 16 people. Those are the things you care about, not just that you want to show off.

Dave: I also find there's this naive tendency to want to communicate to business owners in terms of SLOs and SLO compliance and stuff. They don't care about that. Engineering teams might care, but business owners definitely don't. You have to talk in terms they care about.

When I'm talking to a senior executive about what to expect from their SRE team, we sit down and set up a budget. What is the number of minutes a month the senior executive thinks is acceptable to spend talking to a customer who's unhappy about the reliability of the product? If your exec really thinks that number is zero, then you have a bad exec, and this product is going to fail. Experienced leaders understand that they will have to occasionally talk to unhappy customers. So, what's a reasonable amount of time per month for that? That's the error budget.

Back when Diane Green was running Google Cloud, that was a conversation she and I explicitly had. How many minutes a month are you willing to devote to having that kind of uncomfortable conversation with customers? It needs to be greater than zero. Okay, we can measure that. That's on your calendar. You know what it is. If we're under that, you could broadly feel like the team in the aggregate is doing its job, and if we're a lot over that, then something's broken.

This is a metric that every leader can understand and measure.

Proving the Success of an SRE Group to Others

Dave: Proving the success of SRE to others is not the goal. You're orienting yourself in the wrong way. Asking that question that way presupposes that the SREs want to have a conversation that continues to justify their own existence. That is not the conversation we want to have. We would rather not exist. We would rather have systems that don't require our expertise (at least in a dedicated sense) over time. We would prefer to solve your problem and move on to something else—because there will *always* be something else.

We have this conversation with leaders all the time. Sometimes the leader is sincere: "How do I know it's just not my amazing devs that led to our success this year?" And sometimes the leader is cynical: "I'd like to claw all this headcount back and use it for my devs. Why shouldn't I?"

But whatever the case is, the answer is precisely the same: "Okay, well, we could test that. Why don't we just put your devs on the pager rotation and reassign the team elsewhere?" That's great. That's success for us. That's the thing we're eventually aiming for because there's no shortage of demand for SREs at Google. And 99 out of 100 times, the leader's like, "Ooh, no, I'm not comfortable with that." Well, why aren't you comfortable with that? Help me understand what your sincerely held opinion is here.

SRE doesn't go (or good SREs do not go) into a conversation trying to justify their own existence. They're going into a conversation trying to figure out a path where they don't have to keep doing the job for that service. I think that's an important conversation to have with every leader at least once (probably twice) a year. It's always that our goal is to eventually not be needed. And so we're going to check in a couple of times a year to see if we're any closer to it.

The other thing is that reasonably mature SRE teams keep a near-miss list of the outages we had before and the way we changed the system to make them either occur less frequently or be smaller. And that's another way of showing progress. So you can say, "Look, we had a thing, we changed the system. We probably would've had it seven or eight more times, but we didn't."

Budgeting for SRE

First Budget Request

Dave: Nobody, just nobody, has the conversation about "I want to fund an SRE team" in the abstract. It always starts with, "There's something I'm trying to accomplish that the current feature work won't let me accomplish." Usually, it's because the system has had a series of serious reliability failures and customers are noticing and getting angry. That's almost always where the SRE conversation starts: "How do we dig out of this hole and never get back in it?"

Then, someone discovers SRE as a concept and says, "That's it; that's what we need. We need SREs." Every first proposal to a funder usually comes with one or two really well-thought-out projects. For example, we need three people for four months to go do this thing, and here's the tangible benefit. And then the next question is, "Is this a one-off project, or is it that you really need a team of three to four people to do this project and the one after it, then the one after it, then the one after it." And all those requests kind of bootstrap SRE.

Emergent properties of a distributed system grow faster than the engineers writing code because these properties are the results of (a) a changing codebase, (b) changing users, and (c) changing use cases. So, even if you don't ever change the code, you will have to continuously apply energy to keep the system running well. Because of this, reliability work is exactly the same as any other feature from a budget perspective. Reliability work should *never* be viewed as a tax on development work. It's not. It's a kind of feature work all by itself.

Talking About Funding

Ben: Two ways to discuss funding for teams are related to how services tend to grow. For the first one, some services grow in scale where they get way, way, way bigger. In that case, you don't really want your SRE team to grow. In fact, ideally, your team stays at a minimum size.

One of the things that you want to make sure you communicate is your objective to have a minimum bound as the problem gets bigger and bigger and bigger; that is, the scale of the service gets bigger and bigger. That's appealing to SREs because then their jobs get more interesting and they have more scope, and it's also appealing to the product side because the cost is fixed. It also says something about how the infrastructure is built, that you're confident you can add stuff to it and it's not gonna topple over.

The other way we talk about funding is the most common one where you have longitudinal growth instead of something getting twice as big. It's that they add stuff to it. One product becomes two or adds features or intermingles with another product. And those are places where the interactions of these multiple parts will require attention. You might have one vertical part that's actually reasonably well studied. You can articulate how to scale that with a compact set of people, but it's this longitudinal situation where you're adding products and features and interactions with other services that gets tricky. Those friction points are where things break the most. And there aren't humans who have a foot in each camp.

So part of the description for SREs, and part of the reason why product areas come to us, is they want to use SRE as glue—when there isn't good design or good coordination between working parts. You've got these two systems that all of a sudden need to interact more. Like, oh, this widget's gonna pop up in all of the search stuff now, but it wasn't designed for that. That longitudinal growth is both an opportunity and the part of this conversation where you say, "We're gonna make you do stuff you don't like because you've built two things—two great engineering organizations that have had no reason to be in contact that independently built things that don't quite snap together."

The basic approach really needs to be centered on not making promises about "never having an outage." People want to be told a story about how "SRE is going to make all of your problems go away" and "There's going to be no production pain." The people who don't want to interface with production want you to say that to them. They want to be told a story that they just have to put a dime in the machine and come back in six months and put another dime in the machine. They want you to tell them this— they want to be sold.

When you start approaching people about where to fit SRE in, it's really important to not fall into that trap of selling these promises. If you do, you'll actually get people just nodding along, eagerly lapping it up. You've got to be mindful to avoid this. You have to be able to say, "We're going to cause you a bunch of pain because you have done stuff in a way that isn't gonna grow or isn't gonna scale longitudinally." Generally, I feel like I spend the balance of my time with the business partners, either lowering their expectations or correcting their expectations. It is less about selling them a bill of goods and more about "this is what you get and only what you get" and "here are the things that can and will go wrong."

Re-Up Conversations

Dave: The initial conversation is almost always in the context of some history of pain. You staff a team, they get up to speed, and your pain starts to go down. Things get more reliable and everyone's happy. And then someone comes back and says, "the pain's gone. Why do I have to keep doing this?"

So, you have a couple of ways you can go. My first approach usually is to point out to smart people that no part of the environment they operate in is static. You want more users on your system, not fewer. So, at some point you're going to hit some scaling inflection that you don't know about yet. Your users are constantly using your system slightly differently today than they were yesterday.

The net result is entropy in your system. And so you need to keep injecting some minimum amount of effort or the entropy begins to take over and you go back to where you were before. Now the questions you have are, "Is this the right amount of effort? Is it too much, is it too little?" Those are really reasonable questions. And that's why I beat people up so hard around SLOs and error budgets because I personally think you have to have a quantifiable way to answer this question. In my experience, error budgets are the best way to do it. Just to be able to say, "Look, we can see that we're not burning zero of our error budget, but we're really under, or we're just at the threshold," or whatever. That guides the conversation.

If you're just at your error budget threshold, you should be very careful about adjusting your SRE effort because you're running at some kind of efficient frontier. If you're really underneath your error budget, you should have a real conversation about whether you are overstaffed.

Inside of Google, we run this exercise called Production Excellence (ProdEx). It is a rotating quarterly review of every SRE team. One of the metrics we look at all the time is, "How's your error-budget consumption?" If you were consuming more than your error budget, there was one kind of hard conversation. If you were consuming just under your error budget consistently, it was mostly a "you're doing a pretty good job here" conversation because that is what we want to see. And if you were consuming consistently, meaningfully less than your error budget, then we'd start a real conversation on whether you are overstaffed for this and whether you should be returning some headcount to your partner.

There are a lot of reasons for consuming less than your error budget. Maybe the design you did turned out to have a lot more impact than you thought it was going to have. Yay! Or maybe your product's user growth didn't accelerate the way you thought it was going to. Boo! But still, why should you spend extra resources? And so the sustaining conversation depends on where you're sitting in that spectrum.

Organizations—particularly in tech, particularly in the senior ranks—are not static. VPs come and go; directors come and go. People come into a culture and the first thing they want to do is put their stamp on it, which means they want to reexamine all the first principles. That's healthy, actually. One area that is constantly getting questioned is SRE funding. In a tech company in particular, the two main drivers of cost are infrastructure and headcount. The cost of an incremental headcount is way higher than the cost of an incremental piece of a computer.

OK, so you're a new VP or whatever, you've come into the company, you've inherited this product or this part of a product, and you say, "Well, I'm funding 30 headcount; this thing called SRE—what does it do?"

The answer is going to be something along the lines of "It keeps stuff running." You ask, "How does it keep stuff running?" "We make sure stuff is automated and scalable." So, as you start to understand the cost dynamics, it's really natural for you to say, "Well, if they've written all this automation, why do I still need those people? Can I claw back that headcount so I can build more features?" And so that combination of turnover, and then the dynamics of where the costs are, make it basically a quarterly conversation—or at least a twice yearly conversation.

Funding Models

Ben: Initially SRE was attached just to the one or two areas that were critical to Google's existence, like Search. It started out because if we lost revenue flow, if we lost a service, we lost revenue and we lost reputation. At the time, Google was small, and we weren't really in a position to be able to tolerate that. And so, ironically maybe, when SRE was much smaller, because it was only attached to the thing that produced all of our revenue, it was actually sort of an easier sell. The value was really clear because the consequences of having things not be well organized in the production world were really palpable immediately to the company.

As we grew, the concerns started to change. There were places where you're like, "Well, this is gonna hurt us reputationally, this is gonna have an effect down the road." The trade-offs are less immediate and less existential. And so you actually have to think a little more about, "Is this worth putting people on?" We have to explain that this may not be worth it today, or this may not cause pain or slow down the product itself, but it's actually something that we need to do in service of longer-term goals. The longer-term goals become things like "How do we build a production environment so we can build more products, scale more products, and really have a knob around the cost as it relates to reliability that's more complex and less on/off?"

When SRE first started at Google—I don't think this is confidential—it was centrally funded. It was basically a dollop of headcount that the person who ran all of Technical Infrastructure (TI) said, "OK, I'm giving a hundred heads to SRE—you people running SRE, figure out where to disperse those people in a way that is in line with what is most important to Google."

And it was pretty easy to decide where to put people because there were just a few things that you couldn't screw up. When I took over the reins with Todd Curtiss in 2012, one of things that happened when we first started was that central dollop of headcount went away. The person running TI said, "I'm not going to give you any more headcount for SRE—zero more headcount for SRE—you've gotta get it from each product area. You've got to convince them they have to give up some of their headcount."

So, at that point we had to be able to demonstrate to a VP who's not in our organization that it's actually better for their product, their service, their revenue, their reputation, to take some of their precious headcount and give it away to us to manage in the SRE org. At the time, Todd and I were like, "Oh, that, that really sucks," because we were into running the services and we didn't want to have to have negotiations and plead with 10 different VPs. But it turned out that that wasn't really an impediment because we had come far enough that the folks who ran the products were already convinced of SRE's value. The people developing the products wanted to be involved in reliability, but they didn't want to be woken up by a pager. We had gotten to the point by then that that value proposition was really clear. We had that combination of a team that's spread around the globe that knows how to handle incidents, knows the code base, and can work with all the primary developers.

When we talked with the product areas, we made it very cut-and-dried. Like, if you fund it, this is what happens. And if you don't fund it, this is what happens. Not as a threat, but just, "Here's the knob on zero, right? This is what we can do on zero, and this is what we can do on a hundred. And you can kind of choose anything in between." There's some notches in that knob because you have to have a team that's big enough to have critical mass so that you don't have a single person on call for weeks on end.

SRE Alignment

Models for Engagement

Dave: We actually have tiered engagement models. There's the office hours consultative model, which are for pre- and post-SRE engagements. For example, "I have a service that isn't ready for SRE to support." There's both a drop-in office hours model and a separate consultative model (where we will come in and act as a consultant), which we do all the time. Maybe your service will get to a place where it should have dedicated SRE support, or maybe it won't, and that's fine too. For a long time, we did these things called production readiness reviews, which is a service SRE provided where we would just go in and inspect the service and tell you if we thought it was runnable by SRE standards.

Then there's the swarm model. We're going to get three or four very experienced people to swarm for a quarter and help you dig out, but understand that you're going to keep your pagers. That's a little less common. Then there's all manner of splitting the difference. Not every team is dedicated to just one service.

In Google, the goal of an SRE team is to work itself out of a job, and we ask that of every team roughly every quarter; how close are you to that? That's a success metric for us. And so when you get to the other side of that hill and you've automated away a lot of the really urgent stuff that would wake people up in the middle of the night, the rest can kind of go into a queue for developers during the day. They understand enough how production works, and there's a whole set of services we offer to help on that other side of the hill. That's a very happy day.

Ben: There's a little bit of history there. Early in its days, SRE would only engage with services that were large enough to have a really big impact. SRE teams were expensive, and we were still figuring things out, and there was lots of overhead for running them. And so we would wait until a service really was highly important to Google before we would assign SREs to them. But as a result, we noticed that, because Google's kind of a large, distributed place, the services that they owned were really different. Only the fundamentals would be common. One of the principles of SRE is, *How do we build production in a way that's scalable, where we can share resources where the people can move around.* It's not just that we're funding these different little islands of production. We had discovered that the longer we waited, the more we were guaranteed to find that each SRE team would be planted on something that looked really different than every other SRE team. And this was bad for Google, bad for the SREs. It meant lots of development was happening in overlapping but noncommunicating ways. And so we started to brainstorm about how we could get involved earlier in services where we weren't able to commit a full SRE or a full SRE team, and about how we could influence how things were architected and built such that they either didn't need SRE, or the path to getting SREs was really easy.

They had people working with them and advising them who demonstrated their willingness to make something that was production-ready, independent of whether or not they're assigned SREs. The journey really started out with funding a few very mature teams and actually realizing that wasn't the right model. There were years when we would go around very loudly telling people, "If you ever want to have SREs, if you ever want professional support 24/7 helping write software to make your service better, you need to involve SRE early. If you don't involve SRE early, you're going to have a steaming pile of something really important, and we're not going to be able to help you."

Why Not the Embedded Model? Why a Separate Org?

Ben: Part of it is an early historical choice, but part of it is the principle that if you build lots of services, you believe that having a uniform production infrastructure is better for reliability. It allows people to develop their products more rapidly. When you fragment people as individuals and people as part of a larger team, or when you fragment the technology—that's harder. One person who's responsible for SRE stuff on a team where they're 1 of 20 people, that's sort of a harder proposition. And I think it's a little easier to represent, "If you want SREs, if you want our support, here's how it works," if you are not fragmented.

When you're part of an organization that has lots of people looking at the right way to do X, Y, Z, and there are 10 experts working on it, that interwoven connection makes the individuals stronger. There's a natural inclination of a team to draw borders around itself, which makes it difficult when you implant people in other teams. That connection to some central principle tends to wither over time because that's not what they're seeing where they are sitting, and those aren't the people they are working with every day.

Dave: How do you do career planning for those people? So, I have one or two SREs doing SRE things on a team of 20 developers. It is a natural thing that as those one or two people want to get promoted over time, they're going to gravitate toward the things that get rewarded for promotion. And on that team, it's going to be the very dev feature kind of stuff.

The other thing people don't remember or don't talk about much is that before there was SRE at Google, there was a team called SysAdmin, and it was just a traditional ops team. The whole reason we have SRE is we could see it didn't scale. There was a lot of thinking about what is the way we make sure that SREs, as we are now conceiving them, don't turn into ops teams. The big silver bullet there was the ability to hand back the pagers—to say, "You are not holding up your end of the deal; we're walking away." SRE teams very seldom invoke it. I can think of maybe three times in nine years that I've seen it happen, but it's there, and we all know it exists.

For a long time, the feeling was, "The only way we're going to be able to enforce that is if SRE is its own org. So, let's put these people together so they can share with one another so they can rotate across the services." They support some commonality of what they do so that they are evaluated against peers and cohorts. They have their own job ladder that they can be evaluated against to avoid capture into other teams, and we can make sure they don't slowly degrade orbit and fall back to earth as an ops team.

Is that the right choice for you? I don't know. That really depends on your corporate culture and size.

Avoiding the Pager Monkey or Toil Bucket Traps

Ben: The pager monkey situation, where an SRE is valued only because they will take pages any time of the day, does happen. When we talk to engineering leaders sometimes that's what they are interested in getting from SRE involvement, and they won't say it out loud. There are many times when you will talk to someone about how we can automate infrastructure or move to more common infrastructure that will take less energy and will resolve outages quicker. And people are nodding, and you can just see the thought bubble above their heads: "Dollar sign <ding> can take the pager from my frontend engineer."

There's what people tell you, and then there's what people are really thinking. There's variation in how direct people will be. But the fact that there might be a bunch of experts who will take the pager is really, really compelling. Now, it's not always because they want a pager monkey. Holding a pager is stressful, and you've got to understand the systems really well, and you have to be comfortable with that pressure. You will get chat messages from everyone up the chain when the outages happen on your watch. And you have to have built relationships with not just your team and the other time zones, but also with the other infrastructure or adjacent systems. That requires a bunch of energy and a bunch of time and a bunch of desire to troubleshoot and tinker and socialize. In a way, "Take the pager" is shorthand for a lot of really interesting, good stuff, too, not just "Please react when this device makes a noise." There's a spectrum in there.

That is a very large component when someone says, "Take my headcount." It will often be because the engineers on their team say, "I don't feel equipped to do this… I'm afraid that Google search is going to be down, and it's going to be my fault. I'm not going to know what to do…" So, can we please fund a team that's really good at this, that is built to be under fire and then to make things better. And so there's a large component of taking the pager, but it's not all bad.

The other part, with respect to the pager: I would get excited about this when I talked to the team. You get to be part of one of the world's largest production environments. You actually get to be in the lab. You get to mix the stuff and see how it breaks; and there's no amount of single-person coding in a darkened room that can really prepare you for what happens when a massive system fails for a reason that you would never see in a textbook or in your constrained environment. Building something is sort of abstract, but running it is really fun and appeals to lots of people. You get to run this thing, and you get to see why it wasn't built right.

That's an experience that a very small set of people actually get to have. It's easy to go write software. It's really hard to run it at this scale. That desire to tinker and to take a thing apart or to put it back together when it comes apart—that's a unique combination of engineering: being curious and not just taking "That's how it is" for an answer. You have to understand it because it might come apart on your watch. I find that really compelling.

SRE Teams

Choosing Headcount Sizes

Ben: In the beginning, I would be lying if I said there was much precision there. It was sort of an opening bid. Basically, part of our responsibility was to say, if we allocate this many people, here's what you get for it. Then they could say, that's too many people, or that's too few people. Early on, it was not well calculated on anyone's part. We would sort of lay out a menu of here's what you get with this many people. But headcount numbers are also not static. And so one of the things that was part of the planning process was assuming that the number we got in January was not the number we would end up with in August. Often it would be more, sometimes it would be less.

There is an inclination to try to build an organization, which I don't think is the right thing to do. I think the right thing to do is to understand the exchange (headcount for what you get) and make an informed choice on that. And being able to force yourself to say, "Well, what happens if we get zero?" Not like the dinosaurs have all gone extinct, but business-wise, how do we survive with zero? Being able to paint a picture that did not seem like you were totally biased toward one outcome, but rather that you were simply presenting the consequences of doing these different things—that was something we had to be pretty conversant with.

You need enough people that no one is crushed. You need enough people in enough time zones that the job is one where you can spend enough time running the system and enough time fixing the system. It has to be both a compelling career for someone and worth the money. If you pick the wrong stopping point, if you make the team too small, people get burned out because they're just fighting fires all the time. They never improve the system. And really, you're hiring software engineers or people who are good at software engineering, and they're like, "Well, I'm not actually doing software engineering." You have to make sure that you can get enough critical mass to actually make this a job that people want to do. Which means you can't throw them into the fire. So, there's kind of a minimum number there.

And so if you get that minimum number, you have to shed responsibilities. You say, "Well, if we don't get anyone here, then, instead of doing the five things we're doing now, we can do three things." You can't oversell, right? Because then you just end up with no one, or a bunch of miserable people. So that's kind of stage one: "Let's make sure we have good careers for people." Because if you have people leaving all the time, that's a lot of energy to spend in an organization.

I think sometimes there's a tendency for people to look at spreadsheets and think about the end goal. "I want an organization that looks like this." But sometimes you'll talk to a team and they will be like, "We don't need more people because it gets too hard to communicate." So, we wouldn't pick a team size of more than 13 or 14 people. We'd split services into different chunks because otherwise there's too much to learn and too much cross communication. When we think about why *this* number, it's really about what is the quantum where people can pick up something new and interesting and improve it so that it's worthwhile for the company. Generally those quanta are pretty small.

When you gauge the consequences of getting more or fewer people, I think the best practice is to spend a lot of time talking with people who are on the team doing the work. When people talk about this, there are often three people gradations. Typically, if you're asking for numbers that are like just one person, you're probably not taking a really long-term view of it. But if you're asking for 50 people for something, then you're picking a round number. And so it's best to really consult with the team and say, "All right, what do you wish you could get done? What's holding you back from having this job be different in six months?" Getting a sense from the team is generally the biggest signal.

Dave: Ask yourself, "Why are we having this conversation?" It's always in the context of some recent pain or some ongoing pain. OK. What is the pain you had? What is your tolerance for pain? "Well, just on that metric, we've had three outages affecting 30% of our customers in the last three months" (just making this up). OK. How many outages do you want to see affecting what percentage of the customer over what timeline? "I want to see zero over zero over forever." OK. Well, you know that's not possible. And if you don't know that's not possible, we're not going to have this conversation, because that's physically not possible.

Right. Let's try again: What's better? And so that becomes your first number, and it's wrong, and you know that it's wrong, but that's OK. I would rather have a first number that's a little less wrong than where I am now. What is the minimum number of humans I need to probably get close to that number? And then the first thing we're going to do is set up a pretty lightweight process to measure those three things, whatever it was we talked about. We're going to report on it monthly.

How Do You Know When an SRE Team Might Be in Trouble?

Ben: For warning signals, there's sort of two forms:

- One is on a team level, and that is really where the developers don't want to ever be on call. That's often a signal that this area is going south. There's a culture in the development team where they don't feel comfortable being on call or they don't feel equipped for it. That's a local problem that we've seen. That'll just get worse and worse.

- And the other is an existential problem. As Dave says, part of the purpose of an SRE team is to make themselves not needed anymore. If a team gets into a place where stuff is done so well that it's not needed anymore, then you have to deal with this thing where teams tend to have this life force that they try to protect (whether they are doing it consciously or not).

Dave: Previously, we talked about an exercise called Production Excellence (ProdEx) we run quarterly. We don't touch every team every quarter, but every team gets touched twice a year at a minimum. One of the things we look at is consumption of error budget. So, if you're drastically underconsuming your error budget, you're way exceeding your SLOs; that's a warning sign that maybe the team isn't as needed as it once was. We should go look at that. So, we do. We look pretty hard. Obviously, we also look for the ones that are clearly underwater. You're not meeting your SLOs, but we look equally as hard at the teams that are exceeding their SLOs consistently. That's a warning sign that you're beginning to work yourself out of a job, and maybe we should more formally talk about that because people get comfortable in their roles. And that can be an uncomfortable conversation.

I'll also add a couple of failure modes to the list. The other warning I see sometimes—and this happens when we hire leaders who have come from outside the company and who are used to a more traditional ops relationship—is when we see that the SREs are slowly just becoming toil buckets. You can tell this is happening when the project work developers do with SREs outside of their on-call time is low quality. You see SREs having to invent their own project work, being blocked from adding to the core features of the product when they want to. Things like that signal that the development team is slowly adopting a culture that these are just glorified ops people and it's starting to treat them as second-class citizens versus development peers. And that frog can boil slowly over time until it just sort of collapses one day. So you have to really keep an eye on it.

Alert Noise as a Signal of Team Health

Dave: The percentage of actionable alerts is important. So we ask SREs, "How many alerts did you get? So what's the load? And then what percent of them turned out to be actionable?"

Ben: The two questions in this situation are "How much is it that your monitoring needs to be improved, and how much is it that the system you are monitoring needs to be improved?" Both are super important. Those are actually the first ones I look at for product groups, because if you have a bunch of noisy alerts, you have SREs running around all the time chasing stuff that doesn't matter. Or you have SREs who have built up a callus, and they're like, "90% of these don't matter." Those are both terrible failure modes. It also says stuff about how well the services are instrumented.

Seeing the alert load be low but important, as in "there are always three important things that break that are interesting," is a really good state to be in. Everyone understands the system. The system is growing, and so it's breaking in new ways. Ideally, that's always a different way each time. But if you see an alert graph that increases quarter over quarter, you know you have a team that's going to be in an unsustainable state at some point. You look for either overload or toil overload/under care—neither of those end well.

SRE Promotions

Ben: When it comes time to show evidence for a promotion, most often people who are working specifically on product development have a very specific artifact, as in "I launched this thing" or "I built this thing, and here's what it does, and here's the result." Often SRE work involves making sure things don't happen. And so when you think about promotions and building a case, you have to make sure that you educate the reader of the promotion evidence so that they fully understand and appreciate the value of the thing that didn't happen. Promotion committees may not know much about SRE. And so always at promotion time, you have to assume that you need to do some education, as opposed to just "I built this thing; it looks like this. Here's the money that flowed through it."

Turning Teams Down

Ben: The primary reason that I've seen it done is because they've done a great job in making it economical to run the service at a high reliability without needing as many people. That's sort of the ideal outcome, to be able to say, "Hey, we don't need seven people on this continent or in this time zone and seven in this one to keep this service running alive." So, most often, it's because we've done a good job and we've actually constrained the problem to a point where it actually doesn't make sense to have a full force on it.

In less good situations, it is a relationship issue. In most business relationships, surprises are not a good thing. So the right approach is having communications with the development or product team. If we are getting to a point where the SREs have been signaling for a while that either the operational work is increasing faster than the team's capacity to get on top of it, or that the product folks don't have enough state or experience to ensure that the product itself is actually runnable in a finite way, then this is not a good situation. This often happens when teams don't sit together. Sometimes developers will build things that make perfect sense to them and—people often use this metaphor—they throw something over the wall. The thing that lands doesn't quite fit into production, or it takes a bunch of effort, and that wall prevents good communication between the two of them.

So that picture fails. The sides are not doing a good job communicating, things are just getting worse, and then you have to—with the SRE hat on—say, "Listen, the economics aren't working out. This is becoming unsustainable." And so we need to hand this work back to the product team because it's not economical for us to do it.

SRE teams are not designed to do cleanup work for developers. They're designed to make services easy to run in concert with the people who are building the service. So, when you get to that crossover point, you have to give everyone fair warning, but say, "Hey, listen, we can't actually support this when it looks like this, and we're getting closer to it looking like this." And if you get to that point, you have to say, "Listen, we can't because we're not the team to support what you're in the process of creating. So, we'll give you the headcount back and you need to figure out how you want to operate the service, given that it's gotten to a place where what we've built as an SRE team is not the right environment for it."

It's very rare in my experience that we've gone all the way down the road to where we said, "Sorry." It's happened a few times, but from my recollection over 10 years, it was a single-digit number. It was mostly the case that we would travel on this path toward "this is what this is going to look like in six months." And I think the development team in particular would say, "Actually, we don't want it to look like that."

Ideally you get someone from SRE to sit with the developer side a little bit so that they actually understand the problems that happen when they do X, Y, Z. You get one of the developers to be an SRE or actually join a shared on-call rotation—that is normally how we would address that. "Hey, developer, why don't you do the on call? We'll shadow you while you're in the office, make it pretty easy." You break that wall down brick by brick to the point where the teams are again in a place where everyone's doing the appropriate work.

From the Author: I Would Like to Hear from You

David Blank-Edelman here, back with you again. This is roughly where my conversation with Ben and Dave ended, but it is not nearly the end of what can or should be discussed in this sphere. For example, much of this conversation has an enterprise context as its backdrop. Do you believe the answers are similar in other contexts? We didn't get a chance to discuss what happens when SRE fails in an organization and has to be restarted or when funding is initially denied. What should we do in those situations? I would love to hear from others about their SRE-to-business interactions. Please consider writing and speaking about this in the public square.

CHAPTER 14

The Dickerson Hierarchy of Reliability (A Good Place to Start)

In Chapter 4, I discussed some of the reasons organizations turn to SRE in the first place. By far the most common reason is that they have experienced a spate of bad reliability weather—a cluster of outages, perhaps public and embarrassing. In the least worst case, the news of someone else's reliability issues has traveled to management, and they are scared. The organization is motivated and is ready for someone to take on reliability challenges. Cue the epic trailer music.

I've had the pleasure of talking with a sizable number of people who were at exactly this point, right at the cusp of their organization's entry into SRE. Even though they were just getting started, their biggest issue wasn't finding work that contributed to the reliability of their systems. That was easy. There were so many possible things they could be working on. It wasn't a matter of finding some low-hanging fruit[1] they could start with—they couldn't walk without kicking metaphorical fruit. Their biggest problem was figuring out where to start and in what order they should approach their bounty of possibilities for the greatest possible impact.

In this chapter, I'd like to share with you the best answer I've heard to this conundrum and the way I usually discuss this map for getting started. At the end, I'll also mention a few of the paths I've seen people take that are tempting but highly prone to failure.

---

1 I've learned that farmers often consider the low-hanging fruit on a tree or a bush the least desirable part of the crop. Fun to think about next time you use that metaphor…

The Dickerson Hierarchy of Reliability

The clearest map I know for beginning SRE work in an existing organization with reliability issues is the Dickerson Hierarchy of Reliability. If you have heard of it before, you may have encountered it for the first time in the same place I did, in "Part III Practices" of *Site Reliability Engineering*. Since reading those chapters, my understanding of this hierarchy has deepened from listening to others talk about their practical application of the idea and from having to present the idea to many others. I'll give you my best rendition of how I present it to others, but I highly encourage you to also go back and review the original.

The Dickerson Hierarchy of Reliability is a riff by Mikey Dickerson, ex-Googler and founding administrator of the United States Digital Service, on the Maslow Hierarchy of Needs. Usually it is presented as a pyramid, as shown in Figure 14-1.

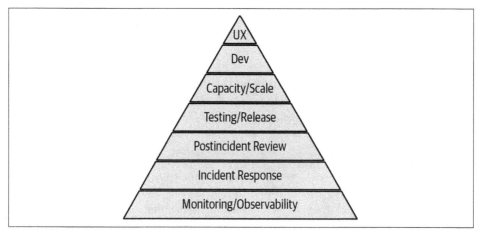

Figure 14-1. Slightly modified version of the Dickerson Hierarchy of Reliability

I've made a few small changes to the wording of the original pyramid found in the *SRE book* based on audience feedback; see Section 3 of that book for the original. As in the Maslow hierarchy (and many other hierarchies), the idea is that you start at the bottom of the hierarchy and only proceed up the levels at the point when the lower level is considered "solid."

Level 1: Monitoring/Observability

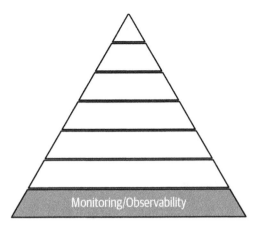

Many in SRE (including me) would claim the first level, Monitoring/Observability, is the most important level.[2] There are a number of reasons this level is so important. Let's look at a few of them.

Determining your position for navigation

The first level is most succinctly described as, "Are things getting better or are they getting worse?" Your monitoring is (or should be) your best source of objective data on the reliability of your systems and the short- and long-term impacts your efforts are having on your reliability. You'll need it to determine whether changes you make (new software versions, configuration changes, environmental modifications, etc.) are having a positive, negative, or neutral effect on the reliability of your systems.[3] It can help you understand what direction you need to head toward next.

---

2 The original hierarchy used just the term *Monitoring*.

3 On some occasions, it will be your indication that you've made any change at all. We all have stories where we thought we had made a change, and minutes, hours, or even days later realized that we deployed something completely different than the thing we modified. whee.

Source of truth and discussion

One thing that SRE brings to an organization is a culture of discussing reliability using objective data. In order for those conversations to happen, there has to be a trusted source of this data; otherwise, your conversations go a little bit like this:

> *Person 1:* So, how well do you think system X is doing these days?
>
> *Person 2:* Hmm, I'm not sure. I get the sense it isn't as reliable as it needs to be.
>
> *Person 1:* That's funny, I was just thinking the opposite since I haven't been paged in a few days because of it.

You've likely been in at least one conversation that sounded like this, where people, at best, were sharing anecdotes. That's the sort of conversation you might have if you have inadequate monitoring in place.

Even worse are the conversations where there is a system in place, but no one trusts it. If people are saying things like "I don't trust that system; it is missing all of the data from Thursday," you know you have a real problem on your hands. See the sidebar "A Red Flag Story" for an example of this in the real world.

A Red Flag Story

Once upon a time, I interviewed at a relatively large company. They were looking for someone to run a medium-sized SRE team that was spread across a number of different time zones. In the interview, I asked what I thought was going to be an innocent question: "So, can you tell me about your monitoring system?"

The answer I got back, as faithfully as I can recall, was something like "Well (sheepishly), we do have a monitoring system. We have two full-time employees who manage it. But it is too noisy, and so nobody pays attention to it."

Apparently my reply of "Well, clearly one thing I would concentrate on first if I were to start this job would be to fix your monitoring" was reasonable enough that I did get an offer (didn't take it, though). But I've never forgotten that person's answer. There's lots to unpack in the answer, including a cautionary tale about curated actionable alerting.

One last comment related to this aspect: we spend a lot of time interacting with the reliability of our systems. Monitoring systems and their alerts are one way reliability interacts with us.

Your monitoring system can be an excellent meeting place (a watering hole of sorts) where people can gather, share a common reality, and talk to each other about it. Don't squander that opportunity.

SLIs and SLOs

An extension of the last item is the role monitoring plays in the practice of SLIs and SLOs, now pretty uniformly accepted in the SRE community as best practices. SLIs and SLOs offer an excellent common language or framework for conversations about reliability. If you are going to use SLIs and SLOs as work-planning tools (perhaps their most important role), it will be crucial that they are fed from a solid and trusted monitoring system. Real conversations require real data.

A mirror

Often, monitoring systems become these (unintentional) mirrors of an organization. What is actually monitored and how that information is treated can say a lot about the organization. If there's little to no monitoring of systems or end-to-end operations from the customer's perspective (rather, it is all component-level metrics), that may say something about what is important to the organization.

If the monitoring/alerting is disorganized, it is like the difference between a chef who keeps a clean work area and one whose kitchen is in shambles. Just by looking at that chef's work area, you can make a good guess about what that chef's internal state is like. Anthony Bourdain famously said, "Messy station equals messy mind."

As a final commentary on monitoring and its connection to the cultural aspects of an organization, I believe it is safe to say that Conway's law is definitely in play with monitoring too. Conway's law is the following:

> Any organization that designs a system (defined broadly) will produce a design whose structure is a copy of the organization's communication structure.
>
> —Melvin E. Conway

If there are two groups in charge of monitoring a set of systems, there's a very good chance that there will be two monitoring systems or, at best, two sets of metrics. If an app is created with three different tiers, each built by a separate team, you can guess the structure of the monitoring system with a pretty high degree of confidence. This isn't to say that this is not actually the optimal structure,[4] but it does provide a good indication of just how critical intentional architecture is to the creation of an effective monitoring system. It's harder than it looks.

That is hopefully enough about monitoring for now. Let's move on to the next level in the Dickerson Hierarchy of Reliability.

---

4 Though it probably isn't the optimal structure, because there's a good chance that the end-to-end customer experience isn't well represented in such a system; but a boy can dream.

Level 2: Incident Response

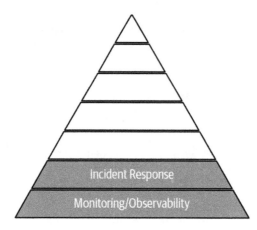

The second level of the hierarchy, Incident Response, is SRE's acknowledgement of the existential truth that virtually every system we encounter will have an unplanned outage of some sort. We wouldn't have very much to talk about regarding reliability if this weren't true.

If we are talking about an outage, we can all agree that it isn't a question of *If?*—it will happen. It isn't a question of *When?*—it will be unplanned. It's hopefully not a question of *Why?*—if we knew why it happened before it happened, we'd like to think we would have intervened before it became an outage. That leaves us with the more useful question of *How?* or *How will we handle it?*

This level in the hierarchy asks us to evaluate whether we have the processes, plans, documentation, etc., that allow an outage to be handled as an operational response we execute instead of an ad hoc reaction. Can we efficiently triage the situation and bring the right resources to bear to remediate it in a cool and considered manner, or does every outage find us running around with our hair on fire?

As funny or unfunny as that last image may be, it is a good reminder that in addition to the obvious business impact of outages, this is the level in the hierarchy that has the greatest possibility for causing collateral damage to the humans in the system by burning them out. All I need to say is the phrase *on call* and everyone has their own story to tell about incident response.[5] This is the level that most strongly correlates with the word *sustainable* in my initial definition of SRE.[6] I'll stop harping on this

---

5 Remind me to tell you about the Father's Day I spent in a data center instead of with my family. On the other hand, maybe don't.

6 Please see the polemic in Chapter 30 of *Seeking SRE* if you'd like a provocative response to *on call* as a concept.

topic now, but please don't stop asking questions about on call for incident response and its impact on the humans you work with.

Level 3: Postincident Review

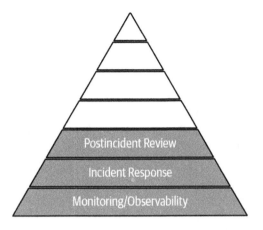

I have to admit, this is my favorite level of the whole pyramid. It has a transformative aspect I find magical. We are all aware that outages are a way for the business to lose money, time,[7] reputation, and employee health (see previous exhortation). This is the "counterspell."

Postincident reviews (or postmortems, postincident learning reviews, livesite reviews, retrospectives, or whatever you call them) are one potential way for us to actually get some value from an outage instead of it being just a cluster of losses. They provide a mechanism like no other for upleveling our operations practice. Here's where we get to learn from failure—but only if we put the effort into doing so. If you have the sense that the best/only thing that comes out of your postmortems is a TODO list or a set of backlog items, I would encourage you to reexamine your process and framing around them because they can and should be so much more. If you are reading this book out of order, Chapter 10 has oodles of my thoughts on the matter.

My biggest influences around this topic come from the academic field of resilience engineering. In relatively recent years, there has been some excellent research and work done to apply what people have learned from other low-probability, high-impact fields like aviation and medicine and apply those lessons to operations and software engineering.

---

7 Outages are unplanned work. I have never met someone who added "Deal with an unexpected disk full situation that caused 40% of our database caching layer to fail—Thursday, 10 a.m. to 4 p.m." to their calendar.

Level 3 is a very rich place with still so much for us to learn. I hope you will spend some real quality time and effort here.

Level 4: Testing/Release (Deployment)

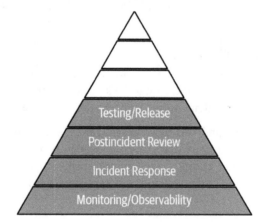

For level 2, I asserted (well, observed, really) that outages are inevitable. Note that I didn't say "all outages are inevitable." This is where level 4 comes in—it asks us to pay attention to deployment and release-engineering processes that have the potential (but are not guaranteed) to prevent outages. We can automate looking for software and configuration issues before they reach production. I use the word *potential* here because there is no software or CI/CD pipeline that you can feed straw into at one end that will yield production gold on the other. Ideally, a pipeline gets "smarter" over time. It is enhanced to catch and repel known issues, keeping them from getting to production in the first place. This only happens if there is a process for identifying and analyzing previous failures[8] and iterating on the development of the pipeline.

This may be a bit strange to hear in an SRE book, but the DevOps crowd has worked really hard on deployment (some, including me, would say it is a central focus). You should spend some time to see what they have to say on the subject. A good place to start is David Farley and Jez Humble's book *Continuous Delivery*.

Level 5: Provisioning/Capacity Planning

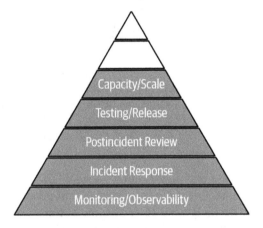

Here's another existential truth, though this one is a little more counterintuitive than the one from level 3: success can be just as much of a threat to your reliability as any bug you hope to catch through your work on level 4 (Testing/Release).

To say it bluntly, your customers can't tell the difference between your site being down because of a bug and your site being down because it wasn't provisioned with enough resources to handle the load when your products became popular.

---

8 Yup, see level 3 in the hierarchy: postincident reviews is one such process.

In my experience, there's considerably less guidance in the world on how to provision for increased load than for the other topics in Dickerson's Hierarchy, and that can make the task harder. Some of the best information on this topic can be found under the heading of "performance."[9]

Levels 6 and 7: Development Process and Product Design

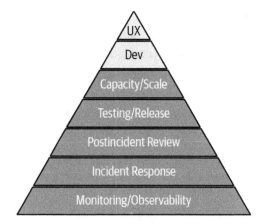

Though Dickerson included these two levels in his pyramid—essentially to focus on the development process itself and product design—I haven't found them as directly applicable to the topic of "getting started" as the other levels for folks just entering the SRE world, so this mention will be brief. There's much to be studied around software engineering, language design, and development processes to assist with reliability, but that's to be found in other books.

The highest level in the pyramid (Product Design [UX]) functions largely as a warning or cautionary tale. It is not uncommon to find people starting their process of building systems by deciding what color blue the buttons will be in the application instead of starting with the lowest level in the hierarchy and asking, "What do we need to instrument so we can get a good signal on its reliability?" Having this question come up in the early design meeting is one sign that having an SRE in the room early in the process is a splendid idea.

---

9 For example, if you haven't done so already, I highly recommend you pick up a copy of Brendan Gregg's book *Systems Performance* (Pearson, 2020).

The Dickerson Hierarchy of Reliability Is Not Enough

You are about to get to an entire section about wrong turns on the journey, but I wanted to get this particular issue in front of you as fast as possible.

The Dickerson Hierarchy of Reliability is great, fabulous, splendid, tremendous in so many ways. It is a lovely map for getting started with SRE—it wouldn't be in this book if it weren't. But it is not, I repeat, not, all there is to SRE, what SREs do, and what they focus on, nor is it the sum total of SREs' to-do/project list or value to the organization.

I say this so forcefully because I am as guilty as anyone else of presenting the pyramid and then moving right along to common SRE practices. But this leaves listeners with the impression that this pyramid is the alpha and omega of SRE. It's not; there are some serious gaps I will mention now, and you should mention them, too, if you are discussing SRE with others or even presenting on the topic.

The first big gap is that there is not an explicit mention of the architectural role SREs can take. Just like having a good security person in the room during an early design/architectural review meeting increases the chances that security will be part of the discussion, having a good SRE in the room does the same for reliability.[10] There are review points all throughout the software life cycle (for example, application and production readiness reviews) where SREs can clearly add value to the process.

Another item that appears to be absent from the pyramid is the role SREs can play in creating "reliability strata" for the organization. They can design and maintain the libraries or best practices that allow development groups to quickly and easily slot into an existing monitoring or remote procedure call (RPC) system. The work SREs do to make the "right way" to use the central monitoring system the "easy way" can have tremendous impact.

Similarly, there's no mention in the hierarchy of "toil" or how SRE efforts can reduce it.

A slightly different and perhaps less visible take on that idea stems from the often unique vantage point SREs have across all of the production environments in an organization. Much can be done from this vantage point, including helping an organization create or maintain consistency in those environments. Or if consistency isn't a high priority, they can, at the very least, help propagate good ideas found in one production environment to others.

I'm certain this is an incomplete list, and to a certain extent, that's the point. The Dickerson Hierarchy of Reliability is incomplete in its representation of SRE as well.

---

10 Though there are some clear similarities between security and reliability (the most salient one here is that you can't effectively bolt on either one of them later), there are also some differences. Chapter 1 of the book *Building Secure and Reliable Systems* by Heather Adkins et al. (O'Reilly, 2020) has an interesting discussion of this.

Wrong Turns

Up until this point in this chapter, I've tried to provide some good on-ramps for a person or a group to get started with SRE. I feel it is only fair for me to describe some of the wrong turns I've seen people take when getting started (or even later in their SRE experience) that have caused their efforts to get lost or even sputter and die. There's a lovely chapter on SRE antipatterns (Chapter 23) in *Seeking SRE* and more on the subject in Chapter 12 of this book. This section is meant to complement the useful advice you'll find in these places.

You Know You've Taken a Wrong Turn When…

…these things happen:

- The main or only benefit to the organization or partner team is that you are handling all of the on call for them. The derogatory term for this is that you have become *the pager monkey* for others. I have seen a number of cases where the SRE or SRE team's perceived value is strictly their on-call work. In many of these cases, this started out innocently enough. The SRE team thought the best way to be immediately helpful and to learn about the systems was to offer to do on call for them. But then the relationship never moved on from there, and that was not a good scene. Even worse was the time I was asked about what it would take to start an SRE practice, only to later learn that management had the notion that SRE would be a "cheaper way of handling on call so their engineers could work on more important things." The flag store ran out of red flags that day.

- All of your time has been spent working on postincident reviews (creating, facilitating, documenting, etc.). I realize calling this situation a wrong turn may come as a bit of a surprise, given how I pledged my undying love for them earlier in the chapter. If it is any comfort, of all the wrong turns, being overly indexed permanently on the postincident review process is the best of the worst. Unlike the previous wrong turn, where it means you have suddenly found yourself unintentionally in the waste management business acting as toil buckets, this is more an indication that SRE is not yet participating at all of the places in the software life cycle where it could offer value.

- There is only "smokejumping" (you get called in to deal with crises), which is not something you signed up for.[11] The reason why this is an issue is threefold:

  — As in the last item, it shows SRE is returning a very limited value.

  — It could be a sign that you are now "Level 3 support" instead of SRE.

---

11 This is precisely what Layer Aleph, the company Mikey Dickerson founded after his time in the United States Digital Service, does for a living.

— It could be a sign that your current job situation is a tire fire with constant crises, and perhaps it would be better for your mental and physical health if you found another workplace.

- All of the SREs are considered just "engineers" and therefore fungible or convertible to generic SWEs. This last item is super subtle, so much so that I almost hesitate to include it, because it could mean that things are going great or, more likely, going poorly (largely for political reasons). I'll try to explain.

On the one hand, as you'll see in Chapter 16, one perhaps desirable state is that we all become engineers who feel responsible for and work toward greater reliability. Google's official party line is that there is precious little difference between an SRE and an SWE in their hiring and career progression, with easy transmutation in both directions. This may be a bit more utopian than pragmatic for most people in most organizations, but the idea still stands as a possibility.

On the other hand, I have also seen cases where an engineering manager hoped to convert existing SRE headcount to just "engineer" headcount so they could gain more engineers for their team to do standard feature work. Google protects against this by maintaining a separate SRE org, so capturing headcount in this way is prevented. That may or may not be the case in your organization. Having SRE headcount be captured like this could be considered a bad thing, a wrong turn.

Positive Signs

Now, after all that doom and gloom, let's talk about some positive signs that SRE is going well for you as a way of concluding this chapter. You know better than I do what success feels like in your organization (beyond the obvious kinds of recognition), and there's an entire chapter on SRE evolution yet to come, but I wanted to share some of the positive indicators I've heard over the years. I feel compelled to mention that if you don't encounter any of these, it doesn't mean SRE is going poorly for you. It just means I haven't heard your story yet, and you should get in touch so I can add it to my list:

Pull versus push.
    It's very common in the beginning for SREs to have to work to be in the room or to be part of an engagement. At some point, you may find that this reverses and people start complaining when SRE is not there or ask, "Why didn't we get an SRE?"

Use of SRE data and phraseology.
    Without any prompt from you, you will hear people quoting statistics from the monitoring system you set up or very SRE-like terms (*common factors*, *what's the SLO for that service?*, and so on).

The number of commits/pull requests to a product repository from SRE becomes noticeable (and appreciated).

SREs are given write access to "the main repos,"[12] whatever that might be for a group, and the amount of contribution to those repos becomes obvious. This is an indicator of collaboration that engineers recognize easily.

"The dogs that didn't bark."

This is a little difficult to spot because we don't always pay attention to absence. But ideally, now there are outages that didn't happen, on-call shifts without escalations, and systems with less toil associated with them. Perhaps even just near misses that are observed by others. People don't always notice this sort of thing, but it is nice when they do.

I wish you all of these things and many other signs of success as you get started with SRE.

---

12 If you are just starting out, being given write access to a partner team's repos can, in and of itself, be a good sign and a positive indication of trust. Just as SREs are protective of production, so too are developers protective of their code base.

CHAPTER 15

Fitting SRE into Your Organization

In Chapter 11, we discussed some of the preparations for a successful SRE implementation in an organization. Let's assume you read that chapter and came to the conclusion, "Yeah, I think this could work." This chapter will address the question, "Once you know you want SREs in your organization, what contributes to organizational fit?" It will do this by covering some potential integration models, points of engagement, feedback loops, and signs of success.

Pre-role and Pre-team Practices

There will be lots and lots more to discuss in a later chapter about how one might scale up SRE teams from scratch, but I still want us to start thinking about this problem at "SRE 0" (i.e., when the org doesn't actually have an SRE). I am a very big fan of trying out SRE practices in an organization even before there is an SRE team hired or a single person holding that title. Unlike, say, civil engineering (where you really want a licensed and certified civil engineer engaged before anyone starts doing any civil engineering), there are no such requirements to begin exploring some of the standard SRE practices. All you need is a healthy dash of curiosity about a service or system and some quality time with a whiteboard to begin to define basic SLIs/SLOs for that service. From there, it is a short hop to keeping track of that SLO in your monitoring system and discussing the results in your regular staff meeting.

In my experience, even pilot or proof-of-concept SRE work[1] can be beneficial. In addition to the actual work, if you pay close attention to the larger picture while the work is proceeding, it will yield some very interesting signals for you about how SRE-flavored reliability work will be received in your workplace. If your colleagues are

---

1 Never denigrate your first steps; celebrate them.

excited, if the stakeholders of that service are engaged and intrigued, if it is easy to track SLOs in your existing monitoring system—those are all encouraging signs. If things don't go nearly as smoothly as this, you may have spotted the source of future challenges or even red flags indicating you should think twice about that SRE thing.

Another similar starting point could be around postincident reviews. If your SRE-less team works to level up their postoutage analysis and learning in an SRE-like way, this is also a significant step in the right direction guaranteed to offer some valuable contextual data around organizational fit.

A practice-first and mindset-first approach is my preferred process when given the option, but sometimes the world doesn't look like that. Sometimes circumstances or personnel will align in ways that will drop you into a situation where the hiring or team composition skips over the experimentation of the sort I suggested—for example, if a senior leader has had some prior experience with SRE and provides allocated SRE headcount you didn't expect, or maybe an SRE team or a set of individual contributor SREs[2] suddenly joins your organization after a merger. If this is the case, I still want to encourage you to frame the situation (internally and in your communications to others) in terms of experimentation. It is just a different set of experiments.

Integration Models

We've talked a little bit about the various models for how SRE is integrated into a larger organization, but it is clearly applicable in this context, so let's do a quick review. I have seen three different models in common use in the industry: centralized/partnered, distributed/embedded, and hybrid.

Centralized/Partnered Model

This is, for lack of a better term, what I consider to be the original model, because it is the one Google adopted when it first created and popularized this discipline. In this model, SRE is a separate organization with its own hiring process, headcount, and job ladder. The SREs work for this organization independent of where they engage in the organization. SREs work on teams. Most teams are partnered with a product (read: development) group and focus on their reliability needs. For example, you will hear about Google Maps SREs, Gmail SREs, Ads SREs, etc. There are also SRE teams that work on centralized tools and services (Borg SREs, BigTable SREs, etc.).

---

2 Here I am trying to be inclusive of both the situation where one inherits either an existing fully constituted team of people or just a number of individuals who do SRE work independent of each other. You will see how this difference meshes in just a moment as we discuss integration models.

The Scarcity Model

This isn't a requirement of a centralized model, but it is core enough to the Google organizational model that it deserves a sidebar. The Google SRE model treats SREs as a scarce resource that is allocated sparingly. New services at Google are developed and then operated at Google by the people who are building that service. A service must get to a certain level of maturity and be able to prove that it would benefit from SRE involvement before the SRE org will partner with it in an official capacity. This is congruent with the Google SRE philosophy of scaling SRE sublinearly.

From an organizational perspective, the centralized model has (at least theoretically; more on that in a moment) a number of pluses and minuses. A centralized org can establish and maintain a common set of practices, processes, tooling, values, etc., more easily than one that is heavily distributed. In theory, the SREs are more fungible and capable of moving around to different teams. Being separate can offer some amount of protection from "headcount conversion/reaping" (i.e., if an engineering leader decides to convert an existing engineer from SRE to SWE); this model makes headcount conversion harder because SREs are treated as a different kind of animal in this context.

In many ways, the flip sides of these strengths are the minuses: SREs are more disconnected from the rest of the org; there can be tooling mismatches between the central org and the local dev group's needs; hiring can be harder and personnel allocation more constrained. An organization may also be much more resistant toward the creation of yet another fiefdom at the top level of the org tree, so new adoption may be harder with this model.

Before I move on to the next model, I want to address the "theoretical" comments. If you talk to enough Google SREs, it becomes very clear that even within Google, the reality of the Google model is considerably more complicated than the pluses would imply. Leaving aside the usual challenges of trying to get everyone in a large enough organization to all march in the same direction (independent of where they are deployed), there are always circumstances and forces that challenge homogeneity that will be familiar to anyone who has worked in a larger setting. For example, when Google (or really any other company with their own established SRE culture) purchases another company, the "assimilation" process and its results can be messy for an extended period of time. I don't think there is any way around the mess—it always complicates the bright, shiny picture of centralized models that usually gets painted.

More information about this model (as implemented at Google) can be found in a number of chapters in the Google-authored SRE books.

Distributed/Embedded Model

The distributed/embedded model[3] is one where the primary modus operandi is the embedding of SREs (titled "production engineers" in the Facebook case) directly within development groups. As in the centralized model, there are also production engineering teams that handle (and create/maintain) central tools and infrastructure, but the key differentiator is the mechanism where SREs join development teams. There are a number of variables that can be tweaked in this model, including the duration of each embedding stint.

The pluses and minuses of this model really stem from the distinction between being a partner to the development team and being a direct part of it. On the one hand, there is a chance to work as closely together as possible; on the other, it means the SREs don't necessarily have the same opportunity to influence their own priorities and roadmap. Just to be clear, the differences I'm highlighting here are matters of degree—they are not binary. Embedding does not mean the SREs lose all identity or independent agency; it's just that the dynamics will be potentially different. Similarly, partner teams in a centralized model can be incredibly close as well.

More details about this model (as previously implemented at Facebook) can be found in Chapter 13 of *Seeking SRE*, authored by Pedro Canahuati.

---

3 Elsewhere in this book, I mention that this model will forever be labeled the "Facebook model" in my head because that was the context in which I was first introduced to it (pre-Meta days).

Hybrid Model

You probably saw this one coming. Some organizations like to implement a blend of the two previous models. They have SREs that work for a centralized organization and individual business units hiring their own SREs to run them independently. This situation can sometimes be the result of the acquisition/assimilation process we discussed earlier where the company acquires a whole SRE org as part of the company they purchase. There might be a decision to leave this org largely alone and independent from the parent SRE efforts. Another circumstance that leads to a hybrid model is the existence of a section of the business that is so very specialized or compartmentalized that it does not make sense to have those SREs be part of a larger organization. I think it is safe to say that the hybrid model is especially prevalent in larger (and maybe older) organizations where heterogeneity on a number of fronts is pretty common.

Leaving aside the idea that this model is sometimes in place due to the circumstances mentioned above (for example, for historical reasons), the plus of this model is that, theoretically, it offers the most flexibility. The minus is that cohesion, consistency, and maintaining a uniform sense of identity can be a real struggle.

How to Choose Between These Models

Can you choose? Not to be glib, but I want to point out that often you don't get a choice. For example, in the context of a larger, established enterprise, starting a new SRE effort might require you to slot your plans into existing hiring or engagement frameworks. If so, the choice might be made for you (at least temporarily), so you can skip to the next section.

Finding the Right Model May Take More Than One Attempt

I know this seems like a big decision (because it is), but I wanted to offer a tiny sidebar of comfort. You might have to get this wrong before you get it right for your organization. I have seen SRE efforts have to iterate a few times (read: fail and retry) before they found a model that worked for them. This is not only OK, but it might also be necessary in some cases, including yours. SRE is all about iteration until things improve, and finding the right model is no different.

If your world is a little more "greenfield" in this regard, then a decision process is in order. My first two questions around this decision are, "Tell me about your organization's existing structure—org tree, etc.?" and "Is there any precedent for spinning up a specialization (for example, a security org)?"[4]

The first question is designed to help you understand placement, both in the appropriate place on the map of the organization and where in the management chain this effort might sit. It can help establish whether the "juice" for the effort will come from the top down in the organization or from the bottom up while this effort is being established. While not uniformly true, I associate the centralized model with representation higher in the org tree.[5] An initial embedded model has the ability to "fly under the radar" a little easier than a centralized model might. Organizational power and influence are required for all of these models, but their source and nature may vary.

The second question here is predictably SRE. If there's data that might be the least bit helpful in predicting success or failure, I want it to be part of the decision process. I don't have any real data to back this up, but my suspicion is that the situation where SRE would be the first real introduction of specialization into an org is somewhere between "never" and "extremely rare." I encourage you to dig deep to find an earlier historical precedent, even if it occurred outside your engineering bubble.

One last comment about model choice before we move along. Not to bury the lede, but if the question of whether to spin up a completely separate thing or create a role that primarily lives within existing structures sounds familiar, that's because it is. Businesses make "Do we spin up a new team for this? Where do we put it/them?" decisions a kerjillion times a day. Making this decision vis-à-vis SRE is not substantially different and is subject to all of the same processes and factors.

Creating and Nurturing the Right Feedback Loops

A key part of what SRE does in an organization is create and nurture feedback loops that are designed (or at least intended) to improve the reliability of the systems, services, and products of the organization.[6] Before I give my abstract thoughts on this, perhaps take a minute or two to contemplate where in your organization SRE can or does have an opportunity to introduce feedback loops into the org in general.

---

4 Implicit in this question, or perhaps the immediate follow-up, is, "So, how'd it go? What did you learn from that experience?"

5 My association here stems from a number of factors. Supporting and defending a separate centralized organization often requires considerable organizational capital and influence. People like that are found nearer to the top of the org tree in most cases.

6 Oh, and probably the org itself, but shhh, don't tell anyone. This is often best left as a hidden agenda.

Feedback Loops and Data

When I think about feedback loops in an organizational context, the first question I like to contemplate is where the data is going to come from. Data is the fuel that is going to keep loops like this spinning. When discussing reliability in this book, there are some obvious sources we discuss time and time again, including incident/outages (captured as postincident analysis) and monitoring data.[7] There are some less obvious sources, including customer support tickets/cases,[8] CI/CD data (test creation/failure trends, deployment results), application/production readiness review results, backlog stats, on-call survey data, and employee exit interviews, to name a few.[9]

It would be possible to stop here in our planning, focus on the areas mentioned, and make tremendous progress toward organizational fit. Let me give what might sound like the tiniest of examples, which, like a lever, could lift huge boulders. How accessible is the monitoring data collected in your organization to everyone in that organization? By accessible, I mean both physically (can other people "log in" and see the data?) and cognitively (once people do get access, is it documented and comprehensible without a ton of specialized knowledge or institutional lore?). One way to sum up that line of inquiry in a single question would be, "If I had a question related to the reliability of X in your org, how hard would it be for me to get the answer?" Data is a huge component of and touch point for the sort of crossroads we hope to create.

Feedback Loops and Iteration

Moving past the data question, the next question to ask when thinking about feedback loops in an organization is either, "How fast can the wheel spin?" or "What slows down the wheel?" depending on whether you are a half-full or half-empty kind of person. A feedback loop that doesn't actually move or a system that doesn't iterate is fabulous for prediction and reporting (you know just how bad things will continue to be) but terrible in all other respects. Not to belabor the point, but entropy will actually start to spin your feedback loops in the opposite direction if you let it.

With this in mind, it is useful to search for all the places SRE can and cannot engage to help iterate (faster, or even at all). Release engineering–related work (including CI/CD and deployment work) is key to software iteration; that's pretty clear. Toil elimination has a similar impact. I would argue that efficient incident handling and

---

7 The cynical pessimists among you might consider monitoring data to be "pre-outage" data. I would be hard pressed to argue.

8 Kurt Andersen, a tech reviewer for this book, points out that a disconnect between customer support and engineering is painfully common and highly regrettable, and I agree completely with him.

9 I'd encourage you to look at the reports from the DevOps Research and Assessment (DORA) research program (*https://dora.dev*), which is always searching for good data/metrics around operations work.

analysis procedures let you experience and then process the learning from outages faster, thus speeding up iteration. A more esoteric area for study and improvement in this category that doesn't get the attention it deserves but still has a strong impact on iteration is service deprecation/sunsetting and retirement.[10]

Antipatterns Are Antifeedback Loops

In Chapter 12 especially, I talk about antipatterns to SRE adoption. Though I didn't mention it at the time, a key way you can identify antipatterns is by studying those practices that impede either the data access/flow or the iteration predicates of feedback loops we've discussed here.

For example, ticket- and tier-based SRE, where SRE is "the new level 3 of support," houses SRE in a tiny ivory tower where cross-org data accessibility and service iteration are highly constrained (at best). Both can miss the point of SRE and have ramifications related to our discussion because they are highly frictional.

Feedback Loops and Planning for Iteration

With one tiny twist, we now take the previous idea of friction on iteration in a very different direction. In the previous section, we discussed a number of sociotechnical factors that slow crucial iterative processes necessary for feedback loops. But here's the killer observation: another way to stop the wheel from turning is to never spin it in the first place.

I have no doubt that there is some sort of planning process for the services, systems, and products in your organization. There is most likely some sort of roadmap for these plans with a comprehensive and detailed description of the new features planned for them. If the reliability work we've been discussing throughout this book is not on that roadmap and there is no easily identifiable process for that to change,[11] you will have a real problem on your hands.

Organizational fit for SRE is going to be dependent on having an open and healthy channel to the people who do control the roadmap. This is crucial to allowing reliability work to have a place there. Any other situation will at best offer a narrow range of benefits from SRE. For example, operations people laboring entirely

---

10 Why do I say this? In my experience, virtually all orgs have some sort of guidelines and processes for spinning up new services. Relatively few have a similar set of processes for making their services shuffle off this mortal coil. This ad hoc approach leads to all sorts of suboptimal behavior that diverts energy and attention away from feedback loops that could use it.

11 "Yeah, there's no way we are going to get on the product roadmap…That's a whole different process we don't have any input into…" or some variation of that sentiment is tremendously common.

---

independently of the main engineering work or trying to fit their efforts into the crevices of that work (both of which are extremely common) can only yield limited results. As much as I want to belabor this point for a few more pages because it is so important, let's move on.

How and Where to Insert These Feedback Loops into the Organization

A key premise of this chapter has been that there are feedback loops that SRE will need to establish and nurture to be effective. The capability for this to take place in an organization is highly predictive of an organizational fit in that organization. So far, we've explored those loops mostly in isolation, as if they'd sprung from the head of Zeus fully formed, without talking about the mechanisms to introduce them into the org. As a way of closing out this section, I'd like to mention one opportunity I have observed for inserting feedback loops that sometimes doesn't get considered until relatively late in an SRE adoption.[12]

SREs have a tremendous ability to influence the reliability of an organization at the point of creation. When they can be in the room for the initial architecture discussions, when they can offer the best practices for resource provisioning (what to provision, how to do it), and when they can provide scaffolding for documentation, propagate reliability-affirming methods, and so on in a *helpful*[13] manner, the organization will be grateful for their presence. Spotify and other organizations use the term[14] *golden path* to describe "the 'opinionated and supported' path to 'build something' in their organization," and I think that's a lovely way to illustrate this touch point. Here we have the chance to set up conditions from the get-go that make positive feedback loops easier.

Signs of Success

As a way of concluding this chapter, I thought it might be useful to consider the question, "How do you know if it is working?" That is, are you achieving the organizational fit you desire? Before I get to my list, it may be the case that you are craving case studies from other organizations to compare your efforts to. My best source for these is the relatively long list of talks given by people in different industries and different organizational configurations at SREcon over the years.

---

12 I have a few nascent theories on why this is the case. The first is "there's lots to do" with activities like incident handling and analysis feeling more urgent. I also wonder if the common perception that operations is a "day 2" activity plays strongly into this.

13 I emphasize this word because the point of creation is fraught with peril if not handled properly. This is also the perfect place for SRE to fall into becoming gatekeepers if not careful. There are a number of places in this book, say, Chapter 16, where we talk about why gatekeeping is an express ticket to terrible organizational fit.

14 See Spotify's discussion of golden paths (*https://oreil.ly/tKvLl*).

There's hours of real-life examples there that may help you see other people's experiences with organizational fit.[15]

If case studies aren't your jam, and you want something smaller to chew on, I'd like to offer a number of highly simplistic questions you might consider asking:

- Are people happy to see you (collectively)?
- Have you moved past or successfully avoided altogether the gatekeeper role?
- Has the relationship changed from *push* (inserting yourself into situations) to *pull* (people asking you to be there)?
- Does the SRE team/org participate in roadmap planning as a matter of course?
- Has the reactive versus project work ratio trended in the right direction?[16]
- Are you seen as removing more toil than adding it?

An SRE reading this list might (correctly) note that this is more of a "vibes check" than a measurable set of objectives. I'm not a big fan of "exercise left to the reader," but in this case I believe that there could be tremendous value in you or your team translating those questions into SLI/SLO-esque indicators and objectives specific to your organization. Like many SLI/SLO exercises, I have confidence this will shine some light into the corners of organizational fit and SRE adoption for you.

---

15 There's also a lovely *Building Effective Site Reliability Engineering (SRE) Practices: A Personal Journey* Google doc (*https://oreil.ly/aBs4s*) (referenced with permission) that contains Caleb Hurd's maturity model. I recommend checking it out for another perspective.

16 Note that I didn't give any specific percentages or time frames. One nuance that is often lost with the 50% figure is that the ratio often fluctuates over time based on external conditions, including service maturity.

CHAPTER 16

SRE Organizational Evolutionary Stages

Talking with managers of a new SRE team, I find that they are quite curious about how their team or organization can be expected to change over time. They have a very clear understanding of what their team is doing now and how it relates to the rest of the organization, but the future is not nearly as clear.

The best conceptual framework I've seen for SRE team evolution comes from a talk given by Benjamin Purgason, formerly of LinkedIn, at SREcon Asia 2018 called "The Evolution of Site Reliability Engineering" (*https://oreil.ly/PUVg7*). In this talk, Ben drew upon this experience leading numerous teams through a set of stages, really nailing five possible stages SRE teams can go through over time (though not in a specific linear order). This chapter draws (with permission) heavily from that talk with my added commentary. It is also worthwhile watching the original talk as well for the extended examples taken from Ben's experience at LinkedIn.

Stage 1: The Firefighter

As you know by now, people often come to SRE after having some bad or worrisome experiences with reliability. Maybe they have a bunch of outages, or perhaps another company in the same field makes it into the press because of some significant spate of downtimes. A slightly cheerier scenario is that engineering management comes to the stark realization that there is no way they are going to be able accelerate their development velocity without things breaking more often. Neither going slower nor experiencing less reliability is a tenable option for the business, so here comes management, hoping SRE can save them. And that's how we get our first SRE role, the firefighter.

This is where almost everybody starts. There are reliability-related problems, and SRE works to fix those problems (ideally in a way such that their contributing factors are addressed so they don't repeat nearly as often). Then there are new problems, and SRE goes to work on those problems next. Rinse and repeat until the size and impact of the fires are no longer existential threats and there is time to work on other things.

The most common question I hear about this stage is, "When is it going to stop?" I'm sorry to say that there is no set timeline for leaving this stage. As Tolstoy wrote, "Happy families are all alike; every unhappy family is unhappy in its own way." I don't know if this is comforting in the slightest, but almost without exception I hear people talk about this stage in terms of years (at best, large fractions of a year; at worst, a number of years). I feel pretty safe saying that the amount of time needed to exit this stage will not be described in terms of weeks.[1]

A more encouraging thought to leave you with for this stage is Ben's suggestion that what you do in between fires can be crucial. I like his idea that in addition to the items on the first two levels of the Dickerson hierarchy (monitoring/observability and incident response, respectively), this is a good time for the team to be:

- Learning more about all the moving parts in the complex system you are caring for (the strengths and flaws, behavior under load, and dependencies—the kinesthesiology, if you will).

- Building what he calls "automatic fire suppression." Besides the poetry of the term in this context, I really like the idea that there is a focus on building the necessary mechanisms to allow the system to respond and mitigate its own issues. Perhaps you introduce autoscaling, load shedding, better load balancing/traffic management, or any number of the tools we have for reacting to and automitigating problems in production. This is another aspect of removing toil as SREs are wont to do.

Stage 2: The Gatekeeper

In his talk, Ben suggests that it is possible (and even desirable) to skip over this stage. My experience talking to many people leads me to a marginally different conclusion. In my experience, even if people have been able to hop over this stage, they have at least thought hard about gatekeeping and how they might implement it.

---

1 Though sometimes people *will* talk about taking a few weeks to stabilize the patient—but that is different from the months it will take to leave the care of emergency medicine entirely.

Here's a human story behind that assertion. See if you recognize even a little bit of yourself in it:

> Our team was brought in to help deal with a ton of reliability problems. We have just spent a year putting out fires and dealing with reliability issues in production. We are finally at the point where things aren't so bad. What do we have to do to keep things this way?

The very natural answer is, "Keep the Visigoths at bay," meaning keep the forces of disruption away from production. Keep not just the forces away but also the people who might be the source or the transport for those disruptive changes away. Control the border.

This answer makes sense from the perspective of the SRE who is tasked with protecting the reliability of the systems after having just righted the ship. However, from the organizational perspective, the whole sociotechnical systems perspective, there's a big problem here: SREs who start acting like gatekeepers tend to make everyone else's life more unpleasant. It is not a great way to make friends or contribute to a pleasant and productive workplace environment. The image I get in my head of this kind of gatekeeper is that of a customs officer at an airport. In my experience, I am rarely excited to see one on my way out of the airport, and they don't look so thrilled to see me either.

If the image of you as a protective customs officer doesn't sound like the best look, you've spotted the problem. When an SRE group becomes the arbiter or enforcer of change control, there's a dynamic at play that will not serve you or the organization well in the long run. It can breed intra-team resentment, impede collaboration, and disrupt productivity.

Gatekeeping (in a long-term, manual, and/or frictional way) is a great way to have SRE sputter and die in an organization. Not only that, but it also doesn't work, and it doesn't scale. People will route around damage, even if that damage is a well-meaning SRE team just trying to keep production from becoming a tire fire again.[2] And when everyone has to go through the SRE team to get anything done, you probably can't hire enough people to mind the gate.

---

2 I've seen this play out countless times with sysadmins or IT people in the starring tragic role.

Not All Gatekeeping Is Poisonous (Yet)

I want to make sure I'm not giving the impression that all gatekeeping (including short-term gatekeeping) is immediately poisonous. Sometimes it is the right thing—given resource constraints or contractual/regulatory compliance—to do. The crucial thing, as book reviewer Patrick Cable points out, is being willing to periodically reevaluate the situation to determine whether you can make it better or at least less onerous.

However, if gatekeeping is all your SRE people are and have been doing, that's also a May Day parade's worth of red flags. More on what to do about that next, back in the main text.

Now what if this book is coming to you too late, and you are already deeply enmeshed in the gatekeeper stage? Having trashed this stage repeatedly, it would not be fair for me to abandon you in this dark place. The best advice I have heard for finding an exit comes from Ben again. He suggests trying to attack the problem, not the people.

If you can work with the others in your organization to identify the problems that led to the walls around production, and if you can then devise clear and objective ways to detect those problems, you can write code to get yourself out of the business of minding that gate. For example, if memory leaks were the source of your last three outages, and if everyone agrees that all binaries that are going to run in production must be checked for memory leaks—have a computer check them before deployment is completed. If someone shows up with a leaky, untested binary and asks to run it in production, code could gently tell that person just what they need to do before deployment is allowed. Everyone agrees on the rules/guidelines/policy,[3] the computer (via code that perhaps an SRE wrote) enforces the rules in a consistent manner, and SRE is free to do other things. Another way to frame this might be, "Here's a thing that will make it easy for you to do what you need if X is satisfied," where X is some condition or standard that is important to the organization.

What other things are SRE freed up to do? Let's get to the next stage and see.

---

3 Book reviewer Kurt Andersen smartly points out that jointly agreed upon SLI/SLOs directly tie into, and could even drive, this idea/process as well (for example, an SLI of "memory leak per unit of time").

Stage 3: The Advocate

As you know, SRE is, by nature, relentlessly collaborative.[4] This is the first stage where we might begin to initiate collaboration intentionally and not just as a side effect. In the firefighter stage, you collaborate by necessity, consulting with expert colleagues while doing the firefighting. If you passed through a gatekeeper stage, your relationship with your colleagues may have been more combative than collaborative. If that indeed was your story, you will need to make time and effort to fix your relationships and the perception of SRE.

In order to move toward a more collaborative place, the next stage involves taking on an advocacy role—advocating for reliability in your organization. You and your team will begin to clearly articulate for, embody the practices of, and build systems to support reliability. (This is in addition to the standard responsibilities I've already discussed, like monitoring.)

So what does advocacy mean in practice? At this point, SRE is starting to engage with reliability at all stages in the software life cycle, not just holding the hose on existing systems that are on fire. They are ideally in the room for design and architecture discussions, just as you might hope security is in the room early in the process. Perhaps they are helping lead application or production readiness reviews,[5] before systems are deployed. They are paying close attention to the activities of their developer colleagues so they can plan to appropriately support new features, releases, etc., before deployment (versus learning about those changes or events for the first time during an outage).

It's in this stage that SREs are also building systems/tools/processes that let others in the organization have greater self-service capabilities to help them develop, deploy and run their services. (Ben talks about "developing systems that empower ownership.") Recall that the bridge out of the gatekeeper stage was the creation of systems that allowed for more collaborative and automated gatekeeping/policy enforcement. This is the other side of that bridge and where it leads to. Ideally, at this stage the policies in place for protecting production are co-created by SRE and developers because everyone is working together to create the production environment desired.

Does that sound like a step toward a richer partnership? I hope so because here's the next stage.

---

4 A comment from Ben Purgason himself on this text: "I think this notion frequently gets lost in early-stage teams and is merely an unspoken assumption once it becomes normal in later-stage teams."

5 Patrick Cable wryly and correctly points out that these reviews can be kind of a gate, too, depending on the organization and its policies/processes.

Stage 4: The Partner

Hopefully, by this point in the discussion, the direction we've been heading in is becoming clear. This is the next step in that direction.

In the previous stage, we had the SREs paying close attention to the activities of their developer colleagues so they could react appropriately. The upgrade to this is the two groups doing their planning/roadmapping together as partners.

In this stage, SRE continues to build systems/tools/processes, but perhaps they become part of the building blocks everyone uses. Examples could include SRE owning and developing the monitoring libraries embedding in all projects or the standard RPC mechanism adopted by the organization. For this sort of foundational role, I like to think of it as SRE becoming responsible for creating and nurturing a common "set of reliability strata" or "reliability platform."

One of my favorite terms in Ben's talk comes when he suggests that SRE could also be building tools that "empower intelligent risk" at this phase. If you like this idea, you may wish to see Chapter 1 in *Seeking SRE* on context versus control, where the idea is to provide enough context (dashboards, scorecards, etc.) such that all employees can make intelligent decisions versus spending time on control mechanisms.

And finally, it is during the partner stage when the idea that SRE and developers share on-call responsibilities really comes into its own. In the partner stage, this practice is something both parts of the organization welcome versus it being a kind of payback that SREs dream of. (No more need to think, "The first time a developer gets paged at 3 a.m. is the last time that bug shows up in production.")

Stage 5: The Engineer

In this final phase, the distinction between the reliability-based priorities of the SREs in the organization and the rest of the engineering staff has blurred significantly. Everyone is participating in the activities necessary to promote reliability at all stages of a system's life cycle, including architecture, various preproduction reviews, on call, postincident reviews, roadmaps, tool building, and so on.[6]

Given prior warnings in this book about the perils of "headcount conversion," where SREs get converted to feature engineers, I have to make an important point here: it's not that SREs become indistinguishable from any other engineers in their day-to-day activities and suddenly all engineers are fungible. SREs continue to work on and hold primary responsibility for separate things than the part of the organization that builds

---

6 Kurt Andersen's summary of Björn Rabenstein's talk "SRE in the Third Age" (*https://oreil.ly/PQbN2*) mentions the term *democratization of reliability ownership*, which I like very much.

features. They continue to hold a perspective with a laser focus on reliability in ways other personnel do not. But what is going on here is a high level of cohesion and collaboration not seen before.

An important question you might be asking yourself at this point is, "Is this stage just a pipe dream—does it ever really happen in the real world?" In my experience, it can and does happen in the real world (rarely), but it isn't stable. This stage is predicated on an alignment of incentives and a specific organizational structure, both of which are easily disturbed by changes as common as reorgs and budget reallocations.

Much has been written in the DevOps community about how feature and operational work are often prioritized differently due to oppositional incentives. Similarly, the longer it takes an org chart to converge before you get to a single person responsible for making decisions, both about reliability engineering (SRE) and the nonreliability engineering (feature dev), the less likely you will see the required alignment in the organization. Both incentives and structure may change for completely unrelated reasons, with an adverse impact on the cohesion and collaboration that are required for this stage.

I say all of this not to discourage you from aiming toward the ideas in this stage but just to offer a bit of pragmatism and empathy should this stage come into and out of reach for you.

Caveat Implementer

Like a number of the other chapters you've seen already, this one, too, will end with a few caveats:

First off, it's important to not think of these stages as a set of uniform states that you or your entire team/organization go through like some sort of DEFCON level. It is entirely possible that some SRE teams in a larger organization are firefighters while others are advocates.

In fact, it is not clear to me that uniformity should even be a real goal. Just like we have an "appropriate level" rubric for reliability, so, too, we may need an "appropriate stage" rubric for SRE team evolution that depends on their unique situation in their organization. In other words, "Stage 5: The Engineer" may not be an appropriate end goal for every SRE team.

Secondly, I am reminded of a story I heard about Elisabeth Kübler-Ross. In her most famous book, *On Death & Dying*, she introduced the "five stages of grief" model that became tremendously popular. One of the misconceptions about this model was the notion that everyone passes through all of the stages in a very specific linear order. Apparently she spent considerable time and effort in her later days trying to combat this idea. She was very clear that this was never her original intention when publishing the model.

It is a little presumptuous to compare the SRE evolution observations in this chapter to the Kübler-Ross model, but the one thing they do share is that lack of linearity. While it could be the case that you or your team will experience the stages in the order found in this chapter, it may not go that way for you. This is why I have shied away from calling this an "SRE maturity model," because people tend to treat that as a state machine where the goal is to make it to the end state. It is entirely possible that your team will be deep in their partner stage and you will still wake up in a cold sweat when you realize that part of what the team is doing is straight-up gatekeeping. Or you may move in and out of stages as partnerships change. And though I hate to say it, there are always fires lurking around the corner that are going to need firefighters...[7]

If you can take the idea that there are different stages that you may or may not pass through, that will serve you well.

---

[7] If you haven't yet read Dr. Richard Cook's short paper on "How Complex Systems Fail" (*https://oreil.ly/l4_Vy*), you should really put this book down now and go do that first.

CHAPTER 17

Growing SRE in Your Org

In this chapter, we are going to talk about scaling. Not the usual scaling of infrastructure or services we usually discuss in SRE, but the scaling of people. We are going to talk about how SRE might go from zero (or part of a single person's time) to a much larger presence in your organization.

I say *might* in the previous sentence because I think of SRE (and operations in general) as highly situational. I believe that the same seed can grow very differently in different soil. As a result, this chapter will be less about prescriptive advice and more about describing some of the more common patterns I have seen work for different organizations. The hope here is that you will be able to choose options from this menu that feel congruent with your existing organization.

How Do You Know When to Scale?

Before we get into actual numbers that are going to increase as the chapter goes on, I want to call out and question the implicit assumption that "scaling bigger is better." It is very easy to read into (and quite frankly, write) this chapter as if the ultimate goal is to grow an SRE org to the maximum size the budget will allow. Just like we discuss "appropriate levels of reliability" throughout this book, there are also appropriate levels of scaling SRE.

For example, it may be tempting to grow or split a team based primarily on the load on that team demonstrated by a rise in the number of tickets or pages that team is expected to handle, but that may not be the best decision. It might be far better to use "scope change" as a leading indicator. This point and other excellent pieces of advice can be found in Gustavo Franco's SREcon talk "Scaling SRE Organizations: The Journey from 1 to Many Teams" (*https://oreil.ly/RcuZU*), which I highly recommend you watch. I'd also refer you back to the discussion on team size in Chapter 13.

With that caveat in play, let's get started.

Scaling 0 to 1

Everybody has to start someplace, so let's begin with the significant jump from 0 SREs to 1 SRE in your organization. The first thing to note is that this isn't as binary a leap as the integers might suggest. It is entirely likely that the hiring of a dedicated SRE is preceded by other individuals within the organization adopting a bit of an SRE mindset (and perhaps some of the practices) well before that dedicated SRE person is hired. Perhaps that is a single individual doing this work[1] part-time, which gets you some fractional number (0.5, 0.25, 0.40?) of an SRE.

But let's assume we want to go for the big "number 1." Like any other specialized position, either this is a new hire or a specialization/transformation of a role. Much has been said throughout this book about how dicey transformations can be (title flips, etc.) and the importance of doing them right, so I won't do more than note that here.

So what is this person going to do for a living? The answer is highly situational, but I can give a few hints. I talk lots about what getting started in reliability work looks like throughout this book (e.g., see Chapter 14 on the Dickerson Hierarchy of Reliability) but very quick and reasonable answers would be something like "work on monitoring/observability" and "engage in the postincident review process." I encourage you to take a quick look back at Chapter 3 for some thoughts on culture so you are fresh on a key factor for supporting your nascent efforts.[2]

Premature SRE

You might think, given how gung ho I am about SRE in this book, that I might suggest everyone should run out and get an SRE if they don't already have one. The first time I was talking with a new startup and I heard the words, "No, don't hire an SRE; not yet" come out of my mouth, I was surprised too. I've now said that a number of times over the years.

The reality is that very early startups and even new groups in a larger organization may not benefit from this premature specialization. Often the priority has to be "just get things bootstrapped." Now, ideally, this work gets done with an eye toward

---

1 Or perhaps it is one of those situations where Clark Kent just has to take off his glasses to be recognized as Superman. It is not unusual to have SRE-leaning or SRE-curious staff who start to look awfully like SREs if you squint at them and the job they are already doing.

2 Hopefully, this person is allowed to amass a bookshelf full of SRE-relevant books (or ebooks) to help support them and their training. One such book that may seem a bit aspirational but could help set this person up for success as things progress is Tanya Reilly's *The Staff Engineer's Path* (O'Reilly, 2022).

reliability (via instrumentation, automation, etc.), but if you spend all your time designing the perfect SLO and never provisioning a working development environment, that's going to be one very theoretical piece of software or service that hasn't yet been written you've got yourself there.

Scaling 1 to 6

Why 6, you might ask? The number 6 happens to be the right number for constructing a humane, on-call rotation (within a single geographic area). I say this with some trepidation (see the section "Contributing Factor 3: On Call and That's All" on page 139 in Chapter 12), but 6 is a natural scaling unit. I'll use that instead of units of 10, but if that drives you nuts, feel free to round up or down to the nearest 5 or 10.

Are Managers SRE? How About Project Managers? Business Admins?

At this scaling level (5+) we are already at the point where we are going to determine team composition. It is very easy when we talk about scaling SRE teams to have this picture in your head that an SRE team of 100 is 100 identical engineers all doing the same thing versus real SRE teams that have some blend of roles, including PMs, managers, business administrators, etc. From this point on, you can assume I am talking about teams as they are constituted in the real world.

Just like SREs have the ability to make other teams more effective, there are definitely important roles that support SRE teams, which are themselves not primarily direct engineering roles. For example, you might have an engagement team of seven people, five SREs, one PM/TPM,[3] and one manager or tech lead.

At this scaling level, the SRE presence in your org is likely taking on small, discrete pieces of work,[4] separately consulting with other teams as requested. For example, individuals or pairs/triads might be improving the monitoring or piloting SLIs/SLOs for a specific service. They might be part of remediation efforts for outages and the subsequent postincident reviews. Depending on the state and maturity of the services in the wider organization, their early days might be a bit more reactive than people in the team would prefer.

---

3 PM is either *project manager* or *product manager*, depending both on what is needed (they are different roles) and how your organization likes to expand that acronym. TPM is *technical PM*.

4 Note: this is only one plausible scenario. In cases where an SRE team was constituted originally to address "the biggest reliability issue we have," chances are the entire team will be heads down working on slaying that dragon first, whatever it is. In this chapter, I am largely assuming that SRE is currently fulfilling a noncrisis driven, nontargeted role. Your mileage may vary.

While doing all of this, they spend considerable time helping other parts of the org understand what SRE is and how it can help. All in all, they are seeking localized wins and building their reputation for success and collaboration.

How Should We Count?

One surprising reminder I received when putting this chapter together was just how many ways it is possible to structure the same organizational-scaling discussion. In this chapter, I chose to striate by absolute numbers, but thinking about bands of (as suggested by reviewer Patrick Cable) "0, 1, 1-a single team, multiple teams" also yields a good discussion.

Or…it can be interesting (as suggested by reviewer Jess Males) to consider ratios, as in ratio of SRE to non-SRE engineers, and how things should go as that ratio increases.

A further nuance, he suggests, comes from the cohesiveness of the organization. Scaling in a balkanized situation where separate groups have very different technical and tool constellations is different from scaling in an environment where it is easy to move from place to place and quickly begin having an impact without prolonged onboarding. This can have a considerable impact on team sizing.

Scaling 6 to 18

There's that weird multiple of six again. This time, we've potentially hit another inflection point, depending on your global plans and hiring practices. At 18, it becomes possible to consider a "follow the sun" on-call rotation that will be less painful.[5] "Follow the sun" is a configuration where 24-7 coverage is achieved by scheduling a team who is in a time zone that is in daylight (i.e., roughly standard business hours for them) to handle the on-call responsibilities for that time period. As the sun moves and their business day comes to an end, a handoff is made to the next team in business hours. This is much more pleasant and humane than having someone be on call to handle incidents impacting or generated by time zones during their deep-sleep hours.

Outside of on-call numbers, we find ourselves potentially passing the magic number of 10 and perhaps even being very close to 20, both of which give us that feeling of "OK, this is a substantial team." In practice, this can mean multiple engagements at once or a larger footprint if you are using the "embedded team member" model I mentioned above. There are, especially in the larger numbers, more opportunities for SREs to begin to specialize at the task level. Perhaps one of the team members is the

---

5 Kurt Andersen points out the implicit requirement here is that the company itself has hired people in multiple geographical locations since having 18 people in the same geo (unless they agree to wacky sleep schedules—bad idea) is not going to help with "follow the sun."

go-to person for a particular set of monitoring expertise. Maybe a pair of people handle most of the (nascent) production readiness reviews, and so on.

Scaling Sublinearly

I would probably have my SRE membership card revoked if I didn't point out that from the start, SRE has always had a goal of scaling "sublinearly." By this we usually mean something like "We don't hire a new person for every new service we take on" or "Increased load on the service does not necessitate hiring more people," to put it crudely. This is one of those easy goals to state but quite challenging and nuanced in real life.

The pseudo dialog can go something like this:

> How many people do I need to move a big rock?
>
> *Well, how much can each person lift?*
>
> But wait, I have a lever! (automation)
>
> *OK, so now we can lift more with fewer people!*
>
> But wait, I have a better lever or more levers!
>
> *Great, more lifting power with fewer people.*
>
> But wait, I found a special rock-lifting lever!
>
> *Great, more lifting power with fewer people.*
>
> But wait, we've discovered steam power; now we lift rocks with steam engines!
>
> *Great, more lifting power with fewer people; now we will train people to use steam engines.*
>
> But wait, we've created a special rock-lifting steam engine!
>
> *OK, we'll teach people how to use this special engine.*
>
> But wait, now we have to lift other heavy objects besides rocks, like trees!
>
> *Hmm, those steam rock-lifting machine operators will have to learn how to lift trees; that will take a little time. We have time, right?*

This obviously gets progressively sillier, but to save you some time, I will point out that factors like automation (and what kind of automation), commonality of tooling/practices, number of different technologies involved, and other contributions to cognitive load all make "sublinear" hard to calculate and plan for. Maximizing an individual SRE's lifting power is still a good goal, but it is not a trivial one.

Not to be too cynical, but I feel compelled to note that when people discuss this goal, they can have multiple rationales. We'd like to think that the rationale is to free up SREs to do more interesting and impactful work over a larger surface area. But that is sometimes replaced with a goal of hiring fewer SREs simply to save money. To the best of my knowledge, the progenitors of SRE had primarily the former in mind, not the latter when they stated this goal.

Scaling 18 to 48

I'm sticking with multiples of 6 because I know if I don't, it will make some readers mad, but we're now past the point where that has any significance. In this scaling band, we begin to talk about the SRE organization composed of several SRE teams versus "the SRE team." How you choose to subdivide into teams is highly situational. I have seen a wide variety of models, including:

- Standard engagement teams with the creation of an additional SRE infrastructure team that focuses on common infrastructure
- Teams created to explicitly partner with larger product groups (the "Google Maps SRE team")
- Teams broken up by their central location (the "Dublin SRE team" or the "Europe SRE team")
- "Fungible" engagement teams composed of N people (Team 1, Team 2, Team 3, etc., even though no one calls them that)

How you choose to segment depends on a whole host of organizational, contextual, and strategic factors. The least subtle and perhaps most obvious of these factors is, "What do you want to achieve via SRE?" This is also highly influenced by the centralized versus embedded frames we discussed earlier in this book. If it makes you feel any better, it is common for an organization to try out different configurations (often sequentially, though sometimes simultaneously) before they find the one(s) that work better for them.[6]

I would also expect the number of "What is SRE?" and "What do we want to do when we grow up?" conversations to increase significantly. We are starting to move to a staffing level where the discussion has the potential to move from "What must we do?" (reactive firefighting in particular) to "What do we want to do?"[7] Ideally, an increase in staff expands the potential for the kinds of things the SRE team can do, so more discussions will naturally occur.

---

6 I say this also so you can brace yourself for a number of reorgs. If it is any comfort, Kurt Andersen suggests smartly that managers should note that the current org tree/reporting structure in an organization isn't necessarily, and doesn't have to dictate, your SRE engagement model.

7 Just so I am clear, there are many factors that go into the potential for an SRE team to move away from reactive work and start to realize their full potential—size of team is just one of them. How long you've been working on the problem (usually measured in years), how good management is at prioritization, and larger org culture are several that come to mind that can be more impactful than just increasing the number of people on a team. It is entirely possible (and I've seen it) for an SRE team to staff up for the sole purpose of throwing bodies at the problem. That hiring "immune response" doesn't in and of itself get you out of reactive firefighting.

An important thing to pay attention to at this band[8] is SRE organization cohesion. We are definitely at the point where mission, tool choice, documentation standards, hiring standards, partner relationships (including what the team versus the partner is responsible for) and cultural norms can start to skew. On top of this, the sharing of lessons learned from failure no longer happens implicitly (since you are all not involved in the same incidents), so methods and practices for doing this have to be explicitly and intentionally constructed for it to happen. This natural "diffusion" of the organization as it gets bigger is also impacted by the centralized versus embedded frames in just the ways you would expect. The choices to keep the people in the organization together or more highly distributed in the larger organization can necessitate intentional efforts to maintain cohesion. This is one of the places where the discussions we had in Chapter 3 on SRE culture really come into play.

Scaling 48 to 108 (and Beyond)

With this jump, we leave the scope of an introduction-to-SRE book like this one. I personally would love to see more writing and talking about larger SRE organizations, but this book isn't the place for that. However, I do think it is useful to give you a very brief peek at where SRE can go as it starts to get larger.[9]

Here are a few things you might expect to see as SRE gets bigger in an organization:

- SRE teams that specialize even further (e.g., an SRE team created just for storage, a more release engineering–focused team)
- SRE teams formed around a technology or core function (the "Kubernetes SRE team")
- Emphasis on effective onboarding (both SREs and partners for SRE teams)
- SRE teams spawned to create and propagate common SRE standards, practices, and perhaps tools/platforms built for both SRE and the larger engineering organization

I'll offer one last guiding principle that I believe is crucial for SRE scaling to be effective (actually at any size, but especially as it grows): SREs must be agents of convergence and connection—not agents of conformity, deindividualization, or removing distinction.

---

8 And, quite frankly, in the previous one, but here's a place where it *really, really* matters, and the pain of not doing this will become quickly apparent.

9 My yoga teacher is fond of saying in class (usually after demonstrating something far out of my current reach), "Give your yoga a future."

SRE Meets Platform Engineering

In my experience, the following idea mostly comes into play when your SRE org gets to a substantial size, but I want to mention some ideas of things a larger SRE org might take on as you look out to the far horizon. A common thread is that an SRE team gets created or allocated to take on more of a pure dev role than we usually discuss when we talk about SRE.

To ease into this idea, let me point out that, well before this scaling point, it is pretty common for an SRE team to create, adopt, or evolve[10] specific tools to get their job done. No surprise there. Sometimes those tools escape the SRE team and get wider use in the organization (and so now the maintainer team has "customers" external to the team for those tools).

An even more explicit version of this is when an SRE team creates, evolves, and/or drives the adoption of some internal platform for running workloads as part of their reliability goals. In larger orgs, it is not uncommon for a team to be created to tend to either of these scenarios. This is one of the places SRE meets the nascent (as of this writing) movement called *platform engineering*.

Building a successful platform to enable the development work in an organization turns out to be trickier than it sounds—hence, the creation of platform engineering, an area devoted to paying close attention to this idea and its challenges. A viable platform has many requirements and potential goals. SREs have the experience and incentives to contribute to the reliability aspects of these efforts. They also have strong opinions on ways to construct platforms that are easy to maintain and operate from their years of dealing with systems in general.

Creating full-fledged platforms can be an all-consuming effort, but there are incremental steps SREs can take. They may construct pieces of what I would call reliability strata for the entire organization. Let me offer a few examples to make this clear:

- An SRE team might be responsible for maintaining the library that makes it easy for a development group to effortlessly onboard and emit data to the central monitoring system. A new service in development just has to link to this library, and they start "doing the right thing" vis-à-vis monitoring. There is near total adoption of the library, as all of the services in the org are expected to use it unless they have a really good reason not to.

---

10 We all know the story of adopting a piece of open source software that we wind up contributing to and, before we know it, becoming a maintainer of it or a fork of the original package.

- An SRE team might be responsible for creating canonical libraries for authorization and access control (any time the code needs to ask, "Can user X do operation Y?").[11]
- An SRE team might be responsible for creating the canonical tools for canary deployments in production.
- An SRE team might be responsible for creating the canonical remote procedure call (RPC) format/libraries for the team.[12]

In all of these examples and the general class of possibilities, an SRE team becomes responsible for coding underlying strata that "everyone uses" and ultimately engenders greater reliability in the org as a result.

Growing SRE's Leadership Representation

As the last point to lead us out of this chapter, I want to point out one other subtlety that may not be clear when we talk about growing SRE. In addition to just thinking about how we might increase in number (and effectiveness by doing so), it is also important to consider how we might scale other things at the same time, like leadership representation.[13] Does SRE have a seat at the table of the business leadership in your organization? Is SRE in the room where important decisions are being made, engineering or otherwise? As you grow SRE, you will need to pay attention to this in order to stay effective.

In this chapter, we've talked about the various axes that SRE can evolve on as it gets introduced into and then grows in an organization. I believe that this only happens through intentional leadership, so being strongly connected to the decision-making process in the organization is critical.

---

11 This example also could plausibly be in the hands of security and privacy engineers, but those are also usually found in larger orgs.

12 Though unless you have a really good reason, it makes more sense to use someone else's work such as gRPC. I didn't quite understand why SREs would want to get directly involved in something as low level as the RPC layer until I saw Gráinne Sheerin's talks at SREcon. For example, watch: "Yes, No, Maybe? Error Handling with gRPC Examples" (*https://oreil.ly/CZvx8*), in which it becomes clear that an RPC layer could "do the right thing" from a reliability perspective instead of every service writing custom code to handle common scenarios. Though not talked about publicly nearly as much, there are some very interesting possibilities for what monitoring and observability (and networking and security…) is possible if the RPC layer could communicate and expose what it knows.

13 While I am focusing on leadership here, I am a big fan of paying attention to other kinds of representation as you scale, including the hiring of underrepresented minorities in tech for your team. It's an important part of creating the best SRE team and organization.

CHAPTER 18

Conclusion

I'm a little sad because it is that time when you, me, and this book have to part ways. You don't have to go home, but you can't stay here because, in a moment, I will stop typing, you will stop reading, and this book will come to an end. Let's take a moment to review where we have been together.

SRE stands for the proposition that it is possible to work as an individual or as an organization, in collaboration with others, toward manifesting systems that can serve others at a desired level of reliability. SREs with a certain mindset, operating within a certain culture, and who have prepared for this role, can effectively use a set of practices within an organizational context that supports their efforts, at different scales, to achieve this goal.

And it is fun. And rewarding (both for the individual and the organization). And fun. Did I mention fun? Not always, but on balance, it can be great. SRE offers a test of your mettle and a chance to work with others to have a real impact at work. The challenges reliability throws at you and the road you need to take to navigate them aren't always obvious (hence this book) and are very rarely boring. I'm hoping you are leaving this book with at least some of the excitement I have for the field.

What's Next?

I'm really grateful that you have stuck with me to this point. I wish I could give each and every reader a gift basket on the way out to show my appreciation. I think the best I can do is give you a virtual "doggie bag" or "take-home container" (whatever you call it in your neck of the woods).

In that container, I would have:

- A little needlepoint sign that says, "It starts with curiosity…How does a system work? How does it fail?"
- A set of Dickerson Hierarchy of Reliability flashcards (perhaps with my definition of SRE in the front).
- A temporary (or permanent—your call) tattoo that says "Relentlessly collaborative."
- A neon sign in the shape of a feedback loop.
- A barrel of SREcon videos.
- A small beach shovel for your toil.
- A cupcake—because who doesn't want a cupcake?

Each of these items will serve you well when you need it as you begin your own SRE journey.

Thank you for reading this book, I wish you all the best.

Letters to a Young SRE (Apologies to Rilke)

Once upon a time, when I published *Seeking SRE*, I asked people in the various SRE spaces I knew if they wanted to contribute to a crowdsourced chapter on SRE versus DevOps, and the response was phenomenal.

For this book, I thought it might be cool to ask the collective wisdom if they had any tips for new SREs or orgs new to SRE that they would want to pass on, knowing what they do now.

I specifically asked, "In two paragraphs (ideally) or less, what advice would you give to either individuals or organizations just starting on the road to SRE? What do you wish your future self could have told you? Things to pay attention to, things that aren't as important as they may seem, practices you wish you started earlier, resources you have found helpful, lessons you learned, and so on."

I'm very grateful for people's willingness to share their experiences for this book. Here are their submissions (names and titles printed just as they were submitted to me):

John Amori

You'll find that not all systems were designed as elegantly as you would have hoped, and even more are outside of your control to improve. It's important to remember that you can't do everything and, despite your best efforts, things will always eventually break. It's here that I'll impart this wisdom: "Be prepared." It's a simple enough thing to consider but difficult in practice to have great up-to-date documentation with clear, actionable tasks that consider every dependency and will enable you with the right tools and resources to investigate an issue should the urgent need arise. Spend some time studying good documentation habits and read some published postmortems, as it'll help you understand many of the challenges that SREs face in practice.

There are a plethora of tools and technologies that are consistently expanding, and while it's great to understand what many of those things do and why they are useful, it's not very important early in your journey to master them until you have a need to do so. My advice to anyone starting in SRE is really just to master a programming language (Python/Go) and a Unix-like operating system (*nix) first before getting too far ahead of yourself and being overwhelmed in the ecosystem. You'll find even the best SREs are consistently using basic command-line tools and simple scripts to get things done, because they are well documented and easy to use. Much like walking before you run and not biting off more than you can chew, take your time and try to learn one thing at a time as many things build on one another. There are plenty of great resources to learn each individual concept, but I've found the DevOps Roadmap (*https://oreil.ly/z32Ao*) to be a great learning path, coupled with all the O'Reilly SRE books and their concise explanation of the practice.

Fred Hebert

Staff SRE, Honeycomb.io

Never forget that all our systems are sociotechnical. Without people to adjust them when objectives, priorities, or pressures change, they grow useless and brittle. Maintaining the human part's health is what keeps things sustainable in the medium to long term. Metrics grow useless and need changing; there's more information available on the edges of the system than what a central decision maker can keep in mind. Keep looking at it as a growing, living system, and not just a technical snapshot; in time, you can analyze at a leisurely pace.

Decision making is contextual. Seek an understanding of how people do their work. There is always a gap between the work as we imagine it to be and how it is done. The narrower that gap, the more effective our interventions can be; all the nitty-gritty details of work and their pressures are fundamental. Try to properly understand the challenges, clarify the goal conflicts that arise in systems (and result in sometimes frustrating trade-offs), and make learning from these experiences an objective of its own. We can't expect change if the goals and pressures stay the same. SREs have the freedom to be a key organizational feedback loop to drive these changes.

That was a dense set of ideas taken from my previous writings:

- *My Bad Opinions* (blog), "Errors Are Constructed, Not Discovered" (*https://oreil.ly/2E7xL*), posted April 13, 2022
- *My Bad Opinions* (blog), "Embrace Complexity; Tighten Your Feedback Loops" (*https://oreil.ly/_sE_9*), posted June 20, 2023
- *Learning from Incidents* (blog), "Carrots, Sticks, and Making Things Worse" (*https://oreil.ly/saQD3*), posted July 13, 2023

Aju Tamang

DevOps/SRE Engineer

Prioritize incident response during outages and participate in on-call rotations for personal and team growth. Runbook documentation is a long-term investment that will help you and your team in the future. It can be a daunting task and requires a specific skill set to do it effectively, which can be underrated by itself.

School of SRE (*https://oreil.ly/AyrAH*) is something I recommend to aspiring SREs. Get into SRE Google Books (*https://sre.google/books*) for comprehensive insights into SRE principles, best practices, and real-world use studies. I also recommend an open source SRE interview preparation guide (*https://oreil.ly/yh1J3*). These resources will help any individual to excel in the dynamic and demanding field of site reliability engineering.

Daniel Gentleman

Senior SRE

Welcome to the world of site reliability engineering. We are bridge builders. We are enablers. We try to give everyone the tools and education to make the best code of their lives. We want everyone to push code to production and participate in incident response without fear. You will use skills in code, infrastructure, automation/orchestration, and incident command to provide tools and education for your teams.

It's important to know the needs of your teams, and they can meet in the middle. For example, developers may not know how autoscaling and container orchestration work. They don't need to know all of it, but they need to know the limitations, tools, and visibility available to them. Likewise, infrastructure engineers may not know the magic of frontend code and job queues, but they need to know how to monitor those systems for load, overload, autoscaling, and circuit breakers. Learn the needs of both sides, find opportunities to build bridges, and automate everything you can. If your organization lacks a robust incident response strategy, involve yourself in building it with a focus on safety and ownership for all stakeholders. Reliability is your job. Develop a culture and strategy to make reliability the default behavior for everyone.

SREs are enablers.

They enable developers to do their best code without having to fear operational tasks, but they also enable developers to understand the operational tasks enough so they don't deploy code that's wrong for the infrastructure. They also provide tools and automation to help the developers manage their own infra.

They enable execs and budget-minded people to make smart decisions on spending and infrastructure.

Ideally, they enable all incident responders to do their best work without fear by giving them a structured, safe environment for incident response. This is through both a mature incident response playbook and disaster simulation exercises with the developers.

They enable infrastructure, automation, and orchestration engineers by giving them a bridge to the developers and providing tools and education for both sides.

Joanna Wijntjes

SRE, Google

The loudest and most confident person in the room may not have the best answer, may not be the most right. Do not mistake conviction for accuracy, and don't let noisy voices silence you from asking the questions you want to ask or investigating the options you think deserve attention. It takes courage to share a differing opinion, but it is a crucial part of your job to voice these ideas. You will often find yourself in a room where you are the only SRE, and your organization is counting on you to be the voice of reliability and good practice. By the same token, when you are the loud, confident person, always pause and make room for the quieter voices to share their ideas and concerns. I have seen senior SREs listen patiently while very junior engineers excitedly share their ideas, and they don't interrupt them or cut them off, but they ask questions and request more details in a way that grows the expertise of the junior engineer. That makes for a great organization.

You can't make progress without an error budget. Call it an SLO, call it your mom, but there has to be a measurable metric for errors that you can hold up and say, "Here's how the service is doing"; and that budget needs to reflect how customers see your service. Management does not want outages and does not want problems—ever. The part of management that wants every engineer at the company working on every outage is the same part of management that refuses to allow a single query to be dropped. Neither of these strategies scale; they just feel safe to the people who report up to the CEO. If there is no error budget, the engineers will not be able to build automation and make improvements. And when outages do happen, they will be so much larger because the service is bulky and fragile. Decide the acceptable budget for errors and then let the engineers build and create and improve within the safety of those rails. You're the engineer; help the managers be confident that the service will be successful by sharing expectations and error budgets so they are not caught off guard, and make sure they see the progress that can be made when there is room for errors to happen on the road to a healthier service.

Fabrizio Waldner

Site Reliability Engineer

Don't worry about having toil, deal with it. When I was a young system administrator, I used to try having everything automated. Although automating is a good thing, it is impossible to automate everything. Dedicating a person to manage the toil is the key to coping with it and detecting patterns in it. Then, create projects to automate the most vexing issues.

Graham Poulter

Site Reliability Engineer, Google

I wish that I had been bolder about asking for help, shadowing other SREs, and engaging in coworking with a project mentor. I came from an academic and smaller-system environment where it was reasonable to jump in and "figure it out on my own" from code, documentation, and group whiteboard sessions. I became discouraged to find myself lost in a never-ending depth-first search through a maze of dependencies and documentation on my first project, with no idea where to start. Large systems are often too big for one person, and I found that it's a crucial metaskill to watch and learn from your colleagues by working together.

The other thing I wish I had learned earlier is the art of choosing and shaping projects. I came from a company with top-down assignments. Moving to a more bottom-up planning environment, I ended up with the "leftover" project ideas, which were often unsuited to me, low value, or unworkable in their proposed form. Over time, I learned about what work engages me, how to state my preferences, generate and filter ideas, make my own independent assessment of feasibility and impact, know my criteria for projects, and identify and remove unnecessary work from the scope.

I may have been over-leveled by half a level at hire—at level 4 (independent) when I was more of a 3.5 (supervised, becoming independent) in the large-system work environment. That contributed to the early struggles, as more independence was expected from me by default than I was ready for.

Jamie Wilkinson

Site Reliability Engineer

A lot of material for new SREs (and old!) will talk about incident response, or automation, or observability, and so on, and you might be wondering how that sets an SRE apart from a platforms engineer, a DevOps, or classic systems administrators from the 90s and earlier. Well, that's easy: the defining trait of an SRE is to measure, and then defend, the appropriate reliability of a system. That's it. That's not to say those other jobs don't also do that—but SRE explicitly makes it the mission.

All that other stuff that looks like "classic operations" are just tools in the toolbox. Going on call isn't a thing that defines SRE, it's just a sometimes necessary behavior to defend a reliability target. Being able to program a computer, automate a process, or reengineer a system to avoid a failure mode aren't things that define SRE, but they are well-understood techniques for improving the reliability of a system and making you *good* at being an SRE. Being able to inspect your system isn't anything more than a troubleshooting tool, but when used to measure reliability, it can be an early warning that a target is likely to be missed. So, you see all of these work patterns, under SRE, are not the job; they're the emergent behaviors that come from the primary mission of measuring and defending the reliability of the system. Knowing this gives you a lot of creative freedom to come up with new ways to work and keep the job interesting.

Andrew Howden

Staff Engineer

There are quite a few things that you can do to make site reliability engineering a success within your organization. My experience is that hiring, team management, goal and purpose, an engagement model, clear stakeholder expectations, a structured organizational change model, and regular check-ins with senior leaders all enable you to drive reliability improvements.

I didn't know these things at the start, though, and even if someone had passed them on, I do not know that I'd have been able to take action on them. Instead, one moment when the ambiguity of "make embedded SRE work" became a clear path was working with a senior leader to define a strategy for my team. This strategy defined that precise purpose and engagement model and set those stakeholder expectations. It also allowed me to inventory the capabilities I had available to me and develop a way of driving change that leveraged both people within my organization and connections outside of it and the broader engineering community. I didn't get it all right, but I did get it more right than wrong. If I were doing it again, step 1 would be writing that six-pager strategy. From there, you can structure, learn, and grow into the rest.

The TL;DR is to "be clear about what you have and intend to do on paper, rather than having gut reactions in response to production issues."

Pedro Alves

Site Reliability Engineer

Bootstrapping SRE in a large company can be a tricky process. Trying to drive a big initiative to change how things are done can be fraught with friction. In a previous company, we chose to plant the seed of SRE by bootstrapping a small team (five engineers). The team operated in a kitchen-sink mode, working on different projects together with other teams as hands-on consultants.

There were two key ingredients that made that team effective: (1) engineers had a broad set of skills (individually and as a whole), and (2) engineers had tenure at the company and enjoyed a fair amount of social capital. The knowledge of the company and the social capital meant that the SRE team could go straight into problem-solving mode, thus skipping any lengthy onboarding into the domain of the team. The broad skill set meant that there were many different types of projects that this team could tackle.

After a number of successful projects, the reputation of the team grew, and with it, also the trust in the SRE model. Building on the results shown, management agreed to grow the SRE team.

Working in a kitchen-sink model allowed our team to achieve success in localized projects. That, however, is not enough to impact a whole company. To get to that level of impact, we had to upgrade the SRE team to a department. But that upgrade only made sense with an engineering vision and strategy that tied together the different teams that made up the SRE department. In our case, the vision and strategy was focused on observability. As such, the SRE department was composed of the teams owning the observability infrastructure, the incident management team, and the original SRE team. The ultimate goal was to expand SRE beyond observability, but observability was the starting point that would guide our organization into its future steps.

Here is a very summarized contribution of the content originally published in a series of blog posts: "Tracing SRE's Journey in Zalando," Part I (*https://oreil.ly/hePvn*), September 13, 2021; Part II (*https://oreil.ly/7xoeS*), September 21, 2021; and Part III (*https://oreil.ly/aXUdt*), October 15, 2021.

Balasundaram N

Senior SRE

Document as much as possible into internal processes and implement them, but don't "boil the ocean." Iterate the baseline process review routinely, specifically for incidents. Documentation should get hosted on a site as soon as you commit it.

Eduardo Spotti

CTO, Crubyt

When we are looking for a path of happiness for our professional lives, we think about looking for a role that entails a set of responsibilities and challenges, with a good salary and a great work team. Working as an SRE is not the beginning of that path, it is part of the result of constantly training in technical aspects, of building work teams that adopt a culture and a set of practices that simply improve the quality of life of those of us who make software. The salary will be a consequence of taking this responsibility and making things happen.

In team building there is no recipe or methodology, but try to correlate active listening, leading by example, Agile principles, DevOps values (CALMS), and the roles of an SRE. I say roles because in an SRE team you can find a world of possibilities, from a site reliability operator who operates, makes available, and knows how our platform and end-user products are working to an SRE who is a specialist in observability, incident management, application performance, business KPIs, or disaster recovery—but all this with a product mindset. Remember that an SRE also builds solutions and provides mechanisms through which we have clear work paths in the face of any unforeseen event.

And on that path, going through step by step, those who find themselves in an SRE role make decisions about using cloud or on-premises systems; developing or managing systems; doing quality testing or monitoring; and developing practices that can be applied among the entire ecosystem, such as SLI/SLO, automation, incident tools, and backup tools. Learn about code, then the operation of that code, and finally the platform where that code lives; from there, you will build the best life-cycle paths for that code.

Ian Bartholomew

Staff SRE

Take notes. Site reliability engineering encompasses so many practices that, especially when starting out, it's hard to know all of the patterns, concepts, laws, practices, ideas, etc. So, take notes on all the things you don't know. Find a note-taking app or personal knowledge base such as Obsidian, and when you run across something that you don't know or that piques your interest, write it down. Then, spend time every day researching those topics, and write down and organize what you find.

As you do this, you will not only learn but also start to build a reserve of ideas and concepts to pull from and reference. When problem-solving or working on an issue in a particular domain, you can refer to your notes and tap into the ideas. It's hard for us to hold everything in our heads and getting them out of our minds and into notes makes it much easier to reference and search for the ideas we need.

Coming from a software background, I had to learn a lot about the IT and networking aspects of the role, and doing this was crucial for me.

Olivier Duquesne

SRE, Techsys

First thing about the road is probably to explain that SRE is not the new DevOps and not the new SysOps name. SRE is not an *Ops* work, it is nearer to improving quality than Ops. SRE is not the superhero who will save the world because they know every new technical concept; this is not the way.

Everything is measured (toil, postmortem, automation, etc.) to argue about quality. SRE will be the missing link between product owners and technical teams. The owner only knows the objectives (SLO), knows the goals, and can provide objectives and key results (OKRs). They don't care about "error budgets," which is a tool for SRE to speak the same words. SRE is a new language to make teams collaborate.

Ralph Pritchard

Senior Platform Engineer

There should be no mysteries. Our software and infrastructure should be transparent and understandable at all times. We want our applications to produce predictable outcomes that we can explain even when something unexpected happens, such as an incident. To achieve this goal, we need to dig deep into why things happen. We may not be able to explain every event on the first occurrence, but over time, we can improve our ability to decompose any event into the sequence of steps that decides the outcome.

Your tools for monitoring and observability will provide the required proof when used effectively. Learn techniques to effectively use each tool and the situations when each technique should be applied. Embrace failure and learn from it—ideally, in a nonproduction environment. Stage experiments, record the outcomes and the steps you took to observe, and understand what's happening. Nonproduction environments provide a place to practice. Use them often to simulate situations such as failovers or performance testing. Record what you learn into runbooks, so it will be easy and seamless when you see similar incidents in production. When we deal with production, we have a paying audience, and our performance at those times—regardless of the task—should be game day ready and proficiently executed.

David Caudill

Staff SRE, Capital One

It might seem like getting your SLI perfect is essential to success. This is a very easy place to get stuck because you haven't yet seen the entire process work end to end, and it's the work you're doing while you have the least experience. In reality, I regularly work with teams that have highly imperfect SLIs and still get a lot of value from them. Site reliability engineering is a systems-thinking endeavor, and your priority needs to be ensuring that the *system* is working for your teams. That means staying focused on the goal: implementing SRE.

This is a lot like riding a bike. It's more important that the teams you work with complete a wobbly full "cycle" implementation than it is to get any one part perfect. A team with a bad SLI can correct it. A team with the wrong SLO can adjust it. A team that does the wrong thing to try and recover their error budget can learn from it in a retro. When an incident happens and your error budgets don't move, you'll adjust them. Once these constructs are in place and entrenched in your culture, they become "levers" you can pull to adjust the functioning of the team. Each one of these is an opportunity for an engineer on the team to shine and contribute. Get off the starting line as fast as you can and manage expectations aggressively. Expect that whatever you do first is wrong. Exactly *how* it's wrong might only become visible once you can observe the system as a whole.

Alex Hidalgo

Principal Reliability Advocate, Nobl9, and author of Implementing Service Level Objectives

Site reliability engineering is an exciting discipline and one that resonates deeply within me. Since initially escaping the cathedral at Google, much has been written and spoken about in terms of *how to SRE*. These teachings often involve a myriad of topics such as principles, tools, approaches, systems, best practices, and more. For a conference keynote I gave at SREcon EMEA 2022, I crowdsourced a list of "Things SREs Do" and ended up with more than 50 concrete, distinguishable items. That's a lot of things! It is a testament to how broad (and deep!) the field can be. However, this also means that getting started on your SRE journey can be intimidating.

Luckily, you have books like this one to help you get started and guide you on your way, but I'd like to offer one concrete piece of advice that has served me well over the years: *be meaningful*. It can be overwhelming when you are faced with all the things it seems like an SRE organization needs to accomplish to truly be *doing SRE*. But, it turns out, you don't actually need to be doing all of those things at all. With every piece of philosophy you ingest, every tool or process you're introduced to, every book (including this one!) you read, ask yourself: "What does this mean for me, my team, my organization, and my users? Do I really need to be doing this at all?" Learn from what others have done and what others may tell you, but always, always make *meaningful* decisions. You won't get far if you just try to copy what has worked for others.

Effie Mouzeli

Wikimedia Foundation

Dear future SRE,

Welcome to the community! SRE is a long, winding road with breathtaking (dashboard) views and the occasional bits of excitement. The technical aspect of the work is something you will learn one way or another; but being a good SRE goes beyond having an aptitude for solving tech puzzles. There is one skill that SREs tend to not pay enough attention to, and that is good communication.

Help yourself learn how to properly express what you want to say, starting with improving your writing. Your peers will always appreciate reading a presentable design document, a clearly written postmortem, or a useful commit message! But writing, sadly, improves only through friction (sorry, no shortcuts here). Get out there and start writing posts about something you like! Any topic will do, as long as you organize your thoughts and put them on "paper." Moreover, improving that skill will, without any doubt, advance your instant messaging (also important) and, of course, your verbal skills. Half of your work is dealing with tech challenges, but the other half is communicating; you owe it to you to give them equal attention.

Advice from Former SREs

It may seem a little strange to include information from people who have exited the door marked "SRE" to those who wish to enter it, but in my experience, the people who have left a field often have a unique perspective that only a little distance can offer. Plus, I have heard that while you could take the person out of SRE, it wasn't nearly as easy to take SRE out of the person.

To hunt down this rare view, I've sought out and talked to some ex-SREs and have asked them about what they are doing now and key questions such as "What things continue to stick even after your departure?" and "Now that you are out, what would you suggest new SREs pay attention to as they are entering SRE?"

Here are some notes they made on the topic that I believe will be helpful to you.

Dina Levitan

SRE background. Google Ads SRE, Pittsburgh, 2012–2014; Google Apps SRE (Gmail/ Calendar), Mountain View, 2014–2017; Google Cloud SRE, 2017–2018; Google SRE EDU, 2018–2019

Post-SRE occupations. Product management; consulting; problem solving to broader societal problems, including opioid epidemic; COVID vaccine distribution/capacity planning: formed a nonprofit (JitVax) at early stage of vaccine rollout; parent (see blog posts on SRE and parenting at *https://www.dinalevitan.com*)

Lessons learned from SRE:

- Reducing single points of failure (SPOFs). Pay attention to when there is a SPOF and what can be done proactively to mitigate it:
  - Systematic/global versus localized SPOFs.
  - Cascade of events leading to failures.

- How to share load and incorporate load-sharing/load-shedding into design upfront.

- Sometimes, you can remove the SPOF; other times, you can introduce mitigations and prevent severity of issues were they to arise.

- "Automate yourself out of a job." How to put into place systems and processes so that ecosystems are more resilient.

- If there are ways to teach someone to fish and get yourself out of the loop, that's good for everyone.

- Playbook. Value of reducing cognitive load in an emergency. See *The Checklist Manifesto: How to Get Things Right* by Atul Gawande (Picador, 2011). When you've learned a thing, help the next person avoid learning it the hard way.

- Eliminating toil. In your life/work, pay attention to areas where you are spending a lot of time/energy but that are not necessarily valuable, and how you can automate/ameliorate them.

- Troubleshooting. "Wheel of Misfortune" approach:[1]

  - Collaboratively deep dive issues.

  - Brainstorm what could be going on in this situation and what you should try next.

  - Good to practice when stakes are low so that you can perform smoothly when stakes are higher/in a real emergency.

- Surviving first years:

  - Be part of an on-call rotation—"Don't hesitate; escalate" for outages:

    - It's better to bring in additional resources rather than let a problem persist.

    - Good for nontechnical problems as well.

  - Know where to find information—developing the ability to troubleshoot from first principles is important, but so is knowing where to look for past learnings/issues.

  - Yes, some day you'll "take down production" or otherwise introduce a bug, and the most important thing is to learn to facilitate a postmortem that people are aware of and have learned from: "prevent—mitigate—resolve"—it's a milestone. "Congratulations, you've done work that has enough impact to affect production." The last person who broke production got a stuffy on their desk, as a sort of acknowledgment that it is normal and not to take it personally.

---

1 Disaster role playing, as described in Chapter 28 of *Site Reliability Engineering* by Betsy Beyer et al. (O'Reilly, 2014).

Sara Smollett

Pre-SRE. Systems/network administration in the *.edu* world

SRE background. Seventeen years at Google headquarters (SRE and later SRE manager for corporate applications, security infrastructure, accounts, Google Reader, Google Calendar, Spanner, etc.)

Post-SRE. Taking some time off

Lessons and things I find still relevant:

- Scaling, scaling, scaling. Applies to everything, not just services. The Google I joined was a ~5,000-person company; the Google I left had ~190K full-time employees. Constant growth and onboarding new SREs. Increased organizational complexity and hierarchy. Many knock-on effects and other changes.

- Skepticism. Identifying possible failure points in services/products/processes. Planning to prevent/avoid problems/failures; be resilient to that which cannot be easily avoided and prepared to recover from predicted and unpredicted problems.

- Learning from failures. Never let a good failure go to waste. Write and share thoughtful postmortems/retrospectives. Role-play failures and learn from those. Read postmortems from other services; you might find things you should apply to your own services. More than once, I've found myself reading incident reports from other fields for fun: utility companies, airlines, medicine, scuba diving, etc. If you abstract away the specifics, there are a lot of similarities.

- Consider the user experience and the end-to-end flow. A query may flow through dozens of (micro)services, each understood by different engineers. A lot of problems arise from no one understanding/taking responsibility for the big picture and what happens between the interfaces. This applies to human processes as well. A lot of fields could benefit from an SRE-like mentality to reduce bureaucratic mazes. If you want a specific example, I could rant about the US healthcare system and disability insurance providers in particular, but there are probably examples that are more universal.

- Data, particularly quantitative data. Years ago, I remember this sticker (*https://oreil.ly/bd8qj*) being popular. I don't endorse the "So *@#& Off" part of it, but certainly the "We Have Charts & Graphs to Back Us Up" applies. So much time spent setting up monitoring and looking at dashboards. I still enjoy a good time series or graphical visualization.

- Learning to be proficient and appropriately confident with systems/environments where you have only partial knowledge because you can't know it all. There are too many systems and they change too frequently. Also internalizing that SRE is not an individual but part of a team, and that asking for help is not a failure mode. I've rarely seen people ask for help too early/often, but many times I've seen people needlessly spinning their wheels when someone else could give them a boost.

Andrew Fong

Pre SRE. AOL System Administrator in Internet Access Operations and AOL Video, including Nullsoft, Winamp, and Shoutcast

SRE Background. YouTube SRE, early Dropbox SRE/SRE manager

Post-SRE. VP at Dropbox Infrastructure, CTO at Vise, Startup Cofounder/CEO

Lessons learned from SRE (technical):

- First-principles thinking.
- Love the problem, not the scale. I love scale and most of the SREs I know love scale. It can be a great teacher. What I've learned is that you can find interesting problems at any scale.
- Stateful versus stateless. Stateless systems are hard, harder than anything else you will ever deal with as an SRE in terms of technical complexity.

Lessons learned from SRE (leadership):

- Start by leading yourself. Your mindset determines everything, and it's easy to fall into the death spiral of believing the world is against you. Too many times I've seen the *us* versus *them* culture; too many times I've been part of teams that don't believe the problem can be solved or think it's outside of their control.
- Own your mindset and realize only you can change it.
- Be optimistic, not cynical.
- Be curious (e.g., "Why are there these constraints?").
- Appreciate the wins; be grateful for the experience.

Scott MacFiggen

Pre-SRE. IT and network engineer at enterprise software companies; did a stint in QA for a few years as well

SRE background. Facebook 2007–2014: first full-time SRE hire; technical lead and manager of the US-based SRE group from 2008–2012; production engineer for API and the Mobile Team; Lead SRE for Snaptu[2] integration; Lead SRE on Tupperware[3] and used that to drive Facebook to move to a cloud-based deployment with Tupperware managed pools versus the hostname-based deployment that was the norm; Dropbox 2014–2018: Lead SRE on Magic Pocket[4] development and deployment.

Post-SRE. Founder and winemaker of Sosie Wines

Lessons learned from SRE:

- Focus on impact. This is one of the core principles of Facebook engineering and is even more relevant to SRE. The SRE/engineer ratio always favors engineering. An SRE needs to consider how to have the most impact with fewer resources. This could involve selecting projects that offer the greatest impact, leveraging engineering resources by driving roadmaps to include operational features, or setting better goals. It's easy to get caught up in low-value work if you're not careful.

- Don't ignore issues. While a reboot might fix random issues on your home computer, at scale, things go wrong for a reason. Investigate every issue and understand what is happening.

- Be a gatekeeper. Be strict about what you allow to co-locate with your services. Engineers love to write global daemons to solve issues, and sysadmins love to deploy the latest, greatest helper process. These can disrupt your service. Don't be afraid to push back and ask the hard questions about why a deployment is needed.

- Relationship building is critical. It's easy to become siloed as an SRE, but SRE is fundamentally a cross-functional role. Building strong connections with leaders across engineering will help you identify issues that span organizations and will have a high impact to solve.

- Get involved in engineering roadmaps early. This is especially true for SRE organizations that are not embedded within engineering teams. The last thing you want as an SRE is to be tasked with operating a service that wasn't built from the beginning with reliability and scalability in mind.

---

2 Mobile application platform, acquired by Facebook. See *https://oreil.ly/q9ldI*.

3 Facebook's cluster management system, now called Twine. See *https://oreil.ly/YP0WH*.

4 Dropbox's multi-exabyte storage system (*https://oreil.ly/N-cyN*). See also the blog post (*https://oreil.ly/RvmU4*) on Magic Pocket.

SRE Resources

One of the goals of this book is to offer you an index of the most helpful resources available to you on site reliability engineering. All throughout, I have pointed to the sources I have personally found valuable as I learned about the topic. This appendix collects the major sources and offers you a little tour of them.

Since this book is largely static, and there is new stuff being produced all the time, this is my point-in-time list. If there is something you have personally encountered that you believe should be in this appendix in future editions, please don't hesitate to get in touch.

Core Books

- *Site Reliability Engineering: How Google Runs Production Systems*, edited by Betsy Beyer, Chris Jones, Niall Richard Murphy, and Jennifer Petoff (O'Reilly, 2016)
- *The Site Reliability Workbook: Practical Ways to Implement SRE*, edited by Betsy Beyer, Niall Richard Murphy, David K. Rensin, Kent Kawahara, and Stephen Thorne (O'Reilly, 2018)

It's pretty well accepted, and I agree, that you have to start here. These are the books written by SREs at Google and published by O'Reilly that really launched SRE into the world. Both are available online at *https://sre.google/books* for anyone to read, thanks to the largesse of Google, so if you haven't read them yet, start here. The first is an excellent reflection of SRE as started and practiced at Google. The second is a substantial expansion on the initial work that is still Google-based, but with considerable effort made to generalize the topic beyond the walls of Google and excise "the Google voice" that rankled some readers of the first book.

When I recommend these books to others, I always provide one piece of cautionary advice that I will provide to you too: both books are heavily steeped in (and often predicated on) the values, resources, and truly unique engineering culture of Google. If you do not currently work there, it is incumbent upon you to read these books with a critical eye to determine the applicability and feasibility of the ideas and practices in your current environment. As much as I have seen people try to do this (and fail), it is not possible to copy what you read in those books wholesale into your environment without taking into account your local values, resources, and engineering culture.

Another core book:

- *Seeking SRE: Conversations About Running Production Systems at Scale* by David N. Blank-Edelman (O'Reilly, 2018)

Full Disclosure

I am the editor and curator of this book, so assume this is a biased recommendation.

By 2018, I had participated in enough conversations to realize that there were quite a few topics being discussed in the community that had not been covered, or covered thoroughly, in the Google books. They included detailed descriptions on how SRE grows differently in different soil outside of Google, additional best practices/thinking, future-leaning topics, and some of the human aspects of SRE (mental health, privacy, social justice, etc.) that should get more attention. I pulled together a book that captured some of these conversations, *Seeking SRE*. My recommendation to others is to first read the Google books to get a good grounding in SRE as defined at Google and then read my book to expand your understanding and conception of the subject.[1]

"SRE and…" Books

O'Reilly has published three books that aren't precisely "applied SRE" but are pretty close:

- *Building Secure and Reliable Systems* by Heather Adkins, Betsy Beyer, Paul Blankinship, Piotr Lewandowski, Ana Oprea, and Adam Stubblefield (O'Reilly, 2020)

---

1 Niall Murphy, one of the reviewers of this book (and an author of the Google books), also strongly recommends *Establishing SRE Foundations: A Step-by-Step Guide to Introducing Site Reliability Engineering in Software Delivery Organizations* by Dr. Vladyslav Ukis (Addison-Wesley Professional, 2022).

- *Reliable Machine Learning* by Cathy Chen, Niall Richard Murphy, Kranti Parisa, D. Sculley, and Todd Underwood (O'Reilly, 2022)
- *Database Reliability Engineering* by Laine Campbell and Charity Majors (O'Reilly, 2017)

I recommend these books for reading after the core set if any of their topics overlap with your job function or interests. They are optional reading with one small exception: the first few chapters of *Building Secure and Reliable Systems* are broadly applicable to anyone who needs to be an advocate for SRE to others (which is probably most people reading this book).

It can be useful to make comparisons between security work and reliability work when discussing SRE since priorities around security are usually well established in peoples' minds.[2] The first few chapters of *Building Secure and Reliable Systems* do a good job of teasing out the similarities and differences between these two emergent properties of systems that are crucial to making a cogent argument.

Events

I am a very big fan of gathering together as a community (in person[3] when practical and safe) to talk to each other about SRE. Conversations about our best practices, identity, success, failures, past and future challenges, and connecting with others in similar circumstances are invaluable.

For SRE, there are on-topic and adjacent conferences that are worthwhile.

SREcon

SREcon is USENIX's wildly popular global conference dedicated solely to SRE for SREs. As of this writing it takes place in multiple locales (for example, Americas and EU), each locale with a slightly different character representing the interests of the organizers in that region. All sessions that are recorded are made available to watch for free[4] on the USENIX YouTube channel (*https://oreil.ly/M4iqj*).

---

2 For example, "If you wouldn't ship this with a known security issue, why would you ship it with a known reliability flaw?" or "We all agree that bringing in a specialist who focuses on security to review this is important, so couldn't a similar argument be made for including SRE in the meeting to review this for reliability concerns?"

3 I say this because some of my greatest learning experiences have been during the "hallway track" (in between sessions, at a meal, etc.) at conferences where serendipitous conversation with others expanded my thinking.

4 Even though the sessions are available to watch after the fact, this is not a substitute for attending. The content is great, but the opportunity to ask questions, mingle with others in the same boat, and participate in the "hallway track" is invaluable.

Vendor SRE Single-Day Events

Over the years, I have seen a number of "boutique" SRE events held in various locations. The vast majority seem to be events created by a vendor[5] for marketing purposes. The speakers are predominantly sourced from that vendor versus community sourced through a call for proposals. I'm usually not a big fan of these events (they feel a bit too marketing-y to me), but sometimes they can have value if that's the only game in town for you.

DevOps Event Tracks/Sessions

As organizers of commercial, high-quality DevOps events realized that there was interest in SRE topics,[6] those events started to grow SRE tracks with curated content that has been pretty decent. Two prominent examples of this are DevOps Enterprise Summit and All Day DevOps.

Similarly, entirely community-led DevOps events like Devopsdays (*https://oreil.ly/cJ7fT*) have been amenable to presenting SRE content in an ad hoc way. Sometimes you can find good SRE sessions at your local Devopsdays event. This is more the exception than the rule, so I would not go to a Devopsdays event specifically for the SRE content (there are lots of other good reasons to go—they are, on the whole, good stuff).

---

5 There are exceptions to this that are more community led. For example, there is a UK SRE Days that on the surface (I have never attended) looks pretty good.

6 And to be frank, they saw that there was money in them thar hills…

SRE-Adjacent Niche Events

As a final recommendation around events, I would encourage you to consider attending some of the "niche" conferences that are forums for discussions about single topics that are part of the SRE space or are clearly of interest to SREs. For example, there are smaller events on chaos engineering, release engineering, incident response, platform engineering, and monitoring/observability[8] that I have found valuable to attend.

SRE Video Content

One of the best byproducts of the events we have been discussing is the largely free[9] video content they produce. As I mentioned, all SREcon recorded sessions are available on YouTube as of this writing. There is a tremendous amount of good information to be found in those videos. One suggestion I have given people over the years is to set up a "book clubbish" learning hour with their teammates or others in their organization when everyone gets together to watch an SREcon session and then discuss it. This (perhaps plus pizza) is a low-effort way to help jump-start a healthy SRE culture.[10]

---

7 One way to increase your luck if you currently don't have one near you is to start your own.

8 Shout-out to Monitorama in particular.

9 With only a few exceptions, the vast majority of the conferences I attend publish their sessions for all to watch free after the event.

10 If watching videos is not your jam, a variation where people get together to discuss postincident write-ups (either internal or external) can also be beneficial and, quite frankly, a blast.

I am preemptively answering the question, "Are there any good online SRE courses?" because I have received the same question for years. The unfortunate answer is that, as of this writing, I have not seen any general-purpose SRE courses that I would recommend without reservations.[11] I would love to discover something I may have missed or perhaps have my mind changed on re-review. If you have any suggestions, please drop me a note.

SRE-Specific Podcasts

There have been a number of good SRE podcasts that have popped up over the years, which can be found wherever you consume your podcasts.[12] I find myself listening to the following podcasts that are active as of this writing:

- *Google SRE Prodcast* by MP English, Salim Virji, and Viv
- *Slight Reliability* podcast by Stephen Townsend
- *SREpath* podcast by Ash Patel and Sebastian Vietz

SRE-Specific Email Newsletters

Many newsletters in this space are strongly marketing-oriented toward whatever vendor is producing them.[13] Some of those aren't bad, but if you would like your SRE information "uncut," I would highly recommend you sign up for the *SRE Weekly* newsletter (*https://oreil.ly/YrP-a*) published by Lex Neva.

Online Forums

So perhaps you believe, as I do, that SRE should be a community activity and you want to stay plugged into that community in between the events we discussed. Where do you go?

---

11 Note: I don't know of any good general SRE courses, but there are plenty that will help you level up as an SRE. For example, the System Design Interview course and Alex Xu's books on the topic (*https://oreil.ly/0bbVy*) are quite good.

12 There are a much larger number of SRE-adjacent podcasts with DevOps, operations, and observability content, such as *Page It to the Limit* from PagerDuty, which is also in rotation in my podcast app.

13 There are a ton of SRE-adjacent newsletters for DevOps, observability, etc., that can be found via a web search. One good example is Thai Wood's Resilience Roundup (*https://oreil.ly/8wWC-*) (for resilience engineering).

Here's my SRE-specific starter list:

- /r/SRE on Reddit (*https://oreil.ly/e96Kk*). Pretty dead from a discussion perspective (posts are often pointers to other places), but I suggest we in the SRE community keep our eye on it anyway.
- /r/SRE on Discord (*https://oreil.ly/qlYpy*). An offshoot of the Reddit subreddit, this is relatively new as of this writing, but I have high hopes because the discussion has been flowing there each time I have checked in.
- #sre on hangops Slack workspace (*https://oreil.ly/k0bYi*). Hangops is a busy Slack workspace for operations people with a ton of channels. #sre is one of those channels, with around 2K members as of this writing.
- SREcon Slack workspace (*https://oreil.ly/2jzxH*), which tends to be more active during SREcon events.

Similar to the SRE-adjacent event idea, there are also SRE-adjacent online forums worth participating in. For example, the Chaos Engineering Slack workspace (*https://oreil.ly/7_Nzc*) is a good place to discuss this important tool in the SRE toolbox.

Historical Document

I realize this inclusion is a little off the beaten track for most technical books, but stick with me for a moment. In January of 2023, many of the larger tech companies initiated several rounds of layoffs that let go many SREs. It was a really rough time. My social media feeds were full of SREs—including many senior SREs who had been employed for many years—who were now looking for jobs. Perhaps cold comfort, but my feed also included many posts from others in the SRE community who offered to help these people find new positions.

Google was one of the companies that fired SREs. To their credit, I saw many ex-Googlers (often called Xooglers) step up to help their colleagues. One particularly impressive effort in that direction was *SRE in the Real World* (*https://oreil.ly/rijid*), written specifically for the Googlers who had been laid off. I reference it here with kind permission of Niall Murphy and Murali Suriar, its primary authors.

I'm giving special attention to this document because I know of nothing else like it. It offers a unique perspective on SRE as a whole by holding up a Google-based mirror to SRE as it is practiced outside of Google.

Two small caveats: (1) there are a small number of names in this document (largely tool and project names) that will not be familiar to the non-Googler. That's OK, you can pretty easily tell through context what those things are, and it does not detract from the main lessons found in the document if you can't; (2) This document is not what I would consider classical beginner-level material, even though I believe beginners will get something from it (and it rewards repeated reading as your familiarity with SRE grows).

You can find *SRE in the Real World* as the original live Google doc or at a mirror blog article (*https://blog.relyabilit.ie/sre-in-the-real-world*), in case the original Google doc is not available.

Curated Link Collections

I have one last recommendation, which is similar to the ending of *Grover and the Everything in the Whole Wide World Museum*.[14] If you are the type of person who likes lists and is on the lookout for more SRE resources, I recommend you check out the curated list of links put together by Pavlos Ratis called "Awesome Site Reliability Engineering" (*https://oreil.ly/LRwvt*). I can't vouch for everything on the list, but this is a great resource for further exploration.

---

14 A fine piece of literature; you should check it out if you haven't already read it or read it to somebody.

Index

About the Author

David N. Blank-Edelman works for Microsoft as a technical program manager focused on site reliability engineering and modern operations practices. He has almost 40 years of experience in the SRE/DevOps/sysadmin field in large multiplatform environments. He is also the cofounder of the wildly popular SREcon conferences hosted globally by USENIX and is the editor/curator of *Seeking SRE* (2018) and the author of *Automating Systems Administration with Perl* (2nd ed., 2009), both with O'Reilly.

Colophon

The animal on the cover of *Becoming SRE* is a greater bamboo lemur (*Ceratophrys ornata*). Living up to the name, approximately 98% of the diet consists of giant bamboo (*Cathariostachys madagascariensis*). The other 2% consists of flowers, leaves, soils, and fruits.

Greater bamboo lemurs are the largest species of bamboo-eating lemurs in Madagascar. The length of their heads and bodies together averages 40 to 45 centimeters long, and their tails are 43 to 48 centimeters long. Their bodies are covered in a coat that ranges in color from reddish gray to olive brown. Two distinguishing features of the greater bamboo lemur are their blunt muzzle and white tufts near their ears. They have specialized molars and a strong jaw that help them break down bamboo.

This species of lemur is endemic to Madagascar, and it is said that they only live on approximately 1% to 4% of their original habitat. The predominance of bamboo in their diet restricts them to living in tropical rainforests with an abundance of large bamboo trees. Due to the threat of slash-and-burn agriculture and competition with humans for bamboo resources, they are considered to be critically endangered. Fossil records show that roughly 90,000 years ago, their population was one million. Now their population is estimated to be less than 1,000. Many of the animals on O'Reilly covers are endangered; all of them are important to the world.

The color cover illustration is by Karen Montgomery, based on antique line engraving from *Riverside Natural History*. The series design is by Edie Freedman, Ellie Volckhausen, and Karen Montgomery. The cover fonts are Gilroy Semibold and Guardian Sans. The text font is Adobe Minion Pro; and the heading font is Adobe Myriad Condensed.

Printed in the USA
CPSIA information can be obtained
at www.ICGtesting.com
JSHW062109260224
58102JS00005B/31

9 781492 090557